The Dead Sea Scrolls

Revised Edition

The
Dead
Sea Scrolls
A PERSONAL ACCOUNT

John C. Trever

William B. Eerdmans Publishing Company

William B. Eerdmans Publishing Company
255 Jefferson Avenue S.E.
Grand Rapids, Mich. 49503

Set up and Printed
Reprinted, November 1979

Library of Congress Cataloging in Publication Data

Trever, John C. 1915-
    The Dead Sea Scrolls.

    Published in 1965 and 1966 under title: The untold story of Qumran.
    Includes bibliographical references and index.
    1. Dead Sea scrolls. 2. Qumran. 3. Trever, John C., 1915-   I. Title.
BM487.T7 1977   221.4   77-10808
ISBN 0-8028-1695-9

TO THREE —
Elizabeth, my wife,
John Paul and James Edgar, our sons —
from whom
the Dead Sea Scrolls have required
incalculable sacrifice and infinite patience

Contents

Photos by John C. Trever, inserted after pages 64 and 96

Preface to the First Edition

DURING the winter of 1946-1947 three Bedouin shepherds happened upon a cave secluded among the rocky crags overlooking the northwest shore of the Dead Sea in Palestine. From a bowl-covered jar the youngest shepherd withdrew three leather scrolls which were destined to create a new era of Biblical studies in the Western world. Through all these many years the story of how those and other scrolls reached the hands of Biblical scholars has remained obscure and confused. As the first American to examine, study, and photograph the documents about twelve months after their accidental discovery, I labored to bring them to the attention of the world. Thus I have maintained an intimate interest in uncovering the details of the drama which surrounded their discovery.

One evening many years ago I was enthralled by the words of the late Dr. Edgar J. Goodspeed, who recounted his experiences with ancient Greek papyrus manuscripts in a lecture entitled "Adventures With Manuscripts." Not long after I became involved in the story of the Dead Sea Scrolls, the full meaning of his title dawned forcefully upon me. These ancient leather manuscripts have produced an adventure as exciting as any mystery story.

When so often during the past dozen years I have been asked, "Why do you not write the full story about the Dead Sea Scrolls?" my stock answer has been, "How can you write a mystery story when the mystery is not solved?" The answer was not entirely facetious. As long as I felt any uncertainties about key points in the story, I hesitated to add to the confusion which already existed from the many conflicting accounts. The knowledge that I had been partly responsible for some of that confusion has further restrained me from publishing anything until the facts could be established.

Several persons who were involved in the original discovery have died; others have chosen to remain silent, while still others have offered information which proved to be distorted or confused, probably from failure of memory. A few have been objectively helpful. Gradually, through the years, I have sifted all the evidence from correspondence, personal interviews, and publications, until now I feel the story can be recorded with a considerable degree of certainty. Sincere and determined effort has been exerted to keep any new errors from creeping into the account. New evidence, of course, will continue to be welcome.

In view of the nature of the story, I have followed the advice of many friends and tried to address this book to as many readers as possible. Since it contains a considerable amount of new information never before published, however, I have felt it necessary to keep the Biblical scholar also in mind. The popularity of the story of the scrolls leads me to believe that the layman will be understanding at those points where some tedious details are included for the sake of accuracy of the record. I shall hope too that the scholar will be patient about the local color and other details which have been included in the interest of the lay reader.

It would be difficult to name all those institutions and persons who have in one way or another contributed to the adventures recounted here, though a few to whom I am especially indebted should certainly be singled out: the American Schools of Oriental Research, which awarded me the fellowship for study at their Jerusalem school in 1947, and which again in 1950 provided additional assistance for manuscript study in England; St. Mark's Syrian Orthodox Monastery and its former Metropolitan, Athanasius Yeshue Samuel, whose telephone inquiry opened the door to my adventures; the International Council of Religious Education (now a division of the National Council of Churches), which generously granted me a six-month leave, with salary, to pursue paleographic research during 1950-1951; the American Philosophical Society, which contributed a stipend to enable me to spend three months of that leave in England and later awarded me their John F. Lewis Prize (1955); Drs. Millar Burrows and William H. Brownlee, who adventured with me in Jerusalem and gave generously of their assistance then and since; Mr. Anton D. Kiraz of Bethlehem, who, through many hours of personal interview and copious correspondence, has patiently endured my incessant questioning and intensive cross-examination to help uncover the facts; the Palestine Archaeological Museum and especially its gracious curators, Mr. Harry Iliffe and Mr. Yusif Saad, who granted me many privileges and generous services during three trips to Jerusalem; Drs. W. F. Albright, Herbert G. May, and Luther A. Weigle, who read the manuscript in an early draft and offered many helpful suggestions.

To my colleagues in the Department of Religion at Baldwin-Wallace College, who have relieved me of extra duties — especially Dr. Ernest Knautz, who voluntarily assumed some of my teaching load during one quarter — I am most grateful; and to the administration of the College, which has provided skilled secretarial assistance in the person of Mrs. Robert Carroll, who has labored over this manuscript without the benefit of adventure.

To one who has patiently endured many repercussions from this adventure, and yet has labored long hours at typing, editing, and research toward improvement of this manuscript, a special measure of appreciation is due — my faithful wife, Elizabeth.

John C. Trever

Preface to the Revised Edition

ALTHOUGH the "untold story of Qumran" was set forth in the first edition of this book, as further details relating to the discovery have continued slowly to unfold, public interest remains unabated. The effort, therefore, to keep the documented record up to date seems justified. To allow space to update chapter 16 and to expand adequately the contents of chapter 17 some less essential details have been condensed or omitted here from chapters 1 to 15. Certain implications of special concern to lay readers of the Bible can now be drawn with greater certainty from the discovery, and thus chapter 17 has been divided into two chapters which enlarge upon academic and spiritual reflections respectively.

The book continues to be the only thoroughly documented record of the history of the Scrolls discovery. Chapters 1-16 have been carefully annotated for the sake of the specialist who must examine the evidence to be satisfied. Much of chapters 17 and 18, intended for lay readers, is footnoted to provide them with references to other sources should they wish to enlarge their study of those areas that are presented here only briefly.

My indebtedness is gratefully acknowledged both to the William B. Eerdmans Publishing Company for making this revised edition possible, and also once again to my wife, whose patient typing efforts and careful checking of details have assured greater accuracy for the finished product.

Claremont, California
December 1976

John C. Trever

1

A Telephone Call in Troubled Jerusalem

THE BOOKS, papers, and note cards piled around my desk left little room to work, but they were all necessary for studying the trees of the Bible. My interest in this subject had been quickened on that beautiful Wednesday, February 18, 1948, a day that seemed to promise an end to the chill winter which had brought much-needed rain, but great discomfort to the drought-plagued Holy Land. It was a day that also marked the beginning of a great adventure.

The part of Jerusalem that could be scanned from my second-floor window had been washed clean by the torrential rains. Lofty Aleppo pines bordering the School property, gray with dust most of the year, were sparkling green, their uplifted branches etched sharply against the blue sky with its cottony tufts of clouds. The dense foliage, darkened by the lengthening shadows of the late-afternoon sun, screened from sight all but a few red-tiled roof tops of this newer part of Jerusalem.

I could not have been at my desk for more than half an hour when a gentle tapping on the door disturbed the unusual period of silence. Our Arab cook, Omar, hesitatingly opened the door and asked if I would come to the telephone. One look at his glum face, usually smiling and radiant, made me start a little. "Someone wants to know about some ancient Hebrew manuscripts." "Hebrew," he repeated solemnly, as if suspecting some conspiracy with the Jews. During those tense days it seemed that every Arab acted as a self-appointed detective to watch for pro-Jewish sentiments, especially among foreign visitors. I reminded Omar that in a school of archeology in Jerusalem a discussion about Hebrew manuscripts was normal. Were not Biblical backgrounds our primary concern? I argued. Descending the stairway, I walked across the courtyard to a small hallway just off the dining room, where the telephone for the School was located. Omar followed close behind, and during the ensuing conversation he kept within earshot.

As I lifted the receiver of the old-fashioned telephone, I was greeted by a friendly voice. The speaker said he was Butrus Sowmy, calling from the Syrian Orthodox[1] Monastery of St. Mark's in the Old City of Jerusalem. As the Monastery librarian,[2] he continued, he had been organizing their collection of rare books to prepare a catalogue of them. Among the books he had found some scrolls in ancient Hebrew, which had been in the Monastery for about forty years, but he could find no information about them. He was inquiring, therefore, if our School could supply him with some data for the catalogue.

His reference to "ancient Hebrew" prompted me to ask, "Do you mean archaic Hebrew?" Yes, he seemed to think it was. This was puzzling, but it sparked my interest. *How could the monks have scrolls in archaic Hebrew in their library?* I thought. That would be incredible. Surely he must be mistaken. I questioned him further, but it was soon obvious that little more could be gained over the telephone. I must see these documents — but how?

A vision of embattled Jerusalem flashed through my mind. The gates to the Old City were surrounded by barbed-wire entanglements, and armed Arab guards challenged everyone who sought entrance. If not obviously an Arab, one was taken for a Jew. The special pass to various Arab areas, received that very morning, would not admit me to the Old City, which was under another jurisdiction. How could I get through to see these manuscripts?

*   *   *   *   *

February was the sixth month since I had arrived in Jerusalem as a Fellow of the American Schools of Oriental Research[3] for a much-coveted year of Biblical and archeological study. After three years of teaching Old Testament at the College of the Bible at Drake University, I had determined that to be an effective teacher in my field I must have a year of study in the lands of the Bible. Applying, therefore, for an A.S.O.R. fellowship, I was one of the fortunate three who were selected for the 1947-1948 academic year in Jerusalem.

With the increased tempo of Arab-Jewish strife in British-Mandated Palestine during 1947, there was much concern among our relatives and friends over my leaving a wife with two small children and venturing into that troubled zone for ten months. My wife Elizabeth and I felt, however, that the likelihood of another opportunity for an experience so basic to my profession was extremely uncertain. It would be better to proceed on faith, despite the dangers and sacrifices, we concluded.

After taking my family to stay with my mother in Pasadena, California, I started on August 5, 1947, for New York by train. There I boarded the American Export Lines converted troopship, S.S. *Marine Carp*. Although a "first-class" passenger, I found sixteen men assigned to my cabin! William H. Brownlee, another of the Fellows, chose "tourist class" on the same ship; he was quartered with 125 men, navy style, in a large dormitory in what seemed like the hold of the ship. The only virtue the ship could claim was that it provided cheap transportation to the Near East.

At dawn on August 30, I joined the cluster of early risers on deck, intense with excitement over our first dramatic view of the Holy Land. In the distance, still shrouded in the residue of the night's darkness and a thin mist, the Plain of Acre spread out like a vast stage whose curtain was being drawn slowly aside. The red morning sun was just breaking through the thin layer of clouds which hovered close to the hills of Galilee. Great shafts of tinted hues darted skyward, as though heralding the adventure that was about to unfold.

Slowly the ship drifted into the broad, sweeping Bay of Acre toward the modern city of Haifa, which splashes over the steep slope of Mt. Carmel. It stands like a sentinel guarding the entrance to what was then the only harbor of Palestine for seagoing ships. The spell was soon broken as the frenzy of docking operations on boat and shore began, accented by the shouts of officers, seamen, and longshoremen.

For the next three months, classes and field trips proceeded normally at our School in Jerusalem. We were quite free to move about and managed to visit every major part of Palestine, drinking in each sight and scene with avid delight. The Bible literally came alive all about us. One of the incredible features of the Bible lands that we soon noted was the amazing degree to which their antiquity had been preserved in contemporary scenes. Apart from the few major tourist centers — Jerusalem, Bethlehem, Nazareth — and the bustling modern cities of Tel Aviv and Haifa, the ancient Biblical stories unfolded as if they had happened yesterday.

Occasionally bombings, snipings, skirmishes, and other evidences of strife among the Jews, Arabs, and Mandate authorities marred the joy of our excursions. We soon became used to the sirens around Jerusalem, which sounded almost daily alerts. When, in early October, the United States pronounced in favor of the *Ad Hoc* Committee's report to partition Palestine, it was answered in Jerusalem with the bombing of the American Consulate. Our movements became greatly restricted. Then, late during the night of November 29, 1947, came the announcement of the United Nations' decision to partition the country. It electrified the tiny land, and the fury of armed strife mounted daily. Concentration on Biblical research became increasingly difficult.

Located on Saladin Road about half a mile north of Herod's Gate to the Old City, the American School was in the Arab Hussein Quarter, a relatively new part of Jerusalem. Nearby, to the west and northwest, lay the Mea Shearim Orthodox Jewish Quarter. Directly to the north, lying in a valley at the foot of Mount Scopus, was the Sheikh Jarrah Arab sector. The Nablus Road, which joined Saladin Road in a sharp V at St. George's Cathedral a block north of our School, separated the two hostile quarters. At a vulnerable point a block beyond the Cathedral stood the American Colony Hotel. Many an evening we watched in darkness at the window of the dining-room wing of the School while tracer bullets flashed between these two newer sections of Jerusalem, outlining the Cathedral and the American Colony.

During December the tempo of hostilities mounted. On the thirteenth the horrendous bombing of loaded buses awaiting departure from the market place at the Damascus Gate numbed us with shock. I shudder to think how narrowly I missed being one of thirty-two injured and thirteen killed when, on the twenty-ninth, the attack was repeated at the same spot. Only five minutes earlier I had strolled leisurely by, stopping to watch a troop of Scottish soldiers parading with their bagpipes past the picturesque Gate.

The strain began to tell on the members of our School. William Beling, the other of the three Fellows, sent his wife to Geneva, Switzerland, on December 18. Millar Burrows, the Director of the School, said little but showed obvious signs of growing concern. Notes of reassurance repeatedly punctuated my letters to Elizabeth, written perhaps as much to convince myself as to ease her mind.

For three weeks during January, 1948, four of us students made a "flight to Egypt," where we rejoiced in the peace and freedom of travel. Beling decided not to return to Jerusalem, but joined his wife in Geneva; the rest of us found our way back with some difficulty. Meanwhile, Sherman Johnson, Annual Professor at the School, had left with his family for Turkey. By early February, therefore, only three students and the Director and his wife, Irene, remained at the School in Jerusalem.

Although I avoided alarming my wife by relating stories about the troubles all around us, I commented briefly about the situation in a letter dated February 15, 1948:

> The situation here is about the same — Jewish attacks, Arab reprisals, or vice versa. . . . Either it [partition] will be enforced by the U.N. with a perpetual state of strife existing, or there will have to be a reversal of policy. . . . The new part of Jerusalem is gradually being reduced to a shambles, and is a tragic sight to behold.

It was early that same Sunday, February 15, that Dr. and Mrs. Burrows, and Ann Putcamp, a student, left the Jerusalem School for a two-week trip to Baghdad. We students had urged the Director and his wife to get away for a respite from the tensions of Jerusalem, for January had been a particularly difficult month there while we had been enjoying Egypt. Shortly before leaving, Burrows handed me a letter in which he appointed me Acting Director *pro tem*. Brownlee and I thus were left alone at the School with the servants. Both of us settled down to the academic projects on which we had been working for some months.

The following Wednesday (February 18) I visited the office of my friend Abdullah Rimawi in Jerusalem's German Colony. He had promised to obtain special passes for us from the Arab High Committee. The pass he gave me was to prove of inestimable value in the weeks ahead. Because it was such a beautiful day, quite in contrast to the several previous stormy days, the desire to take pictures once again possessed me. There was still an hour until lunch. Returning to the School, I hastily grabbed my cameras and drove to the Palestine Archaeological Museum, where a beautiful wildflower garden provided some excellent subjects.

The Palestine Archaeological Museum commands a dominating position on a high prominence overlooking the northeast corner of the Old City of Jerusalem. Its white sandstone hexagonal tower and broad exhibit-gallery wings are glaring to the eyes in the intense Palestinian sunlight. It is an impressive sight from near or far. A gift of John D. Rockefeller, Jr., to British Mandate Palestine during the early nineteen thirties and built at a cost of one million dollars, it is one of the finest museums in the world. With utmost patience and ingenuity Harry Iliffe, the curator, aided by a few others, skillfully planned each exhibit. The two naturally lighted exhibit-galleries, radiating from the large entrance rotunda, spread before the visitor with artistic décor the archeological remains from a vast history of the Holy Land — from most ancient paleolithic to medieval Arabic times, about 75,000 years of human habitation in that area.

We at the American School were privileged to use the Museum galleries and library for study at almost any time without the usual entrance fee. Our travel opportunities having been so greatly restricted, we found the galleries a constant source of challenge and stimulus to our archeological interests. Brownlee and I had examined intently every item in the exhibit cases. We studied carefully the elaborate descriptions and historical information in guide books provided in Hebrew, Arabic, and English. Already I had been allowed to make color photos of almost a hundred objects, a priceless collection of lecture illustrations. The Museum was a part of us, and we almost a part of it.

At the entrance to the Museum one of the guards said that Iliffe had asked to see me. Upon being ushered into his office, I learned that Iliffe wished me to accompany him the next Monday to the excavation at Khirbet Mafjir near Jericho to take color pictures of an Arabic mosaic recently uncovered. Eager for the opportunity to render such a service to the Department of Antiquities, I readily agreed.

Returning to the garden, I set my camera for close-ups of the brilliant scarlet anemones. Hardly had the first picture been snapped when a burst of gunfire shattered the silence of the Old City, just across Suleiman Road from the Museum. Being shielded by the Old City wall, I continued to work, stooping low behind the garden wall for double protection. The skirmish did not continue long, so I was able to return to the School only a little late for lunch.

It must have been about 4:30 in the afternoon when Omar came to my room and asked if I would answer the telephone.[4] As the conversation with Butrus Sowmy continued, I remembered the distinctive garb of the Orthodox Christian clergy, which enabled them to move freely about Jerusalem. I asked him if he could come to our School. He assured me that he could. "If you will bring those manuscripts here to the School and let me study them," I proposed, "I will promise to give you the information you seek." Then, realizing what a hasty statement it was, I added, "Of course, it may take some time to get the information." He readily agreed to come at my convenience, and I suggested 2:30 the next afternoon.

Returning to my room, I pondered the call briefly. Probably the Syrians had a relatively modern Torah scroll or an Esther scroll, I reasoned. On several occasions such documents had been shown to me by friends who thought them highly valuable. I discharged the matter from my mind and returned to the study of trees of the Bible.

2

"Let Your Evidence Lead You . . ."

THURSDAY dawned dark and cold. I had planned to continue photographing objects in the Palestine Archaeological Museum, but a bright day was essential for good color balance. Remaining at the School, therefore, I took care of some miscellaneous duties and continued the flora studies. The activities of the previous day began to tell on me, for after lunch I lay down to rest and fell fast asleep.

At 2:25 I awoke with a start, as though prompted by a subconscious reminder of the promised appointment with the Syrian monk from St. Mark's Monastery. Hardly had I straightened the bed a little and combed my hair when, from the window, I saw a taxi arriving at the School gate. Hastening down the stairs, I arrived at the front door as Omar was opening the heavy steel gates, which were now kept locked. I greeted the smiling Butrus Sowmy, whose flowing black robe, the habit of the Syrian Orthodox monastic order, billowed as he walked. With him was a man in a khaki-colored uniform, wearing a *keffiyeh*[1] draped over his head and shoulders. I took him at first for a British police officer, but soon learned that he was Butrus Sowmy's brother, Ibrahim, a customs official for the Mandate government at Allenby Bridge.[2]

I was genuinely happy to greet them, for regardless of what came of the appointment, I had looked forward to the opportunity to get acquainted with another branch of the Eastern Orthodox Church.

Jerusalem, at 2600 feet above sea level, can get very cold in February. The buildings are stone, and the stone floors retain the cold. Only a part of the School could be heated, for oil was very

— 22 —

scarce; and electricity, necessary to operate the furnace, was lacking much of the time. The wires into the School were repeatedly severed during the Arab-Jewish skirmishes north of us. Frequently we were obliged to study with only the light from kerosene lamps.

On that particular day, however, we had electricity; and I had warmed my room a little by means of a small electric hot-plate that had been purchased for heating water to control temperature while developing color films in the cold basement laboratory. It may have been as high as 65° Fahrenheit in my room by the time the Syrians arrived. Thinking that it would be more comfortable to discuss the documents there, I invited them to follow me upstairs. When we entered the room, they complained almost at once that the room seemed stuffy, and the monk proceeded to fling wide the window. Out went my precious bit of heat! The Syrians, of course, in their unheated Monastery, were quite accustomed to the chilling cold of Jerusalem's winters.

The loss of heat was soon forgotten, however, as I focused my attention on the small leather satchel Butrus was carrying. Laying it on my desk, he lifted the cover and withdrew what looked like a roll of Arabic newspapers. Removing the paper, he handed me a very brittle, tightly rolled scroll of cream-colored leather, less than two inches in diameter. Very gently I pulled back the end of the scroll and saw that it was written in a clear, square Hebrew script, not at all like archaic Hebrew.[3]

Before I had a chance to note more than the somewhat strange character of the script, they lifted from the satchel a large scroll, about 10½″ long and 6″ in diameter, and handed it to me. Removing the Arabic newspaper, I saw that this scroll was made of thinner, softer leather and was much more pliable. It was about the same color as the first one, but with a darkened center, evidence of much handling. It unrolled easily.

Laying the heavy document on my bed, slowly I began to open it. A sheet of leather, containing two columns of text, had become detached from the rest of the document. The linen thread used to bind the sheets together had disintegrated. On the left edge the text was badly blurred by someone who had attempted to re-ink many letters which had been worn away by handling. Obviously this was the end of the scroll. It had been rolled backwards, with the last column on the outside. I continued to unroll another six to eight columns.

Here was not what I had expected! The script was puzzling to eyes more accustomed to Kittel's *Biblia Hebraica* in modern printed Hebrew and a few relatively modern Torah and Esther scrolls. I had expected the identification to be easy, but this scroll was different. It fired my imagination. Suddenly there flashed through my mind the words Burrows had spoken to me several times as I worked on my doctoral dissertation at Yale University six years before: "Let your evidence lead you where it will." My promise to the Syrians, I realized, would take time to fulfill; the evidence must be studied carefully.

The form of the script was intriguing, and it was soon apparent that it was the only clue for dating the document. There was no colophon[4] in evidence anywhere. I went over to my desk and found a box of 2″ x 2″ color slides on the history of the Bible text, and began to thumb through the section on the Hebrew text. I had prepared the slide set myself, for the Methodist Board of Education, just before leaving for Jerusalem. The British Museum Torah Codex,[5] I recalled, had been considered one of the oldest extant Hebrew Bible manuscripts. A mere glance at the photograph of it in my magnifier was convincing enough that the manuscript on my bed belonged to a different category and age.[6]

The next older Hebrew document illustrated was a papyrus fragment (measuring 3″ x 5″) called the "Nash Papyrus,"[7] inscribed with the Ten Commandments and the Shema' (Deuteronomy 6:4). I recalled that W. F. Albright had published an analysis of it in which a date in the first or second century B.C. seemed indicated.[8] In the magnifier only a few of the characteristic forms of letters were clear, but the enlarged final *mem* (M) and the elongated *kaph* (K) first caught my eye. These forms were very similar to those in the manuscript lying before me. The greater irregularity of the bottoms of the lines on the Nash fragment, as well as on the Syrians' manuscript, was also suggestive of a similar date, I thought. The letters seemed to be hung from a line pressed into the leather by a pointed stylus.

My heart began to pound. Could this manuscript, so beautifully preserved, be as old as the Nash Papyrus? Such a thought appeared too incredible, but the similarity to the Nash Papyrus was strong evidence leading in that direction.

Suddenly the story of Constantine Tischendorf's experience at St. Catherine's Monastery in Sinai flashed through my mind. In 1844 that great Greek scholar had found in a wastebasket there some forty-three leaves from a Greek manuscript of the

Bible, older than any other previously known. In his excitement he revealed to the monks their tremendous importance and worth. As a result, it was fifteen years before he was able to see the rest of that now-famed "Codex Sinaiticus," which since 1933 has been the prized possession of the British Museum. *I must not hazard the chance of duplicating Tischendorf's error*, I thought.

Restraining my enthusiasm, I calmly asked the Syrians if they would permit me to take a picture of a column of the larger scroll. They agreed, but then I recalled that the camera I needed was at the Museum, where I had left it the day before, intending to return that morning. All I could do was to copy by hand a few lines from a well-preserved section. The obvious beginning of a paragraph, three lines from the bottom of the fourth column from the end (Column 51), seemed ideally suited for the purpose. Trying to reproduce the form of each letter as carefully as possible, I found my hand unsteady from the mounting excitement. The strangeness of the script to my inexperienced eyes made me especially cautious.

As I copied, the two Syrian visitors began to relate their story of the origin of the manuscripts. It was a former Metropolitan, they said, who had purchased the documents for the Monastery about forty years earlier. Some Bedouins, it seems, had found the scrolls in a cave near 'Ain Feshkha, which is on the northwest shore of the Dead Sea; they were in a jar sealed with potsherds. One of the scrolls, Butrus said, was thought to contain Isaiah, but he seemed vague about it.[9]

Ibrahim remarked that while working at Allenby Bridge he had studied about the history of Jericho and the Dead Sea area. From his studies he had learned about the Essenes who lived in that region during the lifetime of Jesus, and as a result had become very interested in them. He had suggested to the Syrians at the Monastery that these documents might have belonged to that ancient sect of Jews and been deposited by them in the cave during a period of persecution, perhaps when the Romans attacked Jerusalem in A.D. 70. Since the scrolls had been "wrapped like mummies" originally, he added, they must be very ancient, for mummification had long since become a lost art. (Some of his facts were wrong, but his inferences were certainly to prove valid.)

Except for these few strong impressions, much of what the Syrians told me that day was lost in my concentration on the copying. I vividly recall, however, how Ibrahim leaned against the window sill as he related his part of the story, and how Butrus wandered nervously about the room, constantly fingering the string of beads he carried.[10]

With the copying finished, I was bursting with curiosity. I longed for solitude in which to pursue the study of these strange lines of Hebrew. I took time, however, to unwrap the three other scrolls in the satchel to examine them. One was about the same size, color, and texture as the first one. Another was much narrower and on a dark brown leather, inscribed with beautifully clear and large characters. Its entire lower edge had disintegrated or been eaten away. The last scroll they had was too brittle to open. Its advanced state of decomposition on one side gave every indication of great antiquity; it was as dark as the previous one, but much larger. No script could be seen, but a small fragment which the Syrians claimed belonged with it revealed a somewhat different script that was badly disintegrated. (We now know these three scrolls, respectively, as the Manual of Discipline, the Habakkuk Commentary, and the Genesis Apocryphon.)

As we rewrapped the scrolls and returned them to the satchel, I assured the Syrians, with as much composure as I could muster, that what they had was of great interest to me. I re-emphasized, however, that it might take considerable time to gather the necessary information they requested. Primarily what they sought, it seemed evident, was confirmation of their belief in the antiquity of the documents. The evidence for dating such manuscripts would demand a most careful analysis, I explained, and would ultimately require consultation with many scholars. They must be patient, I repeated.

Since they needed a taxi to return to the Old City, I ushered them downstairs to the telephone. Butrus Sowmy made the call, after which we lingered in the garden for a short time as I explained about the work of the American School.

As soon as the men left, I wasted no time getting back to the slip of paper with its precious lines of Hebrew. As I passed Brownlee's room, I noticed his door was ajar. Seizing the slip of paper from my desk, I rushed to his room to unfold the story.

Brownlee had planned to be present for the showing of the manuscripts, but had been delayed by particularly stringent check points while running errands throughout Jerusalem. Now he followed me into my room, as I impatiently sought to decipher the passage. As he copied the lines, we noted the double occurrence of the unusual form *llw'*. Literally, it would mean "by not," which seemed senseless at the moment. It was the kind of evidence, however, which could lead to quick identification if the document were Biblical, I decided.

Having borrowed the large Hebrew dictionary from the School library for my flora studies, I turned in it to the common word *lô*, "not." There were five columns of discussion about it. Quickly I scanned them for the strange form. At the very end was a paragraph which included all occurrences of this form in the Old Testament. A check in my Hebrew Bible on two references in Chronicles revealed no similarity to the context copied from the manuscript. Another reference to Amos 6:13 proved equally futile. The next reference showed *two* occurrences in Isaiah 65:1. With growing expectancy, I hastily turned to it. There, word for word, and almost letter for letter, was exactly what I had copied from the manuscript! It was a scroll of Isaiah, without a doubt! I lost little time communicating the discovery to Brownlee, who was avidly at work on the passage in his room.

Almost immediately my thoughts turned to the task of getting the scrolls photographed. Only by publication and free scholarly discussion could their antiquity be established, I reasoned. We were aware that what two young scholars thought about manuscripts with such a mysterious origin would not be very convincing to the world of Biblical scholarship.

That evening at dinner, our friend Abdullah Rimawi happened to be a guest of Miss Basimah Faris, who was staying at the American School. I told him of the importance of getting into the Old City to visit the Syrian Monastery to see the manuscripts again. He said he would be glad to take me to the Jaffa Gate of the Old City the next morning. There he would arrange to have the pass he had given me two days before stamped by the Old City military official. Then I could get to the Monastery freely.

That evening was spent laying plans for photographing the scrolls, studying the detailed map of the Old City to be sure of the way through the maze of narrow passageways to the Monastery entrance, and recording the details of that eventful day. The certainty concerning the antiquity of the scrolls was growing in my mind, as the words in a letter written that evening to my wife indicate:

I cannot see how it [the Isaiah Scroll] can very well be a fake, however. It would take an artist of extremely skillful ability to produce such a manuscript in modern times. If it is genuine, it may prove to be a sensational discovery. Thus I can't afford to take a chance on it.

Where would the evidence lead me?

The frustration of that night was described in my first published account:

> Sleep was almost impossible that night. Numerous questions flooded my mind. How long was the large scroll? How much of Isaiah was there? Could it be authentic? Those few evidences of a corrector's hand on the last twelve columns seemed a certain argument for authenticity. But how could such a perfect manuscript be as old as the Nash Papyrus? Out of sheer exhaustion I fell asleep, still arguing with myself![11]

Events moved so rapidly after my first view of the scrolls that it was several months before I noticed the ironic meaning of the whole passage which had led to the identification of the Isaiah Scroll. Thumbing through a Gideon Bible one evening in a hotel room, I turned to Isaiah 65:1 and was startled to read the words:

I am sought of them that asked not for me; I am found of them that sought me not. . . .

3

Convictions Confirmed

DEIR MAR MARQOS, as its members call it, or the Monastery of St. Mark, is located in the Old City of Jerusalem south of King David Street in the Armenian Quarter. It is not far from the Church of St. James (Acts 12:1-2). This Quarter occupies the southwestern hill of Jerusalem, mistakenly referred to as "Zion's Hill."

The Syrian Monastery surrounds a small, nicely appointed chapel believed by its communicants to be built on the site of the home of John Mark's mother, where, according to Acts 12:12-17, Peter went after his escape from prison. Visitors to the Monastery are shown an early Syriac inscription beside the entrance to the chapel which links the site with the passage in Acts. Exactly how old this inscription is, however, is not easy to determine. Another tradition associates the church with the "upper room" in which Jesus shared the Last Supper with His disciples.

The Monastery is best known for its small but valuable collection of old Syriac manuscripts. It was to this library that I was determined to go on the morning of February 20, 1948. Eagerly I awaited the arrival of Abdullah Rimawi, who was to conduct me into the Old City. No one from the School had been there for several months, and the very idea now seemed like a new adventure, to say nothing of the anticipation of seeing the scrolls once again.

At eight o'clock Rimawi had not yet appeared. Miss Faris, sensing my disappointment, offered to help me get to the Syrian Monastery. She suggested we take the bus, which would carry us directly to the Jaffa Gate. At Herod's Gate just south of our School we boarded one of the dilapidated buses. Its ancient engine rattled and groaned, and its body creaked under the load of Arabs on their way to market.

Near the Damascus Gate huge conical cement blocks had been strategically placed in the road on either side of the approaches to the broad market place to keep traffic at a snail's pace for careful scrutiny by armed guards. Our patient driver skillfully zigzagged between the obstacles. At the very place where the two frightful bombings had occurred the previous December our bus paused briefly. The vivid memory of my narrow escape tingled my spine.

Jaffa Road, where the bus line ended, sloped gently from Allenby Square down to Jaffa Gate through a line of small shops just outside the Old City. Most of the shops that day had their heavy corrugated-steel shutters drawn tight and locked. Several torn shutters, gaping holes in shattered windows, and charred timbers dramatically justified the owners' fears to continue business. Except for the ever-present uniformed Arab soldiers and barbed-wire barricades, the scenes around the Jaffa Gate appeared almost normal. Fridays always brought many fellahin (farmers) and villagers to Jerusalem, for it was the Muslim holy day. Many thousands came to worship at the El-Aksa Mosque in the Old City and to trade in the bazaars.

At the Jaffa Gate we left the bus and were soon lost in the crowd of Arabs pressing toward the heavily barricaded Gate. Armed guards questioned everyone who sought entrance. When our turn finally came, Miss Faris spoke in Arabic to the guard. I sensed that he was reluctant to let me pass with her. He seemed to be arguing with her, as he cast critical glances toward me. Presently, however, the guard motioned us forward, as another guard took me by the arm and guided me through the Gate toward the Arab Emergency Committee office.

More rapid Arabic followed, and I recognized words that indicated the discussion was centering around our School and the possibility of its harboring Jews. When the officer motioned to me, I stepped forward and, with a greeting in crude Arabic, handed him the pass which Rimawi had given me two days before. He studied it carefully, then talked further with Miss Faris who, I am sure, gave me as fine an introduction as I have ever received. Presently the officer stamped the pass, added his signature, and handed it back with a cordial gesture. Thanking him, I clutched the pass with elation. Now I was free to enter the Old City any time. Once out in the market square, I thanked Miss Faris profusely for what had obviously been a difficult task.

We were soon lost in the crowd of shoppers, merchants, goats, sheep, and donkeys, as we squirmed our way down narrow, shop-lined King David Street toward the small passageway that turned sharply to the right at Christian Street. My study of the route into the Armenian Quarter the night before served me well, for we made each turn correctly in the maze of passageways along the closely packed stone buildings. Soon we came upon the large gray metal doorway to St. Mark's Syrian Orthodox Monastery. As I pulled the iron bar to ring the Monastery bell, Miss Faris wished me success and went about her business.

Slowly the heavy door swung inward, and a small boy peered from behind it. I merely said, "Butrus Salmi" (it was not until sometime later that I learned his correct name, Sowmy), and he motioned me into a small courtyard within. Then he closed and barred the cumbersome door. He said nothing, probably assuming correctly that this stranger from the West could not understand Arabic. He motioned to me to follow him up a stairway that led to a second-floor balcony. On the upper level he disappeared through a doorway, and I waited at the head of the stairs with a vague feeling of uncertainty.

Silently I prayed for guidance, that it might be possible to win the friendship and trust of these people about whom I knew so little. Something within me seemed to answer, "Just be yourself." There was not much time for meditation, however, for within a few seconds the black-robed and bearded Butrus Sowmy appeared at the doorway which led into what he called their "office." His greetings were most cordial, though he expressed surprise to see me so soon again. I apologized for coming at such an hour but said that I had found the passage copied from the large scroll to be from Isaiah. He seemed surprised and delighted.[1] I hastened to add that many questions had arisen to make it imperative that I see the documents again.

Inviting me into the room from which he had come, he said he wanted me to meet the Metropolitan (the Eastern Orthodox "archbishop"). Behind a small desk in the right corner of the small room stood a dominating, portly figure, his black eyes set deep in a round, jovial face draped with a heavy black beard. I stepped forward to shake his outstretched hand, as Sowmy introduced him as His Grace, Athanasius Yeshue Samuel. His handclasp was warm and friendly, and I immediately felt at ease.

The usual formalities in such a meeting in the Near East involved talk about incidentals until demitasse cups of thick, sweet Turkish coffee had been served all around. While the coffee was being prepared, therefore, I took advantage of the opportunity to inquire about the historical background of their church.

In answer to my question about their origin, they emphasized that theirs was the oldest continuously existing Christian church. They mentioned the name "Assyrian" as the usual means of identifying themselves. Did that mean they were Nestorians? Their reply was an emphatic "No!" They belonged, they said, to the Eastern Syriac-speaking church which developed in the area of ancient Assyria, and long before Nestorius. Then I asked if they were Jacobites, feeling sure that would identify them. To my amazement the Metropolitan again said, "No!" Their church, he explained, was much older than the Jacobites. It had begun in Edessa (modern Urfa, which is today in southern Turkey, a little east of the upper Euphrates River) very shortly after the resurrection of Jesus. Theirs was the only church which still used the language of Jesus in worship. Now I *was* confused, for all their descriptions indicated the Jacobite Syrian Christians, with whose Bible, the Syriac Peshitta, I was familiar.

Fearing that further questions on this subject might defeat my purpose, I conceded that their explanation had clarified the matter for me, though inwardly I resolved to find some other way to satisfy my curiosity.[2]

Language seemed to be no barrier, though frequently the Metropolitan and Butrus would converse in Arabic. Many times Sowmy acted as interpreter for the Metropolitan. The quality of Sowmy's English had already so impressed me that I frequently found myself forgetting the language situation, occasionally to my regret.

The coffee having been duly served, it seemed a good time to turn the conversation toward the documents I was impatiently waiting to see again. I addressed some questions to the Metropolitan about the story Sowmy had related over the telephone and again in my presence. What was the name of the Metropolitan who had purchased the documents from some Bedouins? There was no immediate answer, as the Metropolitan and Sowmy conversed in Arabic. The name which was finally given

— Bishop Phalaxinos Yacob — meant nothing to me, but I jotted it down. A new point was added, however: the Bedouins had first tried to sell the scrolls in Bethlehem.

Their reference to the fact that the scrolls had been found in a jar prompted me to suggest that it would be a great asset to the problem of dating if the jar could be found. It was their understanding, they said, that the Bedouins had taken two jars from the cave to use for water. "Could you contact the Bedouins to see if those jars are still in use?" I asked. They promised to try.

I inquired about the library catalogue which Sowmy had originally mentioned as the basis of his telephone call. They showed me a book in which were handwritten entries listing the documents in their library. Sowmy turned to the page on which the scrolls were listed and pointed out the need for additional information. Their entire story seemed to fit together perfectly, with no attempt to conceal anything or make anything up.

Then their key question was addressed to me. Had I determined the age of the manuscripts yet? Inasmuch as the questions that had flooded my mind the night before were still unanswered, I was being completely honest when I pointed out that it would be some time before any statement could be made regarding the age of the documents. With some elaboration I emphasized the difficulties in determining the age of undated manuscripts. One person's opinion would not carry much weight with scholars, especially the opinion of a young (I was then thirty-two) and unknown student. Many scholars would have to be convinced through personal study and discussion.

Here was my cue! Only if the manuscripts were photographed and published could their antiquity be established, I argued. Scholars must debate the evidence before agreement could be reached. I had to restrain myself, for fear of overplaying the point. As casually as possible, I assured them that I would be very glad to invest the necessary time and materials to photograph all the scrolls, adding some comments to the effect that although the materials might prove to be wasted, I was willing to take the chance. Breathlessly I waited while some more conversation in Arabic ensued. Soberly the Metropolitan stated that only very rarely had anyone been allowed to photograph anything in their library. He went on to relate some unfortunate experiences they had suffered as a result of some previous requests.

My heart sank, but a new approach suggested itself. Did they know the story of Tischendorf's discovery of the famed Codex Sinaiticus at St. Catherine's Monastery? Yes, they knew it well, but mostly from the standpoint of that Monastery's dislike for Tischendorf, who, they felt, had cheated them! Quickly I shifted the story to its outcome. Did they know what happened after that manuscript had been published in full facsimile form? Britain paid Russia $500,000 for it in 1933! They appeared not to have known this fact but were obviously impressed, for they asked how the photographing of the scrolls could be done. Would I bring my photographic equipment to the Monastery? It was hard to help them see that such a procedure would be most difficult. I tried to describe some of the equipment that would be needed, and urged that the photographing be done in the laboratory of the American School. At first they demurred, but at last they were persuaded, and agreed to take the scrolls to the American School at 9:30 the next morning.

Having taken this important step, I was emboldened to ask if I might see the documents again. The Metropolitan pulled a large bunch of keys from beneath his robes and unlocked several locks on a door almost adjacent to his desk. He entered the room which he called their library (actually an oversized closet), and soon emerged with the small leather satchel which Sowmy had carried the day before. I suggested that we concentrate on the largest scroll.

Sowmy moved a small mahogany table before me and placed the scroll on it. With the loose end-sheet of the scroll removed, I proceeded to unroll it slowly, watching particularly for evidence of corrections by other hands, which might give a clue to authenticity. There were very few insertions in the first twenty columns examined; several of those were obviously corrections by the original scribe. Only three or four single-word insertions indicated corrections by others. Curious symbols appeared from time to time in the margins, but they offered no clue.

Almost at the middle of the scroll, three large insertions by different hands suddenly appeared (on Columns 32 and 33), two of them projecting vertically into the left margins. I paused to ponder these carefully. They were not made by the same hand. The one at the upper left was by a less skilled hand. The others were in much darker ink, by a highly trained hand with a beautiful stroke (even better than that of the original scribe). The darker ink immediately suggested a much later addition. But the differences between the hands struck me as incontrovertible proof of authenticity! There were indications of later forms of letters, approaching the traditional Hebrew forms. No modern forger could possibly make such corrections on a forged manuscript and design such developmental differences in density of inks and in forms of letters. No modern forger could know that much about ancient Hebrew writing, I reasoned. *There was no doubt that this was a genuine manuscript.* My excitement rose as the thoughts raced through my mind, but the need for caution steadied me. I continued to unroll the rest of the scroll to see if the beginning could be identified.

Column by column the amazing document unfolded before me. More insertions appeared. One large one in a very fine but again much darker ink, by an obviously later hand (Column 28), further strengthened my conviction. A new kind of evidence began to appear, with signs of ancient repairs to the document. A deep tear in the upper left corner of a column (18) had been repaired by gluing a piece of leather behind it. Two columns further, a break in the middle had been sewn together. Another four columns and a huge tear appeared; it had been repaired with both sewing and leather backing (Column 12). *What forger would bother to make this kind of repair?* I argued with myself. The work was obviously too old to have been done by the Syrians, and they assured me they had not repaired the documents.

The last eight columns were badly broken, and I realized there was a repair job ahead before these could be photographed. The darker brown leather was much more brittle than that of the first part of the scroll; the cracks and breaks were numerous. Carefully I worked through the tattered columns, keeping each separated piece where it was, but looking for what might be the beginning column. Finally it appeared, quite badly broken; but its upper righthand corner was among the broken fragments, clearly indicated by the upper margin reinforced by a strip of leather backing. Sewing marks at the righthand edge indicated that a cover had been attached. Fragments of it were present at the time the scrolls were purchased, the Metropolitan said. The writing was not as well preserved, but I began to copy what was on the fragment, not yet quite certain of the words. My mind was too excited by the accumulated evidence to ferret out the words, anyway.

Suddenly I noticed by my watch that it was almost 10:25, and

I remembered a 10:30 appointment at the dentist. The time jerked me back to reality, and I hastily rolled up the scroll and put it back in the satchel as I apologized to the Syrians for having to leave so unceremoniously. They seemed very understanding, and I literally dashed out of the Monastery, and through the narrow maze of passageways out to King David Street. With great strides I leaped from one broad step to the next up toward the Jaffa Gate. I felt as though I were walking on air, but I wondered if my inner joy had been noticed by the Syrians. Had I stayed longer, I am sure I would have burst with excitement.

When the dental work was completed, I picked up the station wagon at the American School and drove to the Museum to get my photographic equipment. Once back at the American School, I lost little time in examining, with the help of a Hebrew Bible, the words copied from the first column of the Isaiah Scroll. There, word for word, appeared the very first verse of the book of Isaiah. The entire book with its sixty-six chapters was included in the scroll! This, too, seemed incredible, for seldom is an ancient manuscript found to be complete.

The afternoon passed swiftly as I made arrangements for the visit of the Syrians the next day and readied the basement laboratory for the photographic work. Brownlee meanwhile searched the School library for resources on Hebrew paleography. Gunfire broke out to the north of the School, and the electric wires were severed once again, leaving us in darkness that night.

After dinner Brownlee brought his kerosene lantern to my room and placed it near mine to provide enough light to study the two fragments of script we now had. Huddled over the two small tables under the pale yellow light, we examined the retouched photograph of the Nash Papyrus in the frontispiece of a book on the history of the English Bible.[3]

Brownlee had succeeded in finding Albright's analysis of the tiny papyrus in the *Journal of Biblical Literature*.[4] The chart of comparative forms of key Hebrew letters from the fifth century B.C. to the third century A.D., including these from the Nash Papyrus, provided our best clues.

My first impression about the relation of the Isaiah Scroll to the Nash Papyrus was gradually confirmed as form after form of these key Hebrew letters seemed to check with those in Albright's chart. Before long both Brownlee and I became convinced that the Isaiah Scroll belonged in the same paleographic period as that small fragmentary document. In his article Albright had concluded that the Nash Papyrus probably belonged to the second half of the second century B.C., and he felt certain that it must be dated in the Maccabean Age (165-37 B.C.).[5]

With the evidence gathered that morning for the authenticity of the scroll, and now the additional evidence to confirm my initial impression that the script belonged to the same period as the Nash Papyrus, we felt completely overwhelmed. Sleep was almost impossible that night as the full impact of our confirmed convictions caused heady thoughts to overflow my mind.

4

A Day of Days

THE KEROSENE lantern on my desk cast its yellow light about the room as I sat writing a letter to Elizabeth at dawn the next morning. Our wires into the property apparently had been damaged by a recent battle to the north of us. The electricians had worked all the previous afternoon on them, without success.

Carefully I outlined plans for the big day. Successful photographing of the scrolls demanded steady, diffused light. Would we have it by the time the Syrians arrived with the scrolls? That was now a major concern. The day was going to be clear. I could use the light from a basement window, if necessary, but incandescent light would be so much better. Besides, we would have to work fast and accurately to finish in the length of time the Syrians had agreed to allow.

A count of my film supply revealed only thirty-six sheets of 9 x 12 centimeter "Panatomic-X" cut film and one sheet of "Commercial Ortho." That was not enough to put each column on a sheet, as it should be done. We would have to measure the documents and count the number of columns to determine how best to use the limited film.

Everything was in readiness in the basement laboratory at the School. A large drawing-board, resting on four color-developer containers and covered with a piece of red corduroy cloth, served as a place to lay the precious documents. Tripod and camera straddled the copy-board, and floodlights in diffusion reflectors were angled down toward the platform from each side. Such an arrangement was awkward and hard on the photographer's back, but it was the most convenient under the circumstances. A special transformer was necessary to reduce the 220-volt Jerusalem current to 115 volts for use with the American-made photoflood lamps, but fortunately one had been brought by a member of the School for his radio. Its capacity was insufficient to carry the high wattage of such lamps; thus, they could be turned on only long enough to take each picture — if there would be any electricity to turn on!

Since the age of twelve my favorite hobby had been photography. It later played a crucial part in my getting through college, seminary, and graduate school. During those years I had to learn every kind of photographic technique, and particularly copy work, both in color and in black-and-white media. While I was in seminary, the Yale Gallery of Fine Arts provided me a job which involved copying pictures and graphs for lantern slides which professors requested for their lectures. The discipline of experience had been my inestimable teacher.

Promptly at 9:30 that morning a taxi arrived with our distinguished guests. Butrus Sowmy, firmly grasping the leather satchel with its priceless contents, was overshadowed by the Metropolitan, who strolled forward, his silver-topped staff of office pacing each step. His jet-black robe parted in the breeze to reveal a gray woolen full-length gown with a row of bright red buttons from top to bottom. A broad silk vermilion sash divided him across the middle, and a jewel-studded gold cross swayed from a heavy gold chain around his neck. His black, silken, onion-shaped miter glistened in the sun. The two men presented a striking picture of Eastern Orthodox religious habits.

With typical American lack of ceremony we ushered them down the stairs to the basement, apologizing for the lack of comforts and hospitality. They seemed to enter into the spirit of the occasion with alacrity, though a little later Sowmy gently reminded us of the Near Eastern coffee custom. Brownlee quickly responded with a dash to the kitchen to ask Helen[1] to supply some. Then we set to work at once to unroll and measure the Isaiah Scroll.

We counted fifty-four columns of text on seventeen sheets of leather sewn together with linen thread. It measured 23 feet 9 inches, as far as we could determine, with the broken columns at the beginning.[2] It was immediately apparent that two, and sometimes three columns would have to be put on each sheet of film. Such a procedure offended my photographic sensitivities, but there was no other solution.

The electricians had arrived about eight o'clock that morning, promising to have the current restored by the 9:30 appointment. Selecting the same column from which I had copied two lines two days earlier (Column 51), I laid the scroll on the prepared platform and focused the camera. The lights flashed on, and we almost cheered — they flickered, and went out again! The electricians seemed to share our disappointment, for one came to explain the difficulty. Quickly we moved the platform, tripod, and camera over near a window, where the sun made a rectangular patch of intense light on the bare floor. It meant readjusting, refocusing, checking for light intensity and exposure. I clicked the shutter for a test exposure. Just then the lights flashed on again. This time they held steady. Back to the original place between the floodlights we moved the equipment again. One more test shot with the precious film had to be taken.

Within five minutes the test shots were developed and ready to examine — both were usable; one was excellent. Now we could proceed with the major task, being careful that the conditions at the copy-board remained the same.

Meanwhile Brownlee had begun to examine and measure the small scroll to see what problems were involved in photographing it. We knew already the repair work which lay ahead with the first eight columns of the Isaiah Scroll. The smaller scroll measured a few inches short of 5 feet (1.42 meters), and consisted of two narrow strips (about 5 inches wide) of a coarse, dark-brown leather, sewn together. The beginning was badly disintegrated, with only half of the first column remaining. The lower part over the entire length had been eaten away to large scallops by insects or worms during its long hibernation in the cave. The text on each column was therefore broken along the lower edge. How many columns were lost and how many lines of the beautifully preserved script were missing could only be conjectured. The document would have to be carefully translated and analyzed to determine that.

It was apparent from our check of the Isaiah Scroll that only two places in the manuscript could be photographed by allowing three columns on a single sheet of film. The rest would allow only two columns each. The fifty-four columns would therefore require twenty-six sheets of film, *if no errors were made.*

Since the tests were made on Column 51, I decided to use the extra sheet of "Commercial Ortho" film on another single column. One of my first thoughts on seeing the scrolls had been to get several prints to W. F. Albright at Johns Hopkins University to see whether he agreed with my conclusion about their chronological relation to the Nash Papyrus. Thus we rolled the scroll to Column 50 and took one more shot. Returning then to the end of the scroll, we proceeded to photograph two columns on each sheet of film.

The process soon became routine; we worked as a team, even employing Sowmy. Brownlee helped move the scroll to each new position and pressed those points which would not lie flat when I was ready to take the picture. Sowmy sat in a chair by the electric outlet to control the floodlights. I adjusted the scroll, centered and checked the focus of the camera, inserted the plate-holder, called for the lights (checking the intensity periodically with an exposure meter), set the shutter and snapped it. When he was not pacing the room, the Metropolitan sat on a tall stool, hands cupped over his staff, watching the whole process with evident amusement.

By noon it was obvious that not even the Isaiah Scroll could be finished before lunch time. We begged the Syrians to remain for lunch. Brownlee hastened to the kitchen to see if Helen could prepare for two guests. As usual, she complied most graciously. When she called lunch about one o'clock, forty-one columns of the great scroll had been recorded. Only one sheet of film had been lost through error, but it was noticed in time to permit a duplicate exposure without delay.

Our guests from the Monastery ate with relish. Helen had prepared macaroni, great mounds of which they readily consumed. The tall pile of coarse brown bread on a plate in the center of the table disappeared with amazing rapidity. Omar brought another; it too was soon gone. Tea was served with the meal, but immediately afterward Sowmy reminded me that "His Grace" was accustomed to coffee after lunch. I persuaded them to wait until we had repaired the Isaiah Scroll, for this task was one I did not want to delay a moment longer.

While Brownlee worked on the floor with the smaller scroll, I stretched the beginning columns of the Isaiah Scroll on a long table. Scotch tape was all we had to use, but I carefully applied it to the back of the breaks to avoid any possible damage to the script. Setting the various pieces in their proper places was like working a huge jigsaw puzzle. The Syrians stood close by, keenly watching every move. The Metropolitan leaned so close to my shoulder as I bent over the scroll that his beard tickled my neck. I dared not complain! With each successful placement, he uttered an ejaculation of delight.

Finally, every available inscribed piece, except one very small piece containing only five letters, was in its proper place. Much to my disappointment there were still six breaks for which no pieces could be found. The edges of two or three showed evidence of recent tears. I asked the Syrians about the possibility of their having them somewhere else, but they assured me that all the pieces must be with the scroll or in the satchel.

Several small fragments of leather from the outer margins of the Isaiah Scroll, bits of ancient repair material and linen thread, remained in the satchel, and a few had fallen to the table during the repair work. There were a few which the Metropolitan claimed belonged to a "cover" which had been attached to the scroll when he first saw it. These I gathered onto sheets of paper, and the Metropolitan suggested that I keep them as souvenirs.[3]

A taxi was to come for the Syrians at 4:15; it was after three o'clock before the repairing was finished. Hastily we returned the scroll to the copy-board to continue the photographing. Helen, meanwhile, served the Syrians the promised coffee.

When finished, the Isaiah Scroll took twenty-nine sheets of film; that left only seven for the smaller scroll. The shape of its columns made it quite unsatisfactory to include two columns on each film. With eleven and a half columns to go, however, there was no other choice. The final six exposures were soon completed.

With half an hour to spare, I was determined to take a few color shots. The special camera and plates had been carefully prepared for the purpose that morning, so the shift could be made quickly. Then it was that I made two exposures of Columns 32 and 33, with the rest of the scroll rolled on either side — a picture which has been published probably more often than any other one related to the scrolls. A similar picture of the first four columns was also made in color, the red corduroy background providing an ideal setting.

The taxi had arrived. Two scrolls and a small fragment of another had not been touched. I urged the Metropolitan to let us keep them long enough to repair and photograph. They would be kept in the School safe and returned promptly at 2:30 Tuesday afternoon, I promised, remembering my Monday appointment at Khirbet Mafjir. Apparently their confidence in us had been won, for they agreed to leave the documents. Brownlee prepared a simple receipt, which we both signed and gave to them.

As the taxi pulled away from the gate, I returned to the laboratory to put things back in order. I was exhausted. It was more than an hour later when I wearily climbed the stairs to my second-floor room and slumped into the chair by my desk. My mind wanted to examine the other scrolls, but my body rebelled. Finally, placing the scrolls in the safe in the School office, as promised, I went to the dining room for a leisurely dinner. About 8:30, after a relaxing game of ping-pong with Brownlee, I could not resist the call of those undeveloped films in the darkroom.

The room in the basement which was used as a photographic laboratory was really a large closet with a bench around three of its walls, some shelves, and a light-sealed door. Most of its equipment I had brought from home. There was no running water, nor any drain; the nearest source for water was a tap in the courtyard about a hundred yards away. Large metal water jugs were used to haul the water to the room, and five-gallon kerosene cans held the waste.

The special fine-grain developer had to be mixed before processing could begin. Only twelve films could be developed in the tank at one time, and it was almost midnight before the first dozen films were hanging up to dry. All were perfect and assured the success for the rest. A sense of elation swept through me as I viewed the sparkling-clear negatives, copies of what I firmly believed was the oldest extant Biblical manuscript.

Once again I wearily trudged the three flights of stairs to bed. It had indeed been a never-to-be-forgotten day.

5

Progress Under Pressure

SUNDAY MORNING I awakened at four o'clock. My mind was racing with thoughts about the scrolls. *I must have more rest,* I argued with myself, and I tried to relax both mind and body. By then I could appreciate the ecstasy of Tischendorf, who in 1859, after fifteen years and two additional trips to St. Catherine's Monastery at Mount Sinai, finally discovered the huge Greek Codex Sinaiticus in a steward's room. He was allowed to have the bulky manuscript in his own room that night, and avidly he pored over the vellum folios. Later he wrote, "... that night it seemed sacrilege to sleep."

In Jerusalem during 1948, however, we could not enjoy the silence and peace of an isolated monastery like St. Catherine's. At exactly 6:24 that Sunday morning a terrific explosion shattered the brief stillness of the Holy City. Our building trembled. I bounced out of bed and with one step reached the west window, where I flung open the shutters. Over the roof tops, like a huge mushroom, rose an ugly black cloud of smoke. Again the sirens began to wail. Pandemonium broke loose. We learned later that two trucks loaded with explosives had been parked in front of a hotel on Ben Yehuda Street; they had exploded with awful destruction and loss of life (forty-nine people were reported killed). What a tragic way to begin the Lord's day.

That morning we attended the Scotch Presbyterian Church, then enjoyed dinner with guests from the American Colony. Within a few minutes of our guests' departure, I hastened to the task of examining and repairing the two remaining scrolls. Looking like altar candles, and not much larger, the cream-colored rolls immediately impressed me with their similarity of length, color, and texture. Carefully I began to open the smaller one, only to find that severe cracks and complete breaks were frequent. It was obvious from the newness of the breaks that the brittle scroll had not been very carefully handled. The unusually high humidity of the winter months, however, apparently had softened the leather sufficiently to allow careful opening.

All the Scotch tape in the School had been used to repair the first two scrolls. Adhesive tape was the only other possibility. It would strengthen the cracks greatly, I reasoned, and if applied to the back it could in no way harm the text. I systematically raided all available first-aid kits. A strip of tape was placed on the back of each major crack, most of which covered the entire 9½-inch width of the scroll.

The first scroll contained only four columns of text on two sheets of leather sewn together with what looked like the same kind of thread as found on the Isaiah Scroll. One sheet had three columns, and the other a partially filled single column, obviously the end of a scroll. The first column was badly broken and required much repair. Its beginning edge was torn and quite irregular, though none of the text was missing. The upper right corner showed some stitching, which indicated that previous columns had been attached. A strange angular symbol appeared in the margin to the left of the first column. Along the left edge of the last column were stitching holes, which indicated that some more leather had once been attached.[1]

The second scroll was obviously longer, for there were more turns of leather to be seen at the ends. Its first column, though broken across the middle, was much easier to open. Stitching holes along the right edge implied the possibility of previous columns, or perhaps a cover.[2] The wide outer margin of the first column seemed to argue that this might be the beginning of a scroll. The first line of the text was unreadable, for scallops cut deeply into the text at the top as well as the bottom. They were not as severe, however, as those on the lower margin of the smaller scroll.

After the cracks in the first two columns were repaired, the rest of this scroll began to unroll more easily. Only small cracks needed reinforcement. While repairing the first two columns, I noticed that the script appeared identical to that on the other scroll. The same scribe must have copied this manuscript! Perhaps the two scrolls were related.

Three columns of text appeared on the first sheet of leather; and the next two sheets, which were opened before me within a matter of minutes, had two columns each — a total of seven columns on three sheets.

Suddenly, at the very end, the final evidence for the relationship of the two scrolls appeared. All along the upper half of the left edge the stitching thread was still in place where another sheet of leather had broken away; a fragment from the adjacent sheet, about an inch long and a quarter of an inch wide, was still in place. Along the whole lower half of the same edge a half-inch strip of leather, also from the other sheet, remained stitched in position. Traces of two letters were on the very edge. Here were the missing pieces from the beginning of the other scroll!

Quickly I placed the end of the second scroll against the broken beginning of the first one. Every piece fit perfectly! Besides, the fragments of two letters completed the letters at the beginning of two lines of text. A marginal mark at the beginning of a paragraph also was completed by the join. There was now no doubt about it — this was all one scroll with eleven columns of beautifully preserved text.

Carefully I pressed the broken beginning edge of the first scroll down onto the left half of the adhesive side of a strip of tape. Then, to match the end of the other scroll accurately, I started at the bottom with the two broken letters. I pressed the broken end gently against the adhesive, gradually working up the column to be certain that every point was joined correctly. The two scrolls were now one! The five Syrian scrolls turned out to be four.[3] Since we then had no idea concerning its contents, we simply called it "Jerusalem Scroll I" (today it is commonly called the "Manual of Discipline," but scholars call it *Serek ha-Yahad*, "Rule of the Community," or 1QS).

There was no time to attempt an identification of the manuscript, for I was eager to photograph it first. Supper would be called within a short while, so I hurried to the basement to prepare copy equipment and films. But then I remembered — there was only one more sheet of the proper kind of film left!

Exactly where I found some more film, my memory and my records fail to indicate. That the entire eleven columns of the scroll were photographed after supper that evening is clearly stated in my records. From somewhere eleven sheets of film appeared.[4] By midnight all the negatives for this scroll were drying in the darkroom.

The Museum station wagon was to stop for me at 8:30 Monday morning for Iliffe's project at Khirbet Mafjir. Somewhat reluctantly I prepared to fulfill this commitment. With gadget bag filled with camera and supplies, I sat on the front steps of the School at the appointed time — no station wagon appeared! As the precious minutes away from the manuscripts ticked away, my impatience mounted.

It was 9:45 when the Museum car finally arrived, the driver quite apologetic over the delay. Besides the driver, only the Museum photographer and a visitor from England were in the car; Iliffe had been detained. I was disappointed, for I had hoped to discuss the manuscripts with him. We had not been long on the way, however, before I bubbled forth with statements concerning my work on the scrolls.[5]

The respite from my long confinement in Jerusalem added to the pleasure of the trip to Jericho. It was my first opportunity to see the spring flowers in their native habitat, a sight for which I had longed. Splashes of green speckled with red anemones and yellow daisies bedecked some of the Judean hills. Soon, however, as we sped down the tortuous Jericho Road, the grass and wild flowers were confined to a narrow strip along each side of the road. The wilderness we were entering was perpetual. This was the rugged terrain made famous by the Galilean Carpenter, who began a parable, "A man was going down from Jerusalem to Jericho. . . ." Deep gorges, rocky crags, barren slopes, and desert sand greeted the eye in every direction. The black ribbon of road twisted like a snake down toward the Dead Sea, with numerous blind corners which might harbor waiting bandits. The speed with which the driver maneuvered the sharp, plunging turns made me wonder if he expected the parable to be repeated. Recent ambushes along that road gave him good reason to be fearful.

Once in the great plain of the Jordan, we continued through Jericho without stopping. The sight of huge bougainvillea vines, etched against the distant barren cliffs of the Judean plateau and surmounted by a brilliant sky, whetted my photographic appetite. On we sped past 'Ain es-Sultan (Elisha's Fountain), which supplied ancient Jericho with water, and Tell es-Sultan, the great deserted mound of Canaanite Jericho. A mile to the north, we left the main road and soon found spread before us the fascinating ruins of Khirbet Mafjir, the eighth-century A.D. Umayyad winter palace of Caliph Hisham.

The archeologists and their assistants welcomed us and escorted us to the great mosaic-floored bath, some ninety feet square, which had just been cleared. It was the smaller mosaic, discovered the year before and a few paces to the west, however, that was my photographic assignment. A temporary gabled metal roof had been erected over the reconstructed walls to protect the beautiful mosaics laid out to simulate Persian carpets, even with corner tassels, on the desert sand.

By the time I was certain that the best possible pictures had been obtained, it was 12:30; the station wagon was to leave for Jerusalem at 12:45. Hastily I took a few general scenes of the large, newly discovered mosaic, promising to return at a later time to do that mosaic more carefully for the Department of Antiquities (that promise could never be fulfilled). Under the circumstances there was no time to talk with the archeologists about manuscripts.

We arrived in Jerusalem in time for a late lunch. Soon I was back in the darkroom to develop the rest of the negatives of the Isaiah Scroll. By dinnertime all the films had been processed and readied for final washing. There had not been a single mishap!

Washing and hanging large numbers of sheet film is a tedious process, and hazardous without special frames; it is easy to chip and scratch the delicate emulsion. Thus after dinner it was late before all the negatives were safely hung to dry. There was still one project that had to be done before morning, when I planned to make color photographs of the repaired scroll which had to be returned to the Monastery that day. The color films taken of the Isaiah Scroll had to be developed first, so that I could be certain the factors being used were accurate.

Experience had shown that to obtain accurate color pictures, one must develop the latent images as soon as possible after taking the pictures. To process color films, however, an exacting series of fourteen steps must be followed. It had never before been done in Jerusalem. The previous September I had assembled the necessary equipment in the American School basement. A trunkful of supplies and equipment had been brought to process the 150 rolls of color film and twelve dozen sheet films I planned to use. Since all the required solutions must be held to an exact 68° temperature, the fall months had posed a major problem of chilling the water which came from the tap and was far above the required temperature. During the winter, on the other hand, the water was too cold. By February, processing of color films had become a routine, so that I could count on completing each batch — either four rolls or twenty-five sheet films — in a little over two hours.

It was already after ten o'clock when I started the process on twelve sheet films, including the ones used for the Isaiah Scroll the previous Saturday afternoon. Brownlee meanwhile was in his room trying to decipher the difficult script on the small fragment of leather which the Syrians had left with the two scrolls. Periodically he came to the basement to report on his progress and interpretations. By midnight I was so weary that I appealed to him to help with the final steps on the color films, particularly to bring water from the courtyard tap and to haul the heavy cans of waste water to the garden.

As one by one I pulled the transparencies out of the final fixing bath, my weariness was overcome by elation. Every one was perfect! There was the Isaiah Scroll in full natural color!

6

More Problems

MY LAST DAY before leaving Des Moines, Iowa, the previous July had involved the usual frenzied scramble any family with small children experiences before a major move. To complicate matters, an important discussion about a new position had to be scheduled for that last morning. The officers of the International Council of Religious Education,[1] who were then in Des Moines for a convention, wanted to discuss with me an opening which had developed on their staff. In anticipation of the appearance of the Revised Standard Version of the Bible about 1950 (it actually appeared September 30, 1952), they were seeking the services of an "educational representative" to the Protestant churches. They wondered whether I would consider such a position.

With my mind focused on my forthcoming trip to Palestine, I found it difficult to evaluate the sudden proposition. To give up my trip to the Holy Land to begin the job at once was unthinkable, I emphasized. The position could wait, they said. It meant leaving teaching; I had been engaged in it for three years, and I loved it. At the time, therefore, I could only assure the officers that the proposition was interesting and that I would give it careful thought while in Jerusalem. On August 9, while on the way to New York, I stopped in Chicago for another brief discussion with them.

During the subsequent months I had weighed the idea carefully and decided it was the kind of service I would like to render. In the meantime, some doubts had arisen about my being invited to the position after all; others were also being considered. Perhaps an awareness of the competition served to sharpen my enthusiasm, for I began to feel some apprehension over the long delay in the matter. By February no decision had been reached in the Council headquarters in Chicago.

All thoughts concerning such matters had now been erased from my mind by the appearance of the manuscripts. It was while I was hard at work Monday afternoon (February 23, 1948), developing the negatives of the Isaiah Scroll, that a cablegram was brought to the darkroom door. It had been sent from the States on February 18, five days earlier, the very day my adventure began.[2] In it were the words which a week before I was anxiously awaiting — an invitation to join the Council staff. Now, however, the message came as another interruption in the midst of an exciting discovery.

After a rapid reading I set the cablegram aside to continue the all-important developing. My decision would be seriously complicated by the manuscripts, I realized. Such a position with the Council would require much travel and frequent lecturing, leaving little time for the research and quiet study that the manuscripts would demand. But the idea of being related to the Standard Bible Committee and sharing with the members the oldest known Old Testament manuscript seemed to lend an element of providence to the proposition. I decided to "sleep on it."

By 6:30 Tuesday morning I was in the darkroom gathering up the finished negatives of the Isaiah Scroll and the color transparencies. Each negative had to be identified, labeled, and filed in its proper order, a task more complicated than I had anticipated. Without the original scroll before me to determine the proper order, it became necessary to match overlapping sections of columns near the edges of the negatives. Repeated examinations of the negatives led to a growing conviction that they would not produce adequate prints for a quality publication. *Would it be possible,* I pondered, *to get some 13 x 18 centimeter sheet film to rephotograph each column on a sheet? Even if the film could be secured, could I persuade the Syrians to let me have the Isaiah Scroll long enough to do the job properly?* Such a request would take diplomacy, and time was running out. These thoughts gave birth to a determination to begin the diplomacy that afternoon, when we had promised to return the other scrolls.

The Isaiah Scroll color transparencies developed the night

before had proved that my data for color-copying were accurate. It was a routine matter, therefore, to make a full-color record of each column of "Jerusalem Scroll I."[3] The small leather fragment with disintegrated script was also reproduced in color at the same time.

To be doubly certain of a safe return of the precious manuscripts to the Syrian Monastery, I had arranged for the Syrian *kawas* (footman) to meet Brownlee and me at the New Gate to the Old City, which entered off Suleiman Road just north of Allenby Square. By using that entrance we could avoid the hazardous Jaffa Gate so near the embattled Yemen Moshe Quarter. Brownlee carried a large, thin volume of the published Chester Beatty Papyri,[4] with which I hoped to impress the Syrians concerning the need for quality publication.

Bypassing the perilous Damascus Gate, we cut across the open field opposite the School, crossed the Nablus Road, and continued through another vacant field to the Arab Musrara Quarter along Godfrey de Bouillon Street. This street joined Suleiman Road about a hundred yards north of the New Gate and almost adjacent to the property of the huge Convent of Notre Dame. At this point the Old City wall reaches its most westerly extension and surrounds an area dominated by Christian monasteries and churches, as well as the Latin, Greek and Armenian patriarchates.

The New Gate was a huge, steel, double door which could be opened to allow large vehicles to enter the market place just inside. Now, however, the Gate was barricaded with masses of coiled barbed wire; only a small door, a section of the large one, was used for admittance. As we emerged onto the stone-paved market place, two men dressed in khaki stepped forward to greet us and motioned to us to follow. The rough, narrow corridors between towering stone walls provided a feeling of security. Our guides seemed to know almost everyone we met. No one questioned us. The guides knew no English, and our few words of Arabic were soon exhausted, so we walked in silence. Aware of the diplomatic move I was planning and the need for restraint, I sought guidance in prayer.

At St. Mark's Monastery we were greeted with extremely cordial expressions by Metropolitan Samuel and Butrus Sowmy. With the usual formalities (including demitasse coffee) ended, I launched into a discussion of the scrolls and the next steps to be taken. Unrolling before them the repaired scroll, I explained how the two scrolls had fitted together. They seemed delighted with the news.

One thing they most wanted to hear, of course—what we really thought about the antiquity of the scrolls — was the thing I most cautiously refrained from revealing. I reiterated a promise, made earlier, that I would provide them with a written progress report as soon as possible.

With appropriate introductory remarks, I showed them the Chester Beatty volume. This is the kind of publication that should be undertaken with their scrolls, I emphasized, and then added that such work demands patience and considerable investment. To avoid revealing my firm convictions, I punctuated every sentence with *insha'Allah* (a common Arabic expression meaning "If God wills") and such expressions as "providing your manuscripts prove to be what I hope they will." Brownlee sat discreetly silent, or occasionally added a word of endorsement to my remarks.

Another prime concern about the scrolls was their safety in wartorn Jerusalem. It seemed strategic to discuss this matter, too. They argued that their Monastery was as safe as any place. I was not at all convinced. The library in which they kept the scrolls was separated by a wall only three feet thick from the Jewish Quarter of the Old City, one of the worst trouble spots in Jerusalem. They assured me that there were rooms down beneath ground level in the Monastery where the documents could be secreted without possible danger, but I thought of the dampness of such places and what it would mean to ancient leather. Further discussion of this problem seemed fruitless.

Turning the conversation to the tightly rolled scroll from which it was believed the small fragment had come, I urged upon them the importance of having it opened by experts in America. Its advanced state of disintegration would demand the most careful treatment, I stressed.

With the main items of discussion completed and the scrolls returned to their satchel once again, the Syrians invited us to examine their library of rare books. It was indeed an impressive collection, though most of the volumes were late medieval Biblical and religious treatises in Syriac, the sacred language of their church. A Syriac copy of the Gospels, with eight colorful miniatures, dated 1222, whetted my photographic appetite. Its illustrations of medieval art, I urged, should be photographed in color. A similar request had been denied a staff member of the Palestine Archaeological Museum, Sowmy said, and then added, "But we may give Dr. John the privilege." This testimony of their confidence made me hopeful.

Of passing interest at the time was a large dark leather scroll, the only other manuscript in scroll form that we saw in their collection. About twice the size of the Isaiah Scroll, it was quite similar to several Torah scrolls I had previously seen.[5] It was clearly not related to the ones on which we were working. Sowmy commented that this scroll had not been found with the others.[6]

Bidding farewell to the Monastery *kawas* at the New Gate, Brownlee and I returned by the route we had come. There was much to discuss. We were certain that the events of the afternoon had been providential. The warmth of feeling expressed by the Metropolitan's handshake as we parted convinced me that his confidence had been completely won. My prayers had been answered! An overwhelming sense of responsibility gripped me, and an awareness of the need to maintain strict confidence and absolute integrity.

On Wednesday evening the tedious task of printing three copies of each of the manuscript negatives was begun. Brownlee developed the prints while I manned the printing-box. By eleven o'clock, when I sensed that my uncomplaining assistant was catching cold from the chill of the basement room, we stopped. Dozens of prints were ready for washing. Those from the test negatives were washed and put on plates to dry, to be ready to send to the United States the next day.

The next morning I sent a cable to the General Secretary of the International Council of Religious Education accepting the post that had been offered, and one to Elizabeth informing her of my decision. Having posted the letters, I sought a quiet corner of the building to write the good news about the manuscripts to W. F. Albright. In a scrawling hand and with cautious reserve, I wrote to the world-renowned scholar:

> Enclosed are some sample prints from a manuscript which I have discovered here in Jerusalem in Dr. Burrows' absence. . . . If you are right about your dating of the Nash Papyrus, then I believe that this is the oldest Bible document yet discovered! . . .
> My first thought when seeing these scrolls was to get them

photographed and a copy to you for study. I firmly believe the script cannot be later than the 2nd Cent. A.D. (Dura Fragment), and it has some indications to show it may be earlier than the Nash Papyrus. I am so busy with the photographing of them that I can't take time now to make the careful study that they demand for more accurate dating. I am personally convinced that their age is great. . . .

. . . I know you will understand my concern about the safety of the MSS, so will keep this absolutely confidential. Should there be an announcement now, there is great danger that they might be destroyed.

With less reserve I also wrote the same day to my good friend in California, Edgar J. Goodspeed:

The most exciting thing, however, is my chance discovery of what I am convinced are the oldest Bible documents yet found. The most important one is a complete scroll of the Book of Isaiah with very few lacunae! If Dr. Albright is correct in dating the Nash Papyrus in the 2nd century B.C., then this is as old or older!! . . . Unless I am entirely no good as a paleographer this discovery should create a sensation in the United States. It is for one thing the first ancient Bible MS. found *in Palestine*. Its provenance is claimed to be from the Dead Sea area. I am tracing the story as best as possible. . . .

The first news of the discovery was now on its way to the United States, but not for publication.

7

A Frantic Search for Film

APPEARING much like the bar of a British pub, or an American tavern, the darkroom shelves at our School were stocked with all the liter-sized wine bottles I could beg or borrow for the chemical solutions. Some of the corks still wafted an odor of the contents they once sealed; many of the labels still proclaimed this or that brand of fine vintage.

For the sake of economy I had purchased gallon-sized containers of the three key chemical formulae required for color developing. Once the dry powders were put into solution, the two developers and bleach had to be used within two weeks to assure quality results. Even then, they had to be sealed in tightly stoppered bottles to prevent oxidation. Wine bottles proved to be the only proper-sized ones available for the purpose in Jerusalem. The rest of the chemicals needed for the process could be easily weighed out as needed from bulk supplies.

The time limit on the last batch of chemicals had almost expired. To utilize the remainder of these chemicals, therefore, it was necessary on Thursday and Friday (February 26-27, 1948) to concentrate on color developing.

Some studying could be done during the processing, I had found, as long as one hand could be free to agitate the films in the tanks. A timing clock prevented me from getting too engrossed in study. A new theory was growing in my thinking about the date of the Isaiah Scroll, and I sought every possible moment to consider it.

During Thursday afternoon, while developing some more of

the sheet films, I began another review of W. F. Albright's article about the Nash Papyrus. The peculiar "looped *alephs* and *taws*" of Nash were puzzling. They did not appear on the Isaiah Scroll, so far as I could tell. Was this a scribal idiosyncrasy, or a later development, or possibly an earlier?

When developing sheet films, I seldom knew which pictures were involved until the first development had been completed. Turning on the lights for the second exposure, I discovered among the films some columns of "Jerusalem Scroll I" (the Manual of Discipline) and those of the small dark fragment. On the latter I noticed evidence that the disintegrated script seemed to show more clearly than on the original fragment. Since the script was reversed on the transparency and still opaque, however, such an impression had to await completion of the process. During the final fixing bath, when I eagerly drew one of the transparencies out of the tank and held it to the light, my impression was confirmed. The script was clearer than on the original fragment![1] Perhaps now we could make out the contents. The words *'nsh' l'r'* clearly marked the beginning of a sentence, but what did they mean? These forms were not familiar from Hebrew. Could they be Aramaic? There was no time to check. The processing had to be finished.

That evening, while processing two rolls of pictures taken the previous morning at Haram esh-Sharif,[2] I returned to the further study of Albright's article. His "Class IV" discussion included some fourth-third-century B.C. Hebrew Papyri from Edfu in Upper Egypt.[3] Some of the letter forms from these papyri, included on Albright's chart, impressed me as being closer to the Isaiah Scroll than to the Nash Papyrus. The *aleph* (A), *kaph* (K), perhaps *mem* (M), *nun* (N), and especially *taw* (T) seemed to suggest that our scroll might be somewhat older than Nash. This might put it as early as 200 B.C., I reasoned.

What was going on in Palestine about 200 B.C. that might account for manuscripts being hidden in a cave by the Dead Sea? The name Antiochus Epiphanes presently came to mind. A Seleucid ruler of Syria in the early second century B.C., he hated the Jews and persecuted them. I seemed to recall that he particularly sought to destroy Hebrew manuscripts. It was he against whom the Judean Maccabees arose in revolt. Could those manuscripts have been secreted in the cave by some Jews who feared the destruction of their sacred scrolls at that time? It seemed like a perfect historical situation to account for the early script. This would really make the discovery fabulous![4]

The bell on the time clock suddenly jerked me out of the age of Antiochus. Color processing had to be exact! A few minutes later the two rolls were finished.

It was late, but I had just remembered the negatives of "Jerusalem Scroll I." Nothing further had been done to identify it. Tired as I was, I set to work with magnifying glass held against the back-lighted negative of Column I to try a translation. The first two lines were so broken, I started in the middle of the second, where the text became continuous. "To do the good and upright before him, according as he [the subject was obviously God] commanded by the hand of Moses and by the hand of all his servants the prophets . . . ," I laboriously deciphered, checking and double-checking the form of each letter in each word. With only consonants and no vowels to be sure of the pronunciation of the words, the first reading of an ancient Hebrew manuscript is often tedious.

As more words became clear — "evil," "doers of good," "to do truth and righteousness and justice" — sayings in the Wisdom literature seemed to be suggested. I thought of Proverbs and Ecclesiasticus in the Old Testament and the Apocrypha. The documents sounded like Scripture; but after repeated checks, I could find nothing in the Bible that followed the exact words. It was well past midnight when my eyes would focus no longer on the fine script, and I dropped into a heavy sleep.

A more practical problem continued to plague my mind. The Isaiah Scroll must be rephotographed. Where could the proper film be found? Suddenly that night I remembered a scene in the Palestine Archaeological Museum the week before. While photographing artifacts from Jerash in one of the offices there, I had noticed in the nearby shipping room a long wooden box being unpacked. Dozens of packages of fresh 13 x 18 centimeter film had just arrived from England! It was a British film ideally suited for copying manuscripts. I had been told that it was ordered for the detailed copying of the huge mosaic floor uncovered at Khirbet Mafjir. Could I persuade the Museum authorities to let me buy some of that new film to rephotograph the Isaiah Scroll?

I decided to approach Iliffe the next morning. Since I had done him a favor by taking the Khirbet Mafjir mosaics in color, I reasoned, perhaps he would return the favor now. Taking the beautiful mosaic transparencies, a half dozen or more prints of the Isaiah Scroll, and some of the small scroll, I set out for the Museum shortly after breakfast the next morning.

Although my conversations with the Syrians had revealed a reticence on their part toward the government Department of Antiquities (whose offices were in the Museum), I saw no reason to refrain from discussing the manuscripts there. The logical question — why the documents had not been known to the Department of Antiquities before — failed to enter my mind. I was not a detective.

When I inquired for Iliffe at the outer office that Friday morning, I was informed that he had left suddenly for Baghdad. R. W. Hamilton, Director of Antiquities, was in, and I asked whether he could see me. In a short time one of the guards ushered me to Hamilton's office. The guard politely announced my arrival as we entered a large paneled office made cozy from the chill of winter by a briskly burning fire on an open grate. A chocolate-colored dachshund, curled on a rug before the fire, stirred as we entered.

Hamilton, whom I had met casually on several previous occasions, arose from behind a heavy walnut desk well stocked with books and papers which bespoke a scholar at work. A rather slight, wiry, sandy-haired Britisher, he had impressed me as a dedicated scholar without the usual distant austerity. His cordial, personable greeting made me feel at ease.

We wasted little time with formalities. Handing him the color transparencies from Khirbet Mafjir, I asked if he would see that they were delivered to Iliffe. He expressed much delight over the results and thanked me profusely, all of which encouraged me to launch into the manuscript story.

Placing several of the prints of the two scrolls on his desk, I began to unfold with unrestrained, youthful exuberance all I knew about them. The fact that it was my understanding that the scrolls had been in the Syrian Monastery for many years was of course included. I emphasized my conviction that, on the basis of paleography, the scrolls must date from at least as early as New Testament times, and even mentioned my new theory about Antiochus. He examined the photographs closely and seemed to be pleased with what he saw and heard.

Pointing to some of the prints containing more than one column, I explained the problem of enlarging them to their natural size for adequate publication. Then, with some hesitation, I mentioned having noticed the large shipment of fresh film received by the Museum a week earlier. Would there be a possibility, I inquired, of my buying about seventy sheets of this film to redo these two scrolls? Hopefully I awaited his reply as he examined the prints further. He took a few sips of coffee, then began to explain the importance of that shipment of film to the Museum. It was probably the last they could obtain from England, with the circumstances in Palestine so rapidly disintegrating. There was barely enough, furthermore, to complete the Khirbet Mafjir mosaics. My heart sank.

As I shared more of the story, and he examined print after print, I continued to hope that he might, after all, change his mind about the Museum film. He suggested several places in Jerusalem where he felt certain I could obtain the necessary film. Finally, after almost an hour, I was convinced that there was no more hope. Thanking him for his suggestions, I returned to the School.[5]

There was just time to finish the rest of "Jerusalem Scroll I" color films. The results were perfect; that scroll was now thoroughly recorded. Always my concern for the safety of the scrolls lent an urgency to the photographic process. Perhaps the original scrolls, lying so close to the disputed Jewish Quarter, would be victims of the repeated bombings any day, I reasoned.

Except for some further translation of Scroll I late that evening — now with the aid of the color transparencies — the rest of that day had to be devoted to letters, following up the cables sent the day before. Many personal problems, greatly complicated by the manuscript discovery and the acceptance of the new position, had to be discussed with my wife, who was eight thousand miles away. To record all that was happening in Jerusalem as well demanded many hours of writing.

Washing and drying the great mass of prints we had made Wednesday evening continued into that same day. The primitive method we were forced to follow for washing prints made it a laborious chore. Many changes of water on the prints required frequent interruptions of whatever I was doing. Among the last prints put out to dry that afternoon were the rest of those from the smaller scroll (then called "Jerusalem Scroll II").

That evening I gave a set of Scroll II prints to Brownlee. He immediately went to work on a translation. It was then he discovered the key to the scroll which linked it with the book of Habakkuk. The second line on the first full column (Column 3) begins, "For this is what it says . . . ," and follows with the last phrase of Habakkuk 1:6 and all of verse 7: ". . . to seize habitations not their own. Dread and terrible are they; their justice and dignity proceed from themselves." Then comes the phrase, "Its meaning [or interpretation] concerns the Kittim . . . ," and it continues with an application apparently to contemporary history. At intervals Brownlee came to my room to report his discoveries of quotations from the book of Habakkuk scattered through the columns. Each quotation was followed by an interpretation. The scroll was apparently some type of commentary on Habakkuk! During the next weeks Brownlee spent many hours of work on the translation of the entire document.

By nine o'clock the next morning I was on my way to the Old City to begin the search for film. On Jaffa Road, midway from Allenby Square to the Jaffa Gate, was a small photo shop owned by Mr. C. Raad. He was the logical first contact, Hamilton and I had agreed; his skillful photographic work was much appreciated by scholars and laymen alike. Having been a photographer for Allenby's army in 1917, he knew Jerusalem like a book. He could converse with almost anyone who entered his shop, for he knew the basics of about fifteen languages. Already I had come to appreciate him as a trustworthy and warm friend, as well as a helpful merchant.

As I entered his shop (one of the few still doing business along Jaffa Road), the stocky, gray-haired Mr. Raad was bustling about, waiting on a number of customers. After the last customer left, I related to Raad the important project for which I needed his help. He had some 9 x 12 centimeter film, he assured me — enough to do all the Habakkuk Commentary properly — but he had no 13 x 18 centimeter film. He very much doubted that any could be found in all Jerusalem. He suggested, however, that I visit a certain shop in the market place inside the Jaffa Gate.

I asked him to hold the 9 x 12 centimeter film for me and continued on down Jaffa Road to the Gate. At the shop no encouragement for my quest could be given. Another shop was suggested, down King David Street and among the suqs (covered streets in the bazaars, a characteristic feature of many oriental cities). There I was told the same story, but this shopkeeper said he thought he could get some film for me if I would come back in a few days. At each photo shop among the suqs I stopped with the same request. Several dealers assured me they would get some film if I would come back in a few days. Footsore and discouraged, I finally made my way back to the School.

That afternoon I persuaded Brownlee to abandon his study of the Habukkuk manuscript photographs and assist me with the rest of the prints of the Isaiah Scroll and Scroll I — the "Sectarian Document," as I began to call it, since it was religious but obviously not Biblical. We chatted and theorized about the scrolls as we worked, following the same system we had used the previous Wednesday evening. Suddenly we heard the crunch of tires on the gravel driveway — it must be the Director returning from Baghdad, we agreed.

Leaving Brownlee with his hands deeply immersed in developer, I hurried out through the garden to find Dr. and Mrs. Burrows emerging from Mr. Abudayeh's green Studebaker. Without consideration of their feelings after the long, wearisome trip, I urged Burrows to come to my room at once. It was very important, I insisted. He seemed a bit bewildered by my sudden outburst. He complained of being tired and pleaded for a chance to get a cup of tea.

Stopping by the darkroom, I announced their arrival to Brownlee and told him that I was going to my room to prepare for Burrows' visit. Brownlee agreed to continue developing the exposed paper. Bounding up the stairs three at a time, I hastily laid my plans. Already I had begun to assemble a set of Isaiah Scroll prints into a small scroll by trimming a group of the prints to match, attaching them with Scotch tape. About a third of a scroll was in one continuous strip. This I laid out on my desk. Then a set of Habakkuk Commentary prints were laid side by side in proper order. Only a few prints of the "Sectarian Document" were available, but they were laid out with a miscellany of others, including some color transparencies. With lamp adjusted for best light and a magnifying glass ready, I impatiently awaited the sound of steps along the corridor.

Remembering the efforts Burrows had put forth on my behalf in connection with the new position so recently accepted, I located the cablegram. Just then I heard the sound of steps outside my door. Offering Burrows the easy chair placed beside the desk, I handed him the cablegram.

Hardly had he finished the sixty-six words of the message when I launched forth with the manuscript story, much of which I am sure was lost in the torrent of words. When I paused momentarily, Burrows inquired, in a fatherly tone of voice (perhaps trying to calm my flow of words), "What have you done about this?" and pointed to the cablegram. The decision to accept, I began, was complicated by these manuscripts, but I had finally sent it. "Remember, John," he cautioned, "you cannot eat these documents."

He began to examine some of the prints with the magnifying glass, as I returned to their story and my reasons for believing that they represented the most ancient manuscripts of their kind known. Finally I paused to give him a chance to respond.

Continuing to examine them, slowly and quietly, and with characteristic scholarly caution, he questioned some points concerning the paleographic basis of my enthusiastic claims. Pondering some of the prints further as I pressed the paleographic arguments, he finally terminated the discussion by pointing out that certainly the manuscripts were important and should be published as soon as possible. He assured me that the A.S.O.R. would back such a publication. Agreeing to go with me to see the manuscripts at the Monastery the next Monday, he turned the conversation to other matters relating to our two weeks alone at the School.

As Burrows left, I suddenly remembered Brownlee still at work in the basement and returned to the darkroom to relieve him of the monotony of developing prints. We finished the printing after dinner that evening. A total of almost 250 prints from seventy-eight columns on the three manuscripts and one fragment had been completed. We now had three complete copies of each of the scrolls, even though for two of them I was still not satisfied with the quality. The search for more film had to continue.

8

The Truth is Revealed

JERUSALEM'S weather seemed to be trying to hold back the mounting fury of strife, as winter continued to delay the approach of spring. Another blanket of cold settled over Jerusalem on Sunday, the last day of February. At St. George's Cathedral I huddled close to a small stove beside a great pillar in the bone-chilling stone structure. Despite the din of gunfire just north of the church, I found the solemn prayers and intoned chants of the formal service quieting to my overcrowded mind.

After the service Mrs. Bertha Vester of the American Colony invited me to lunch. Brownlee joined us for a pleasant afternoon with the members of the Colony. It was a day of much-needed rest. Not until that evening did I turn again to the matter of the scrolls.

To satisfy Metropolitan Samuel's impatience for the results of our study, I had promised him a written preliminary report as soon as possible. It now seemed important to prepare it. That evening I started to draft a statement which would give some of the information he sought, but emphasized mainly our continuing interest and assurance of full cooperation. Brownlee's and my convictions concerning the antiquity of the scrolls, however, I deliberately omitted. Since it appeared that Burrows was unconvinced, my earlier concerns about persuading scholars had already been confirmed. It would not be dishonest, I reasoned, to refrain from revealing my own convictions to the Syrians. The document was completed early the next morning (March 1).[1]

*Oldest extant Torah Codex copied by Aaron Ben Asher about A.D. 900.
(British Museum, Or. 4445, courtesy of the Trustees.) See Chapter 2.*

*Dr. Millar Burrows and three students in the library of the A.S.O.R. in
Jerusalem, 1948. See Chapter 1.*

St. Mark's Syrian Orthodox Monastery on "Zion's Hill" of the Old City of Jerusalem (telephoto view). See Chapter 3.

Butrus Sowmi (with 1QpHab), Metropolitan Samuel, and the author (with 1QIs⁽ᵃ⁾) at the A.S.O.R. on February 21, 1948. See Chapter 4.

The A.S.O.R. on Saladin Road north of the Old City of Jerusalem (in the Sheikh Jarrah Quarter).

The Great Isaiah Scroll (1QIs^a) opened to Columns XXXII-XXXIII containing Isa. 38:8–40:28. Lines 2 and 3 on the left contain Isa. 40:3 which inspired the founding of the Community that produced the Scrolls.

1QIsᵃ Column 6 with small fragment that added five letters to the last three lines, where Isa. 7:14 appears. See Chapter 14.

1QIs^a Cols. XI-XIII showing evidence of the long use of the MS in ancient times. The boxed word in Col. XII, l.7 provides a correction for the text of Isa. 14:4.

The "Genesis Apocryphon" Scroll with (a) some small fragments, (b) a large fragment from the softer back side.

(a)   *(b)*

The second-century-B.C. Nash Papyrus with the Ten Commandments and Deuteronomy 6:4. (Courtesy of the Cambridge University Library.)

An end view of the "Genesis Apocryphon" showing the white interleaving leather. See Chapter 14.

The *"Rule of the Community"* (1QS), Column VIII, on the right margin of which can be seen the joining point of the two sections. See Chapter 5.

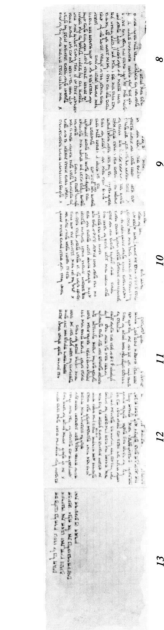

The "Habakkuk Pesher" including the fragment recovered on March 25, 1948. See Chapter 10.

Before leaving for the Monastery to show Burrows the scrolls, I finished splicing together the prints of the Isaiah Scroll. This miniature scroll, I was certain, would impress and delight the Metropolitan. In the meantime Burrows went to get a pass from the Arab Higher Committee to gain admittance to the Old City.

At the Monastery we were most cordially received, as usual. Presenting my statement, I explained that it was merely a "preliminary report" to keep them informed of our progress. The Metropolitan's enthusiastic reaction to the miniature scroll made from the photographs justified my efforts to construct it. Though less than a third the size of the original, it made an impressive scroll which could actually be read if one's eyes could stand the strain. A set of prints of each of the other scrolls was also presented to him.

The Syrians readily offered to show Burrows the scrolls. He examined each one intently but with very little comment. When he came to the small fragment belonging to the fourth scroll, he noted the letters *l'r"* and exclaimed, "This is Aramaic!" What I had thought might be true while examining the color photograph the previous Thursday, and had failed to follow up, now was confirmed. The large, tightly rolled scroll, to which I was still confident this fragment belonged, must therefore be Aramaic. The full import of that little discovery was to be long in coming to light, unfortunately (see p. 131).

Having been assured by a photo dealer in the Old City the previous Saturday that a supply of large film could be obtained, my next move was to convince the Metropolitan that a second set of negatives for the Isaiah and Habakkuk scrolls was necessary. Opening the small scroll of photographs to illustrate the great magnification that would be necessary, I urged him to allow us to redo the two scrolls with large film. Dr. Burrows agreed that we should strive for a high-quality publication and lent support to my urging. He assured the Syrians that the A.S.O.R. would provide the necessary funds to carry out the project properly. The Metropolitan maintained some hesitancy, but we left feeling that the point had been won.

With the manuscripts now available to us in photographic form, we agreed that the courses begun the previous October should be dropped, except for Burrows' lectures on the topography of the Bible. On alternate days, therefore, we concentrated all our academic efforts toward translating the scrolls. Brownlee worked on the "Habakkuk Commentary," and I on the "Sectarian Document." Since October, Brownlee and I had studied Hebrew epigraphy under Burrows' guidance. We had worked through the Mesha, Siloam, and the other earliest-known Hebrew inscriptions. The Christmas holidays intervened just as we had begun to translate the Ugaritic Keret Legend[2] from photostats made for us at the Museum. All these sessions had been a valuable prelude to these new studies. Now we met every other afternoon for almost two hours to discuss the scrolls. Seldom has a graduate seminar had the exciting privilege of analyzing ancient Biblical manuscripts never before translated. Ours was unique.

Sometime early that week an incident occurred in the School library which assured me that Burrows was rapidly becoming convinced about the antiquity of the scrolls. While seeking some published Hebrew paleographic evidences, Burrows and I were checking the shelves when he found a reproduction of the Dura Fragment.[3] Pointing to some of the letters, he remarked, "Your scrolls are certainly older than this." His cautious approach to the matter was a testimony to his pre-eminent scholarship.[4]

Between classes that week I spent most of my time in the Old City making the rounds of the photo shops to see if any 13 x 18 centimeter film had been found. It soon became apparent that every photo dealer was scouring every other photo shop to get the coveted film. Monday afternoon and Tuesday morning (March 1 and 2, 1948) I heard the same story — "We will have some by tomorrow." Discouraged by the series of unfulfilled promises, on Tuesday I went to Raad's shop to get the 9 x 12 centimeter film he was holding for me.

Early Wednesday morning I was again in the Old City. One shop had been particularly certain that the film I wanted would be available. As I entered the shop, the proprietors were beaming with cordiality. Their smiles soon gave way to apologies; the film was not there yet. They pleaded with me to wait a little while; a boy had just gone to get it. They served me coffee and tried to make conversation, but I paced the shop impatiently. Presently the boy burst into the shop, gleefully waving two boxes of film.

I examined the unfamiliar gray boxes. "Gevaert, Studio-film,

Ultra Panchro Normal, Made in Belgium," the labels read. "This is portrait film," I exclaimed, as once again my heart sank. Furthermore, I needed six dozen, not two. This was the only kind of film available in all Jerusalem, they claimed. They had scoured the city thoroughly. Four more boxes would be there the next day, they assured me. But then my eye caught a stamped date on one of the boxes — "Sep 1947." My disappointment exploded. This film was long outdated, besides being good only for portraiture! Whoever heard of photographing ancient manuscripts on outdated portrait film?

Trying to conceal my disappointment, I groped for a decision. *Should I give up, or try using such impossible film?* I had worked with films unsuited to specific jobs before. Perhaps this film could be adapted to the situation, I reasoned; and six months was not too long after the expiration date, if the film had been in a cool, dry place. I decided to take the chance.

How much did they want for it? I inquired. One Palestinian pound (about $3.65) per package was the immediate reply. I was dumbfounded. Normally, outdated film could be purchased for half-price in the States, and film as far outdated as this would be thrown away by any respectable dealer. But here they were asking twice the normal price! I wondered if they had stated this price to begin the usual Oriental bargaining. Offering them half a pound per package, I emphasized the worthlessness of the film; but they were adamant. They did not want to bargain, I could quickly see. Realizing that business was at a standstill without tourists in troubled Jerusalem, I did not have the heart to press the matter. They were as desperate as I was. I paid the £P2 and promised to return for the other four packages the next day.

Shaken with discouragement, I made my way to St. Mark's Monastery to deliver a special cardboard box I had made the night before to protect the "Fourth Scroll," as we called it. The Metropolitan was alone in his office when I arrived, Sowmy having left for a few days of vacation. This was the first time he was absent from our interviews, and I missed his help as interpreter.

With the scroll and small fragment lying before us, I cautiously approached the problem of opening the poorly preserved document. Burrows and I had agreed that in view of the rapidly disintegrating circumstances all around us, we should make the attempt to photograph whatever could be preserved from the scroll. Who could tell what might happen to it any day? The reasons I advanced seemed to impress the Metropolitan, and we concluded that I should proceed with the work as soon as possible.

First, however, the Isaiah and Habakkuk scrolls must be rephotographed. Would he bring the scrolls to our School on Friday? I inquired, assuring him that at last the film was available. Carefully concealing my trepidation concerning the nature of the film, I showed him the two boxes purchased earlier that day. He agreed to bring the scrolls to the School on Friday. Gleeful over both the promise to let me work on the Fourth Scroll and the assurance that I could soon rephotograph the others, I hastened back to the School to begin the necessary preparations.

Early on Thursday I was again in the Old City to retrieve the rest of the film. To my confoundment the drama of the previous day was repeated: again the film was not there; again there was a long delay as the shopkeeper tried to smooth my ruffled feelings with the usual excuses; finally the boy arrived with the four packages of film. Hastily I examined each one. Two were of similar make to the ones purchased the day before, but the date was "Jul 1946," almost two years outdated! Two others were a Kodak portrait film of about the same vintage. Again I remonstrated over the price, for I was sure that only a portion of such old film would be usable. Again they were adamant, and reluctantly I gave them the £P4. As much disgusted with my own inability to cope with Arab business methods as with being robbed in such a way, I stomped angrily out of the shop. I strode rapidly toward Raad's shop on Jaffa Road, wondering if I were destined for failure in this most important task.

Having found a photo tank of sufficient capacity to develop these large films at our School, I sought Raad's help for an adequate quantity of developer in which to immerse the films. Furthermore, I must have a high-contrast, yet fine-grain developer to overcome the low contrast of portrait film. Raad did not have the formula for "D-11" developer which I suggested, but he assured me he could mix up a good fine-grain developer of adequate contrast for my purpose. He would have a gallon ready Friday morning, he promised.

A cold, steady rain was falling Friday morning (March 5), but I determined to go to St. Mark's Monastery anyway. Folding some newspapers to make a semblance of an umbrella (an item not to be found at the School), I started toward the door. Burrows followed me, trying to dissuade me from going; he was concerned for my safety as well as for my health. I argued with him. I had to get the scrolls and the developer to proceed with the rephotographing. Then he told me that the American consul general had advised us all to leave, in view of the mounting hostilities. Our safety was in jeopardy, and the consul could not help us.

I was still determined. As I opened the door, Burrows said, "Remember the word *Mesichi*, John." As I hurried off in the rain, I wondered why he had told me that Arabic word. Suddenly it dawned on me — it is the same as *Mashiach* in Hebrew, the word for "Messiah"; it is the equivalent of "Christian," a Greek word. I found myself saying on numerous occasions thereafter, *Ana Americani Mesichi* ("I am an American Christian").

That day I did not need to use the word. It was not even necessary to show my passes, for the barriers were mostly deserted. The officials must have reasoned that no one would start trouble on such a nasty day. By the time I reached the Monastery, I was dripping wet. The Syrians lighted a kerosene stove in the Metropolitan's office and brought me hot coffee.

My discomforts were soon forgotten, for early in the conversation I mentioned what Burrows had told me — that all Americans were being asked to leave Palestine. Their response jolted me. They began to plead with me not to leave; for, they said, they were counting on me for further help. I was amazed, for I had assumed my work would be finished as soon as the scrolls were rephotographed. Some moments passed as the Metropolitan and Butrus Sowmy, who had returned the day before, conversed in Arabic. I waited expectantly.

Slowly and deliberately Sowmy began: "We have been keeping something from you, Doctor John, until we were certain we could trust you. The scrolls have not been in our Monastery for forty years, as I told you. They were purchased last August from some Bedouins who live near Bethlehem."[5] He went on to say that Father Yusif, a priest of the Monastery, had gone with the Bedouins to visit the cave from which the scrolls had come. Its location he designated only as "near 'Ain Feshkha by the Dead Sea." There he had seen one of the jars in which the scrolls had been found, and many fragments of broken ones. Also, there was a pile of small fragments and cloth wrappings which the Bedouins had tossed aside as worthless.

Two of the jars had been taken to Bethlehem by the Bedouins and were being used as water jars, he continued. Ever since I had mentioned the value of the jars for dating the manuscripts that first day when I visited the Monastery, they had been trying to obtain the jars, he said. They had contacted the Bedouins, but had failed to get the jars.[6] It was their plan, the Metropolitan interjected, as soon as things quieted down in the country, to go to the cave again, and they were eager to have me go with them! The cave, which had previously appeared so remotely significant, suddenly rocketed into prominent focus.

All the more like a tale out of *Arabian Nights,* their story threw me into a state of confusion. Questions flooded my mind, but until I had time for reflection, little could be gained from raising them. Thus I turned the conversation to the major purpose of my visit that morning — to take the Isaiah and Habakkuk scrolls to our School for rephotographing.

Sowmy decided to accompany me, for which I was most thankful. I had not relished the thought of carrying such valuable documents alone through the Old City of Jerusalem so fraught with dangers. Departing through the Jaffa Gate, we went to Raad's shop for the gallon of developer. It was ready, as promised, so within minutes we hailed a taxi and were on our way to the School. With the scrolls safely secluded in the office of the School, Sowmy bade me farewell, promising to return for them on Monday.

Racing across the courtyard, I burst into the Director's apartment to unfold the latest news to Burrows. He, too, seemed dazed by the revelation. If the cave had been so recently discovered by Bedouins, it was a matter of archeological urgency to get there to prevent further damage. Excavation would require the permission of the Department of Antiquities. What should be our next steps?

9

Planning an Expedition

BEING VERY much occupied with the affairs of the School on his return from Baghdad, Burrows left the negotiations concerning the scrolls in my hands. I kept him well informed of my discussions with the Syrians, but there were many details which did not seem important enough at the time to communicate. The new revelation about the scrolls received on March 5, however, prompted much discussion in the Director's apartment the next morning.

Excavation of the cave was now imperative, but excavations take time to prepare. Much careful planning is necessary; yet we were already being asked by our American consul to leave. This was no time to plan an expedition. Time was running out.

Even if there had been no dangers, our position, we realized, was difficult. The scrolls were the possession of the Syrians. Our privileges with the documents depended on their good will, which we had carefully cultivated. They alone knew the location of the cave; that it was somewhere in the vicinity of 'Ain Feshkha was all we knew. As an archeological institution the American School could not conduct an excavation without the permission of the government Department of Antiquities. The Syrians, however, were clearly opposed to working in cooperation with that Department.[1]

To publish the manuscripts, we needed to preserve the friendship of the Syrians. The country was reaching a state of anarchy as the Mandate Government was withdrawing. Many functions of the government had been turned over to the Arabs, as I had discovered when I went to get a bread ration renewed more than two weeks before. Were the antiquities laws really in force? Saving the scrolls and their place of origin for scholarship seemed of primary importance. One conclusion was clear. We must try to get the Syrians to take us to the cave. It was agreed, therefore, that I should discuss the procedure privately with Director of Antiquities Hamilton.[2]

Further discussion regarding an expedition to the cave had to wait. We could have the scrolls at the School for only three days. Every effort must be bent toward getting the kind of negatives that high-quality publication demanded — with outdated portrait film! The rest of Friday and all day Saturday (March 5-6) were devoted completely to that task.

The School was equipped with a fine Zeiss 13 x 18 centimeter view camera for archeological purposes. With its excellent Zeiss lens, high-quality copies could be made, given the proper film. Everything was now in readiness for the first tests. A sheet of film from the oldest box was loaded in a holder. With one exposure made, I immediately developed it in total darkness, using the tray method. When the negative was fully developed, black fog penetrated some two inches into the film, leaving only the center usable, and even there the contrast was very poor.

A sheet of film from the very center of the same package, however, provided only a very narrow strip of fog around the outer edges. My hopes began to rise. About half the films in that box could be used. There would be barely enough film, assuming that the two more recently dated boxes would be entirely good. Hopefully I figured on eight usable sheets from each of the other boxes.

Soon twenty exposures were ready to develop in the large tank. But when the films cleared in the hypo bath, it became obvious that even the usable ones were very much lacking in contrast. Perhaps it was Raad's developer. Another test had to be run.

With the holders reloaded, I made another test exposure. This was developed in a tray of D-76, the only other film developer available. To my amazement and joy, it showed a marked improvement in contrast. But there was only one way to proceed — develop six films at a time in a tray. The process would be tedious, but it promised results.

Except for carrying water and a few other minor jobs, there was little anyone else could do to help me in the exacting task. Therefore, I worked mostly alone. By 10:30 that night I could go on no longer. All the next day the same arduous procedure continued. It was a relief, on Saturday afternoon, to use the smaller film and camera for the Habakkuk Commentary copies. With each column of that manuscript on a sheet of film, beautiful negatives resulted. Besides, Raad's film was not outdated.

With only one more day to keep the scrolls, there was yet another project I was determined to complete — a full-color reproduction of the Isaiah and Habakkuk scrolls. The color transparencies of the "Sectarian Document" had convinced me that similar transparencies of the other scrolls were imperative. For detailed study they would be priceless, perhaps as valuable as having the scrolls themselves.

I still had on hand fifty-four color sheet-films, exactly enough to do the Isaiah Scroll. With no chemicals mixed, not even a test exposure could be developed, for that would take four hours. There was hardly time to do that and make all the exposures before the manuscripts had to be returned. All fifty-four sheets would have to be exposed without developing even one.

For the Habakkuk Commentary it was necessary to start using a supply of another film, Kodak Ektachrome, which had been on the market for only a few months. Several packages had been ordered the previous summer but failed to arrive by the time I left New York. Interminable difficulties arose over getting the film to Palestine and through customs at the Lydda Airport, where it finally arrived. Now, perhaps, it would prove worthy of the efforts we had expended to get it. Sunday evening I studied the instructions which accompanied each box, realizing that there would be no chance for test-developing or retakes. By the time the Syrians came for the scrolls Monday afternoon, therefore, the Habakkuk Scroll had also been recorded in color, but without certainty of the results.[3]

When the Syrians arrived to pick up the two scrolls on March 8, they brought "Jerusalem Scroll I" (the "Sectarian Document") and the "Fourth Scroll," as we had requested. We wanted to check some points on the former, raised in the course of class discussions of our attempted translations. Furthermore, our plan was to begin to work then on unrolling the "Fourth Scroll." In the meantime, however, Sowmy had urged the Metropolitan to withdraw his permission to unroll that scroll. We were disappointed when they announced their decision, but agreed with their claim that we had plenty to keep us busy. They did consent to leave the scroll with us until the end of the week.

That evening I examined the "Fourth Scroll" in minute detail, attempting by measurements to calculate the extent of its contents. There might be as many as 400 lines of text, I estimated, if the scroll could be opened without too much damage.[4] Though it would be a delicate task, I felt confident that it could be opened without too much loss.[5] A peculiar kind of disintegration along the inscribed lines was particularly puzzling, for none of the other documents exhibited a similar phenomenon. To what extent the interior had been affected by it, we could only speculate. At many points deep cracks penetrated several layers of the thin leather.

For the next two days I remained at the School, unable to do more than attend classes and study, with intermittent periods of rest. Having broken out with boils, which called to mind a serious abscess I had suffered the previous October, I felt weak and enervated.

Since we could not open the "Fourth Scroll," I spent much of Wednesday studying it as I rested, wondering if there might be a place on the tightly rolled scroll where some of the script could be clearly seen. While gently probing the softer side near the center, I discovered a jagged vertical crack two inches long which formed a line of demarcation between the brittle, disintegrated part and the softer part. It joined an irregular horizontal crack which ran almost across the width of the scroll to another irregular vertical crack. As I gently lifted the thin brown leather at the point where the two cracks met, the leather at the other end of the vertical crack suddenly gave way, and a fragment 2 inches wide by 3½ inches long broke loose from across the entire width of the scroll.

Five lines of text plus fragments of two other lines from the right half of a column, including the right margin, were now exposed. The script, written on the hair side of the skin, was clearer than on the small fragment we had puzzled over and failed to decipher. It was obviously the same script. The expression *wl' mn kwl* ("and not from any") appeared three times on the fourth line and seemed obviously Hebrew, but there were other clearly

Aramaic words on the fragment. Several words defied decipherment. The script ran together at crucial points, where the leather appeared to have taken the ink like a blotter. All the script was quite different in this regard from the other scrolls, for its lines were heavier, as though the scribe had used a dull-pointed reed pen.[6] The usual lines of ruling, made with a pointed stylus, both for the margins and to guide the script, showed prominently.

An earlier hasty conclusion that this manuscript might be somewhat older than the Isaiah Scroll I could now clearly see was wrong. The script was paleographically more developed. It represented a later period, more like the late corrector's hand on the Isaiah manuscript. Closer scrutiny left the impression that it belonged chronologically with the Habakkuk Scroll. Nothing on this fragment seemed to provide any clues for identification. That it was not Biblical became clear as soon as I tried to trace some of its phrases through a concordance. Here was apparently another sectarian document.

By Thursday morning (March 11) I felt well enough to photograph the "Fourth Scroll" and the newly removed fragment. With both color and black-and-white film, end views as well as back and front views of the scroll and both fragments were recorded.

Meanwhile the formidable task of making four sets of prints from the new Isaiah Scroll negatives prompted me to appeal to Burrows for help. He agreed to provide funds to have the prints made, if Raad could undertake the task. There was no question about the reliability of Raad, but the location of his shop on Jaffa Road gave me some concern for the safety of the negatives. The great respect which he commanded among both Arabs and Jews, however, was in itself a protection. With a boxful of the Isaiah Scroll negatives in hand, I walked to his shop that same morning to discuss the project with him. He was, of course, most happy for the business and assured me that he could handle the large number of prints safely and quickly. It was agreed that the negatives should be delivered to him in groups, as he was able to work on them.

The rest of that day and evening were spent working on the translation of "Jerusalem Scroll I." Gradually the nature of this scroll was becoming clear. In our class discussions we struggled particularly with the meaning of the word *yaḥad*, which occurred repeatedly as a noun. No meaning found in Biblical usage seemed to fit. Brownlee suggested the translation "community," and Burrows "communion." Burrows had suggested that the document read considerably like the book of Deuteronomy, but now we concluded it was a sort of code-book of some esoteric community or Jewish sect, perhaps the Essenes. Later, Burrows likened the document to the Methodist "Discipline," and that name seemed to fit best. Thus we began to call it the "Manual of Discipline."

During our class discussions the problem of the paleography of the scrolls arose repeatedly. Brownlee had examined some ossuary[7] inscriptions at the Museum that week and claimed that they convinced him the scrolls could not be later than the first century A.D. This, too, made me eager to visit the Museum again.

Friday morning was my first opportunity to get there. While waiting for an appointment with Hamilton, I examined the ossuaries in the Roman section of the North Gallery and found two with names incised in Hebrew. One of them had been inscribed by a semi-skilled hand, the other with a crude cursive. A similarity to the script on our scrolls was immediately apparent, especially the final *M* and *T*. Later that morning I examined many other ossuaries stored in another part of the Museum. The great irregularity of the script, the obviously unskilled hands that produced most of them, and the medium in which they were incised made comparison difficult and conclusions from them hazardous. There was no doubt, however, that here was important additional evidence to consider.[8]

When I saw Hamilton, unfortunately I failed to tell him about the newly revealed date of the discovery.[9] Our discussion centered around the problem of excavating the cave, not its discovery. Referring to the apparent reluctance of the Syrians to cooperate with the Department of Antiquities, I emphasized the dilemma created by our working with the Syrians in this project without permission from his Department. We considered it very important, I continued, to maintain the friendship of the Syrians; and thus my visit with him was without their knowledge. My main question was, how could we proceed without violating the law? Though many other details of that discussion are lost to my memory, I vividly recall these points and his suggestions: he said that I should go with the Syrians to the cave and "photograph everything *in situ*," i.e., without disturbing anything. Then, if there were any potsherds or other objects on the surface, we should gather them together carefully and take them to the American School. Finally, we were to report back to him so that he could go to the School to see what had been found.[10]

With the way cleared for us to visit the cave legally, I hastened to St. Mark's Monastery to discuss the matter with the Syrians. At the same time I returned the "Manual of Discipline" to them, as promised. Cautiously I approached the subject of going to the cave as soon as possible. Soon we would have to leave Palestine, I emphasized, and we were anxious to see the project through to completion. Their response was one of concern for our safety; they did not think it possible at that time to get to the cave without serious danger. We would have to go through Jewish-controlled Kallia near the potash factory by the Dead Sea. I recognized, of course, that they knew more about the circumstances surrounding the cave than I; therefore, I decided not to continue the discussion that day.

Interruptions in the pursuit of matters relating to the scrolls and their study were now frequent as the urgency to leave the country became pressing. Our efforts to arrange for transportation were almost frenzied. No word had reached me since October about my reservation from England. Our state of confusion increased with all the confusion around us. We jumped from one thing to another, trying to take advantage of what opportunities were open to us. Research was decidedly intermittent.

During that week, as a result of some further study on paleography, I had abandoned my theory about the scrolls being deposited in the cave during the persecutions of Antiochus between 175 and 168 B.C. That would have meant that the latest of the scrolls, such as the Habakkuk Commentary, the "Fourth Scroll," and the corrector's hand on the Isaiah Scroll, must also date from before 175 B.C. These latter certainly were not that close to the Edfu Papyri, or even the Nash. From a paleographic standpoint the period of about 100 B.C. to A.D. 50 seemed much more feasible. Also I began to feel that the Isaiah Scroll was not as old as the Nash Papyrus, contrary to what I had suggested in my letter to Albright. Association of the deposit, therefore, with the revolt of the Jews in A.D. 66-70, as suggested by Ibrahim Sowmy, now seemed much more likely.

At noon Saturday, as had been agreed the previous day, I met the Syrian guard at the New Gate. I was carrying the "Fourth Scroll" snugly in its box under my arm. When I handed the scroll to the Metropolitan, he informed me that plans were already being made for him to visit the Syrian communities in the United States. At that time, he assured me, we could arrange for proper treatment of the scroll. It was then agreed that I should retain the two fragments, which I had mounted between pieces of glass, for further study and preparation in the United States.[11]

Again I had hoped to bring up the matter of visiting the cave, but on arrival I had been introduced to a British officer who was making a routine visit to the Monastery. He was in charge of the Mandate forces at Jaffa Gate. A lively conversation ensued, quite unrelated to the scrolls. By the time the officer was ready to leave, it was so near lunchtime at our School that I left with him. As we sauntered up King David Street toward the Jaffa Gate, he continued to relate stories about the interminable problems involved in his administration of that troublesome sector of the Old City. His experiences punctuated the frightful dilemma which the British were facing as they prepared to relinquish the Mandate. I felt a new admiration for them in the face of such a thankless, heartrending task.

Further insights into local problems came from a discussion that evening with Anwar Tamimi, Secretary of the Muslim Supreme Council and a temporary resident at the School. Strange sounds from underground were being heard each night near the Haram. The Supreme Council officers were worried about the possibility of Jews tunneling under the Haram from the Jewish Quarter. Together, in the School library, we examined detailed archeological maps of the Old City, and the many underground channels which we discovered on the maps appeared to justify their concerns.

A bitter cold rain again descended upon Jerusalem during the night, and I remained at the School for the next two days, devoting my time to study, completing the color-developing, and writing letters. On Monday morning (March 15) the mail arrived with the long-awaited reply from Albright (my letter to him had not arrived in Baltimore until March 8). Starting on the wrong side of an air-letter, he wrote:

Dear Trever,

Your air-letter of Feb. 25th, with its enclosures, arrived this morning and I immediately got out my magnifying glass and started in. I am now having the prints enlarged so I can study the script to better advantage. My heartiest congratulations on the greatest MS discovery of modern times! There is no doubt whatever in my mind that the script is more archaic than that of the Nash Papyrus, standing very close to that of the third-century Egyptian papyri and ostraca in Aramaic. Of course, in the present state of our definite knowledge about Hebrew paleography it would be safe only to date it in the Maccabaean period, *i.e.*, not later than the accession of Herod the Great. I should prefer a date around 100 B.C. The script is in every respect older than that of the Dura parchment fragment.

In my excitement I began writing on the wrong side of the sheet! I repeat that in my opinion you have made the greatest MS discovery of modern times — certainly the greatest biblical MS find. The spelling is most interesting, resembling that of the Nash Papyrus very closely. The tendency to hyper-correction in writing כי as כיא is most extraordinary. Burrows will now have a chance to forget the events in Palestine for a while. Let us hope that nothing happens to your precious finds!

I don't anticipate any very significant textual corrections of the text of Isaiah, but the new material will revolutionize our conception of the development of Hebrew orthography. And who knows what treasures may be concealed in the remaining rolls!
. . . .

It is a very fine thing that you have been able to get such an important result as this discovery from your difficult year in Jerusalem. You can imagine how my eyes bulged when I saw the script through my magnifying glass! What an absolutely incredible find! And there can happily not be the slightest doubt in the world about the genuineness of the MS.
. . . .

Cordially,

W. F. Albright

His exuberance amazed and delighted me. Racing down the stairs with the letter, I burst into the Director's apartment. Breathlessly I read it to Burrows. His response, as usual, was reserved but obviously enthusiastic.[12] When I read the words about forgetting the events in Palestine, however, his comment was, "Little does Albright know." That very day it was rumored that our water supply had been poisoned! Bombings and gun battles by then were nightly affairs, as anarchy seemed to be closing in upon us. Every day we were forcefully reminded of the troubled present as we ventured into the exciting ancient past.

That evening as I examined a map of the area around 'Ain Feshkha by the Dead Sea, a sudden inspiration struck me. We could avoid the danger zone south of Jericho which worried the Syrians. Nebi Musa, an isolated Muslim sacred shrine in the desert northwest of 'Ain Feshkha, was within walking distance of the cliffs among which the cave was located. If we could make our headquarters at Nebi Musa, we could approach the cave from the plateau above. Hastening to Anwar Tamimi's room, I broke in on his study to share the idea. He looked at the small map I carried and agreed that such an approach was possible. He said he knew the man in charge at the Nebi Musa shrine and was certain he could arrange for us to stay there.

In the School library were large survey maps showing clearly every feature of the country in detail. Examining the area on these, I found a trail leading from Nebi Musa directly to the point above where I thought the cave must be. There were some steep parts, but with donkeys we could maneuver the terrain. With this plan, perhaps, the Syrians might be persuaded to take us there.

Again I sought Burrows. He looked at the detailed maps and exclaimed, "There must be a hitch in this whole thing somewhere." He would unfortunately be proved right.

10

First News Released to the World

A SNOWSTORM in Jerusalem is a rarity, but the cold drizzle that had persisted all day (March 15) turned to snow during the night. Jerusalem and the Mount of Olives, blanketed with snow the next morning, were sights of amazing beauty. Our cameras were swiftly put into action.

Arab children, on their way to school, exhibited an ecstasy of delight. Mahmud, frustrated with concern over the School garden, went about with a broom, knocking the fluffy white from bushes and hedges. Some of it he gathered into a small snowman, complete with simulated corncob pipe, for another servant's children,[1] who danced around it with ecstatic glee. As the sun broke through the clouds, about mid-morning, the fairyland all about us soon evaporated. It was winter's last thrust, for by the end of the week we were favored with the full bloom of spring.

With letters to mail at the post office, more Isaiah Scroll negatives to deliver to Raad, prints to pick up, and another visit to St. Mark's Monastery on my schedule, I set out for town. At the Monastery I was deterred from plunging immediately into discussing our plans for visiting the cave. The Metropolitan had just purchased a camera from Raad and wanted me to show him how to use it. Eager to be cooperative, I proceeded with a lesson in the fundamentals of candid photography.

Confident that our new plan for getting to the cave would win the full cooperation of the Metropolitan, I outlined it in detail, tracing on a small map the proposed route of approach from Nebi Musa. My enthusiastic presentation met with a cool reception.

The Metropolitan, it seemed, wanted to accompany the expedition to the cave; for the spiritual leader of the Syrians, such a route would be too arduous and hazardous, Sowmy explained. Furthermore, he reiterated, if we waited until the troubles were over, we could approach the cave quite easily from the Jordan Valley. Discouraged, and puzzled by their reluctance, I returned to our School.

Immediately I discussed the situation with Burrows, and we decided that probably the time had come to reveal to the Syrians the importance of their manuscripts. We decided, therefore, to work out a typed statement about the scrolls in the form of a news release. Burrows then invited the Metropolitan to the Director's apartment Thursday morning.

Wednesday evening (March 17) I prepared a suggested draft of the statement, in which our convictions regarding the great age of the Syrians' scrolls were emphasized. Burrows revised it and typed several copies for the meeting the next morning. As we worked, several thunderous explosions followed by gunfire north of our School reminded us that time was running out.

Metropolitan Samuel arrived promptly at 10:30 the next morning and was ushered into the Director's sitting room, where Burrows and I awaited him. When the Metropolitan was comfortably seated beside a crackling fire, Burrows handed him a copy of the news release to read. He explained that we would like his permission to release the statement to the press in America. Silence ensued as the Metropolitan looked over the words for more than a minute. Returning the paper to Burrows, he asked him to read it aloud; he could understand it better that way, he said. As Burrows read, the Metropolitan's eyes began to sparkle with obvious delight. Slowly he lifted himself to an erect position on the edge of the overstuffed chair; when Burrows had barely finished, he exclaimed proudly, "I want you to know that these are *my* scrolls!"

Recovering from our amazement at the nature of his response, we indicated some of our reasons for believing that the Isaiah Scroll was the oldest known existing copy of a book of the Bible. Again we raised the matter of the safety of the scrolls, which once before had failed to make an impression on the Syrians. Such valuable scrolls were not safe in their Monastery, we emphasized. Remembering their monastery near the Jordan River at the traditional site of the baptism of Jesus, I suggested that perhaps there was some safe place there to secrete the scrolls from wartorn Jerusalem. With our joint emphases and his sudden awareness of the great value of the scrolls, our concerns obviously registered more deeply. He assured us that the scrolls would be removed to a place of safety.

Burrows then pursued the matter of publishing the scrolls and invited the Metropolitan to the School library to see some of the publications of the A.S.O.R. The library deeply impressed the Metropolitan. Burrows drew several of the many A.S.O.R. volumes from the shelves to show him. Then, opening the huge volume of government survey maps lying on a large table, I traced the route from Nebi Musa to 'Ain Feshkha and again urged the importance of visiting the cave as soon as possible. Burrows stressed the urgency of gathering materials which might strengthen our dating of the scrolls before the scholarly world. Since the weather seemed to be breaking, we said we would like to make arrangements to go the following week. Again the Metropolitan seemed hesitant.

Burrows that afternoon dispatched the news release with a letter of instructions to the A.S.O.R. office in New Haven, Connecticut. The first public announcement about the great discovery was on its way to the United States. (It was not released, however, until April 11.)

Again that night a furious exchange of gunfire took place close to our School, following a violent explosion. During the morning's interview a call had come from the travel agency reporting that they had at last obtained a reservation for me on the *Queen Elizabeth* from London to New York. Amid the din I now pondered my return schedule, and the next morning tried to arrange for transportation to England. Complications were endless; communications with the outside world were poor, and demands for transportation out of the country were many. Visas were required by every country, and took time to procure. Any schedule was at best only tentative.

Arriving in the office of the Metropolitan Friday afternoon (March 19), I found him very agitated. He was worried about the safety of Butrus Sowmy, who had failed to return from Jericho as promised. Furthermore, a Syrian layman had come from the Y.M.C.A. that very morning with a request which greatly disturbed him; he seemed reluctant to talk about it, but made some vague allusions to Jews trying to get the manuscripts. Finally he divulged that Judah Magnes, President of the Hebrew University in Jerusalem, was urgently requesting the Metropolitan to take the scrolls to the Y.M.C.A. for him to see.[2] The Metropolitan seemed to fear that it was some kind of a trick to get the scrolls. Once before an allusion to some Jews' knowing about the scrolls had led me erroneously to think that E. L. Sukenik, Professor of Archaeology at the Hebrew University, was perhaps involved.[3] Wondering if the Syrians were secretly negotiating a sale of the scrolls to the Hebrew University, I asked the Metropolitan directly if Sukenik knew about the scrolls. With some hesitation he revealed that Sukenik had not only seen the scrolls, but also was trying to buy them.[4] The matter had been dropped for some time, he continued, but now Magnes was making new overtures. What should he do?

Knowing nothing of the complex background to the Metropolitan's statements (see pp. 108-110), I could not understand the reasons for his expressed concerns. For him, it seemed to me, the solution was relatively simple: he should report to Magnes that the scrolls were being handled by the A.S.O.R. and that Burrows was the one with whom to discuss the matter. Since both the A.S.O.R. and the Hebrew University, whose opening ceremonies we had attended the previous October, were academic institutions, such a method of handling the problem seemed most logical. Suddenly aware of what a sale of the scrolls then would mean to all our efforts toward publication, I emphasized to the Metropolitan that such a move would be a serious disservice to the A.S.O.R. Thus I laid additional stress on the importance of letting us handle the arrangements.

Seemingly relieved by my suggestion, the prelate voluntarily turned the discussion to visiting the cave. He had a theory, he said, which made him particularly anxious to visit the cave personally — he was confident that the original "Ark of the Covenant"[5] was in that cave! Utterly amazed, I groped for words. What could possibly have led him to such a conclusion? Father Yusif, he explained, when he visited the cave the past summer, had reported seeing in the cave a piece of wood under which was a stone. His theory had developed from this bit of evidence, and he wanted to investigate the matter personally.

This kind of conclusion is always somewhat irritating to one trained in making enthusiasm wait upon proof, and I emphatically warned the Metropolitan that such a procedure would be a

violation of the law. We would have to withdraw all our cooperation if he persisted in such a scheme, I continued. It was then
that I revealed to him the fact that I had already told the whole
story to the Director of Antiquities and had received specific
instructions about how to conduct the visit to the cave.[6] Furthermore, I emphasized, it was impractical to think that anything
else as valuable as the scrolls might be found in the cave. Certainly the Bedouins had already removed the best materials, and
the most we could hope to find would be only fragments and
other insignificant items. The fact that the scrolls clearly showed
the late sectarian nature of the deposit would preclude the discovery of anything belonging to Solomon's Temple, I added. My
torrent of arguments obviously convinced him, for he agreed that
the visit to the cave should be done with the cooperation of the
Department of Antiquities.

Just then Butrus Sowmy arrived from Jericho with reports of
fighting between Jews and Arabs in the region near the cave.
In fact, he added, the Arab tribes in the region were feuding
among themselves. The fears of the Metropolitan were renewed;
my hopes for a visit to the cave began to dwindle. During the
somewhat heated discussion that ensued, a gunfight broke out in
the Old City, not far from St. Mark's Monastery, reminding me
that I was supposed to be back at our School by four o'clock; it
was then five. It was not safe to leave then, so I continued to try to
allay their fears about going to the cave. The conflict so near
their Monastery, furthermore, provided another opportunity to
emphasize the importance of getting the manuscripts to a place of
safety.

As the din of gunfire subsided about 5:30, I insisted on leaving. Again they sent their *kawas* to usher me safely out of the Old
City. We walked in silence along the deserted streets. The steel
corrugated shutters of all the shops along Christian Street were
drawn tight and locked. A deathly stillness pervaded the entire
city, broken only by the echoing clatter of our hard-soled shoes
on the stone pavement. This time the *kawas* insisted on accompanying me outside the New Gate as far as the barbed-wire entrance to the Musrara Quarter midway along Godfrey de Bouillon
Street. There the armed Arab guards checked my pass as we
exchanged the usual friendly greetings, and I hastened alone
toward our School.

Following my usual route between a row of apartment buildings at the north edge of the Musrara Quarter, I emerged onto the open field which separated the buildings from the Nablus Road. Hardly had I taken twenty long strides out into the rough, rocky field, when suddenly — zing! — a bullet whined a few feet above my head. Another zing! — and another! — followed closely. Puffs of smoke from the snipers' guns dotted some buildings directly ahead on the edge of the Mea Shearim Sector. Terrified, I dashed with all the speed I could muster toward Nablus Road and the shelter of the Palestine Pottery Works. My dash was spurred by the sudden fearful recollection that a British woman, on her way to worship at St. George's Cathedral the previous Sunday, had been killed by a sniper within a few feet of the very point where I heard the first bullet pass overhead. Several Arab boys returning from the Ibrahimiyeh College joined me behind the same wall, and we tried to comfort each other with senseless chatter as we crouched there, trembling in fear. The School was plainly visible across another open field. I watched to see if anyone appeared at the gate, so I could signal my dilemma to them. No one appeared.

Some minutes later the shooting subsided, and I made another dash to the gate of our School. Once in my room, I slumped into the chair by my desk, a cold sweat moistening my brow. Psychologically, we were living in Bible times!

With my equilibrium regained, I reported the discussion at the Monastery to Burrows. He suggested trying to contact Magnes immediately, but I urged him to let the Syrians follow my instructions and to await a call from the Hebrew University. Magnes never called.[7]

All Jerusalem was buzzing with excitement early Saturday morning (March 20). During the night, word was broadcast that the United States had reversed its decision regarding Partition. Everyone I met was jubilant. Brownlee reported seeing some Arab boys waving American flags as they raced on scooters down the street near the Y.M.C.A. Besides, the warmth and beauty of spring was in the air.

When I called Anwar Tamimi at the Haram esh-Sharif, he informed me that the Arab in charge of the Nebi Musa shrine was in his office. Burrows and I hastened to Herod's Gate, where we were met by a guard whom Anwar had sent. At the Haram we were ushered into the great Council Chamber; Burrows was offered the seat of honor. Presently Anwar ushered in several Arabs in long robes and *keffiyehs* — obviously men of the desert. Tea and coffee were served before a word was said concerning the purpose of the meeting.

With Anwar as interpreter, we outlined our plan for visiting the cliffs west of 'Ain Feshkha, via the shrine at Nebi Musa. We were deliberately vague about our exact purpose. The Arabs assured us it would not be difficult; the trip could be made in about an hour and a half by donkey, they said. The man in charge of the shrine offered to arrange for donkeys and other needs to be brought from Jericho. He would personally make the trip the next day, he said, since he wanted to investigate a shepherd's complaint in that region, anyway. Thus by Monday he could give us a firsthand report. In answer to my query about Sowmy's reference to Arab feuds, he assured me there were none. He claimed he knew every Bedouin throughout the area. Encouraged by the assurances of the Arabs that our mission from Nebi Musa could be accomplished, Burrows and I returned to the School before noon.

The rejoicing of the Arabs was short-lived, for Partition soon again appeared to be inevitable. The brief respite, however, enabled Brownlee and me to walk to St. Andrew's Church in Zone "A" for their service and for dinner with their pastor on Palm Sunday. The walk both ways was without incident, quite contrary to what we were destined to experience on Easter Sunday.

Impatiently I awaited the report from Nebi Musa on Monday (March 22). None came. Metropolitan Samuel arrived about noon with the Syriac New Testament to permit me to photograph its colorful miniatures. He was having trouble with his camera and left it for me to fix, a task that took the entire evening.

Tuesday morning the Syrians sent a taxi for me to return the New Testament. Having arranged to take a series of pictures in the Monastery, I also carried all my color equipment. On arrival I was surprised to find the man from Nebi Musa talking to the Metropolitan. He had not been able to make the trip, he explained, for it had rained. Discussing the situation with a number of Bedouins, however, he had learned that the Jewish Haganah army occupied all the region around 'Ain Feshkha right up to the base of the cliffs. We would be completely exposed on the cliff if we attempted to descend, he asserted. It was now clear that the expedition would have to be abandoned until peace was restored to the area. The Syrians assured me, however, that they would cooperate fully with the A.S.O.R. when the opportunity to visit the cave became possible.

Discouraged by the frustration of our hopes, I stopped at Raad's shop to find that he had completed all the prints of the new Isaiah and Habakkuk Scroll negatives. This was good news, at least; our photographs were now completed without mishap. Except for our class session, that entire afternoon was devoted to assembling the sets of prints, one for each of us — the Metropolitan, Burrows, Brownlee, and myself.

During the next two days efforts to obtain visas and other details related to our leaving consumed almost all of our time. Thursday (March 25), after a particularly frustrating morning when I tried to secure a visa for England, I returned to the School shortly after noon to learn that the Syrians had again sent their *kawas* with a taxi to conduct me to the Monastery. It was urgent that I go at once, the servants claimed, concerned more about my safety than the Syrians' request. Helen offered to fix lunch forty-five minutes early, so I could be safely back by three o'clock. (By then the almost daily skirmishes began as early as three thirty or four o'clock.) Visions of some tragic accident to the precious scrolls occupied my mind as I hurried my lunch.

Arriving at the Monastery out of breath, hastily I glanced around, almost expecting to see evidence of bomb damage. Then I spotted the Metropolitan standing at the head of the stairway to the balcony; a broad smile lighted up his face. My fears melted into curiosity. As I followed him into his office, a portly stranger in Western clerical garb arose from the settee. He was introduced as the Rev. John S. Malak, formerly of Oregon, and a good friend of the Metropolitan. Little was said, however, for from his desk drawer the Metropolitan drew forth a folded sheet of paper and handed it to me. Opening the paper, I was startled and delighted to see a dark brown fragment of leather, its edges irregularly chewed and several gaping holes breaking its inscribed text.

Immediately its script reminded me of the Habakkuk Commentary. Parts of two columns were inscribed on either side of a margin. The left part, I was sure, would provide the right half of the broken column at the beginning of the scroll, which Brownlee had by then completely translated. Recalling how Brownlee had bewailed the absence of a portion of Habakkuk 1:6, about which a scholarly dispute had arisen, I wondered if this fragment would provide the missing words. The scroll had at least one more column, we now knew.

The Metropolitan said that he had opened a book to read that morning and had discovered the fragment, about which he had completely forgotten. Sowmy, moreover, had left that morning for Beirut with the four precious scrolls. The safety of the manuscripts was by then assured, he said confidently. It was a great relief to know that at last the scrolls were out of strife-ridden Jerusalem. By what route or means of transportation Sowmy had departed, I was not informed. That the manuscripts would be placed in a bank vault in Beirut was all the specific information revealed to me. The fact that removing antiquities from the country without an export license was technically illegal, was totally foreign to my thoughts. I rejoiced to know that the scrolls were safe.[8]

11

Jerusalem, Jerusalem!

EASTER SUNDAY (March 28) dawned clear and warm amid thunderous explosions and exchanges of gunfire not far from our School. Efforts to establish a truce for this holiest day of Jerusalem's Christian calendar had failed. Brownlee and I joined the handful of Christians at the Garden tomb for the traditional sunrise service. Normally, on that occasion, thousands of pilgrims crowded the lovely Garden, which formed a natural amphitheater around the sheer stone cliff with its rock-cut tomb.

Plaintive music from a wheezy reed organ provided little support for the joyous Easter hymns, as halfhearted singers solemnly rendered the victorious notes. Myriad bells from the Old City pealed discordantly during much of the simple service. While a British Army chaplain intoned solemn words of prayer, distant dull thuds of bombs, mingled with the clatter of small arms and machine-gun fire, emphasized his pleas for divine assistance. The urgent words of the Rev. Edwin Moll's sermon were mostly lost amid the sickening jumble of battle and bells.

Hoping once again to attend the St. Andrew's Church service, Brownlee and I started at 10:30 to traverse the city by the route used successfully on Palm Sunday. Descending a broad stairway connecting Jaffa Road and the lower Mamillah Road, we were crossing the latter when suddenly a barrage of gunfire streaked across the Mamillah Cemetery a few hundred yards to our right. Bullets whined above our heads; Arabs, from the tops of the buildings opposite us, returned the barrage. Like dozens of others caught in the cross-fire, we darted into the nearest open doorway. Within a few minutes the firing ceased. Cautiously we emerged from our shelter, hoping to reach a stairway where we could descend into the bombed-out no man's land of the Jewish commercial center. From there we thought it would be safer to get around to Julian's Way and up to the Y.M.C.A. a half mile farther south. We hugged close to the buildings as we approached the Mamillah Cemetery.

We were barely ten paces from the stairway when once again the firing broke out above us. We could see the puffs of smoke near the housetops across the Muslim cemetery. Again we raced to the nearest building entrance, joining a considerable crowd gathered for refuge. Presently, on a stairway directly ahead, who should appear but our good friend Anwar Tamimi! Amazed to see us in the crowd, he motioned us up the stairs. He led us into an office where armed Arab soldiers, whose checkered red *keffiyehs* revealed their Trans-Jordanian origin, were seated along three walls.

Anwar queried us about our purpose in somewhat scolding tones. A little sheepishly we explained our hopes to attend the Easter service at St. Andrew's Church. Promising to help if he could, Anwar chatted in Arabic with the soldiers nearest his desk; a good deal of head-shaking by the soldiers indicated their opposition to his proposal. Being in an office of the Muslim Supreme Council, surrounded by armed Muslim soldiers on Easter Sunday at churchtime, suddenly struck me as ironical. I might have laughed except for the tension of our plight.

In rushed another armed Arab, who spoke excitedly with Anwar. Turning to us, he explained that the battle had now spread to the Montefiore District, making it impossible for us to get to the church. Declining his offer to send a guard with us to the School, we retraced our steps. As we started to cross the Nablus Road by the Palestine Pottery Works, where I had sought refuge from snipers ten days before, Brownlee left me to return to the School. I continued on to St. George's Cathedral.

The service was well under way as I found a seat near the rear of the great nave, whose heavy stone wall seemed particularly welcome. Presently, to my delight, Bishop Stewart rose to preach. It was a brief but pointed sermon, based on the Johannine phrase, "They have taken away my Lord . . ." (John 20:13). Stressing the uniqueness of our experiences, which enabled us to share intensely the frustrations which the disciples must have felt that first Holy Week, the Bishop's consoling words touched each worshiper deeply. After the turmoil of the morning, I felt a strange peace within as I walked slowly back to our School. Still another battle broke out later that day, ending one of the most tragic holy days I have ever known.

Meanwhile our intermittent studies of the scrolls had progressed slowly. Brownlee was pleased to have the additional Habakkuk Scroll fragment, which supplied certain words he had hoped to find. Some scholars many years before had proposed that the book of Habakkuk was written in the late fourth century B.C., and referred in 1:6 to the "Kittim," meaning the Greeks under Alexander the Great; the present reference to the seventh-century B.C. "Chaldeans" (*Kasdim*), they claimed, was a later emendation of the original text. The new leather fragment now provided a first-century B.C. – A.D. testimony to the accuracy of the text as it has been preserved — *Kasdim* was clearly in the text used then by the copyist. The next line, however, begins, "Its interpretation concerns the Kittim. . . ." The modern theory had already been propounded by the ancient community two thousand years earlier!

Saturday, March 27, we held our last class session, during which we discussed the final two columns of the Habakkuk Commentary. Brownlee had, in the meantime, prepared typed copies of a transliterated Hebrew text and his provisional translation for each of us. I regretted my inability to do likewise for the Manual of Discipline, only a few columns of which we had been able by then to translate. Other responsibilities relating to the scrolls had cut too deeply into my study time.

With our plans for an expedition to the cave abandoned, I sought all possible information from the Syrians concerning the cave. One day I questioned Father Yusif at length regarding his visit to the cave with George Isha'ya during August 1947. He reported that there was only a small entrance to the cave, which he said was due to the collapse of the front of the cave during an earthquake.[1] Consequently, he claimed, the scrolls, wrapped in many layers of cloth, were originally found protruding from the debris. He saw the piles of cloth, one complete jar amid much broken pottery, and some fragments of leather scattered on the floor of the cave. He and Isha'ya spent the night just outside the entrance to the cave. The next day they tried to take the one complete jar but found it too much to carry in the August heat.[2]

After repeated interviews with the Syrians, I still found many gaps in the story about the early history of the scrolls. It was to be many months before sufficient evidence could be gleaned to piece together what probably had happened (see the next chapter).[3]

Last-minute preparations to leave were by now underway. Brownlee left from Lydda by plane during a downpour on Tuesday, March 30; Dr. and Mrs. Burrows left in a convoy for Haifa early Friday morning to await a small Norwegian freighter, which failed to dock for two weeks. Scheduled to leave by plane on April 8, I continued to work alone at the School.

On Saturday afternoon the Metropolitan, Butrus Sowmy, and their friend, John Malak, arrived for a final conference. They had come to work out the contract with the A.S.O.R. for publication of the scrolls, they announced. Having been left with no authority, I could do no more than write down items which we agreed should go into the document, with a promise to communicate them to the A.S.O.R. officers in America.

With great solemnity they outlined the various points which they expected to be included in the contract: "1) The owner of the manuscripts is His Grace, Mar Athanasius Yeshue Samuel, Metropolitan of the Jerusalem Syrian Orthodox Church; 2) publisher, the A.S.O.R.; 3) period of agreement, at least three years; 4) the total number of copies printed must be indicated in the volume, and each one must be numbered; 5) several copies should be supplied to the Syrians to use as gifts; 6) if there is a profit from the sale of the volumes, what percentage would revert to the owner?; 7) before publication a copy of the prepared materials is to be sent to the owner for approval."

For the sake of the A.S.O.R. I suggested we add two more points: "8) During the period of the agreement, the rights for publication shall not be transferred to another institution without the consent of the owner, and likewise the owner will not grant any publication rights to any other party or parties during the period of the contract; and 9) if any or all of the manuscripts are sold during the period of the agreement, the purchaser will be bound to allow the same publication rights to continue."

Considerable discussion developed around the sixth point, for the Syrians wanted the matter made specific. It was hard to communicate to them the fact that the kind of publication that would be prepared could not be expected to produce profits. No large volume of sales of such technical books is common; seldom are more than a few hundred copies sold, and those have to be mostly subsidized. The possibility of any profits, I emphasized, was very remote.

Before they left, I urged again the importance of full cooperation with the School on any future visit to the cave. Failure to have an official of the School accompany them, I warned, would be a violation of the agreement worked out with the Department of Antiquities. They assured me that they would cooperate fully. Thus I felt confident that the best possible arrangements had been worked out for the publication of the scrolls and that the cave would suffer no further damage. With many warm and friendly farewells and fond hopes that the strife would soon pass, we parted.[4]

That same day the airline office called, asking me to be ready to leave early Monday morning. If my luggage were reduced to 100 kilograms (about 220 pounds), they said, they would carry it on the same plane. This meant giving Sunday over to repacking. Most of the books I had bought thus had to be sent by mail, despite the uncertainty of postal service, which by then had almost completely collapsed.

At the airline depot near the Y.M.C.A. early Monday, preparations to leave for the airport were complicated and time-consuming. At last I climbed into the airline station wagon for the trip to Lydda. Cautiously the driver made his way through the almost deserted streets of Jerusalem as I craned my neck to gain last fleeting glimpses of the Holy City. The evidences of the many battles were everywhere. Once-beautiful buildings, some barely completed, were now reduced to rubble or filled with jagged holes where windows had once been. Maneuvering the station wagon skillfully through the cement cones that marked the entrance to the Sheikh Jarrah Quarter, the driver nervously hastened through that hotly disputed zone and up the switchback on the south slope of Mount Scopus. At the top, well out of range of Jerusalem's danger zones, he stopped and allowed us to get out for a few minutes. Perhaps he felt the need of a respite after traversing the treacherous route.

As I stood scanning the scene in which I had been engulfed for almost eight months, I was sickened by the sight. There before me lay the results of those incessant conflicts near our School. The new part of Jerusalem was reduced to a ghostly shambles: not a building was unmarred; most were roofless, gutted frames of what once had been homes and shops. I could have taken a picture, but I did not have the heart to record the tragedy of this city which had become such an integral part of my life. Once again, as on a previous occasion when I stood on the Mount of Olives, the words of Jesus, weeping over Jerusalem, seemed to come forth: "Would that even today you knew the things that make for peace! But now they are hid from your eyes" (Luke 19:42, RSV).

Were it not for the grass and wildflowers which grew in rich variety along the side of the road, it would have been hard to believe that this was the height of spring in the Holy Land. Many fields, normally lush with growing grain by this time, were still barren or unkempt. Perhaps their owners had been too busy laying plans to defend their lands from warfare. Down the steep road that follows the rocky, terraced Valley of Aijalon, where once Joshua chased the five kings of the Amorites (Joshua 10:6-14), we plunged toward Lydda on the open plain.

Inside the heavily guarded barrier at the Lydda Airport, the usual complications of travel quickly dispelled my reflections on the tragedy of Palestine. At the customs post my carefully prepared list of contents did not dissuade the official from a thorough search of my luggage. Handing him the papers given to me by Iliffe at the Museum, I explained about the large sealed box of antiquities in my trunk. Looking over the papers, he inquired where my export license was. These were all the papers given me at the Museum, I countered; surely they must include an export license. For a while the situation seemed hopeless, but then he noticed that the Museum had placed a value of less than five dollars on all the items, so he decided to pass the matter by.[5] Later, on boarding the plane, I found my luggage securely strapped directly behind my seat.

With its supercharged motors roaring, the small DC-3 Middle East Airlines plane slowly rose from the runway. Almost immediately the pilot banked toward the west as though impatient to reach the safety of the open Mediterranean Sea, out of range of snipers' bullets. As the ribbon of sandy beach by Tel Aviv swept past below, a wave of relief engulfed me. Suddenly, for the first time since January, I felt safe!

Months of silence now descended upon the story of the scrolls.

12

What Had Happened Before

THROUGH MANY retellings, the fragmentary early published accounts concerning what transpired in the scroll story prior to February, 1948, have become legendary.[1] To gather the evidence and sift the often contradictory information about those obscure events has required many years, but what were probably the essential facts can now be related with a fair degree of certainty. Many details, therefore, are published here for the first time, others are corrected, and still others can now be further clarified. Still other details may never be recovered from their obscurity.

Late in 1945 or early 1946, according to the evidence,[2] a controversy arose among the Syrian Orthodox Christians of Palestine over the handling of a piece of Monastery property located between the Street of the Prophets and the Russian Compound in the western sector of Jerusalem. A small school had been operated there by the Syrian community, but certain business interests wanted to develop the area into commercial buildings. The priests at St. Mark's favored the latter as a source of income for their Monastery; most of the laity, however, wanted the school improved. The priests were planning instead to develop a new school beside the Monastery in the Old City. Considerable heat was generated over the matter, and as a result many lay members of the church became alienated from their religious leaders at the Monastery.

In order to keep harmony in their church, a layman by the name of Anton D. Kiraz attempted to mitigate the tension. A

Cave II   Cave I   Entrance from South

Site of Caves I and II along cliffs above the plateau, one-half-mile north of Khirbet Qumran.

The three Ta'amireh Bedouins who discovered the Cave I Scrolls. L. to r., Jum'a Muhammed, Muhammed Ahmed el Hamed and Khalil Musa. See Chapter 12.

Original entrance to Cave I is to right and above the man's head. The larger entrance below was made in late 1948. See Chapters 12 and 14.

Interior of Cave I where Muhammed found 8-10 tall jars standing to the right and left of the Arab boy. See Chapter 12.

The community kiln and other facilities for making pottery. Excavated at Khirbet Qumran during 1954. See Chapter 16.

Reconstructed jars from Cave I with other artifacts recovered by the excavators in February, 1949. See Chapter 16.

(a)   *Column II*   (b)

(a to d) Liturgical prayer scroll pieced together from the mass of leather fragments. The last line on fragment "d" is the beginning of a "prayer for the Day of Atonement." See Chapter 14.

Mass of nine layers of leather fragments as discovered during the summer of 1948.

(c) Column I (d)

Daniel "A" (1QDan^a) fragments from the two bottom layers of the mass, containing parts of Daniel 1:10–2:6. The Aramaic portion of Daniel begins on line 4 at the left with 2:4b. See Chapter 14.

The area beneath the "Scriptorium" which was on an upper level at Qumran.

Telephoto view of Kh. Qumran (lower right) with Mount Nebo across the Dead Sea (upper left). Did the men of Qumran choose this site to be in the shadow of the place where they believed Moses had written the Torah (Deut. 31:9-13; 24-26)?

*Air view of Qumran community center after completion of five seasons of
excavation, and an official archeologist's sketch of the site. (Courtesy of
Palestine Archaeological Museum.)*

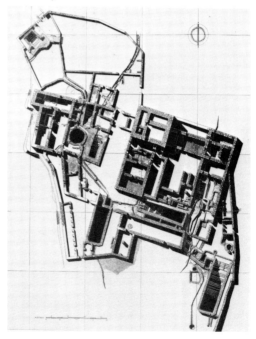

Cave II   Cave I   Cave III   Cave XI

Telephoto view from Kh. Qumran showing cliffs where Caves I, II, III, and XI were discovered.

Cave IV across the ravine to west of Kh. Qumran. Cave V is off the picture, to the right, and Cave VI is in the cliff at the upper left.

dealer in secondhand cars and an operator of a fleet of taxis under the title "Imperial Taxi Service," he had developed a prosperous business and owned one of the finer homes along the old Bethlehem Road just south of the Talpioth Sector of Jerusalem. A great deal of publicity centered around his property in 1945 when E. L. Sukenik excavated a first-century tomb there and found what he then believed to be Christian remains.[3]

When Mar Athanasius Y. Samuel — who had been associated with St. Mark's for many years — was consecrated Metropolitan of Jerusalem by the Patriarch in Homs, Syria, on December 22, 1946, Kiraz was the only member of the Syrian Orthodox community of Jerusalem who attended the service. To honor the newly consecrated Metropolitan, he gave a dinner party at the Villa Rose Marie in the German Colony of Jerusalem on January 22, 1947. Some forty members of the community, including the monks and priests of St. Mark's Monastery, were invited to the gala occasion. Thus Kiraz endeared himself to the Metropolitan, who sought his counsel repeatedly on business and other matters. They were frequently together during 1947 and early 1948, and Kiraz often provided his taxis to assist the Monastery people.

At the extreme northwest shore of the Dead Sea, which lies 1,285 feet below sea level, a modern hotel had recently opened at the popular resort of Kallia, about six miles southeast of Jericho. Many tourists frequented the resort to enjoy the amazing properties of the highly saline Dead Sea water. On October 25, 1947, some members of the American School (myself included) formed one such group of curious tourists.

From Kallia a broad, barren plain stretches for two and a half miles westward to sheer cliffs which mark the eastern edge of the rugged Judean wilderness. Six miles to the south the rapidly narrowing plain is brought to a sharp point where the cliffs plunge to the Dead Sea at Ras Feshkha. Less than a mile north of Ras Feshkha warm, somewhat brackish water emerges from a copious, bubbling spring at 'Ain Feshkha, around which reeds, marsh grasses, and other flora grow abundantly. A well-worn path follows the shore of the Dead Sea south from Kallia, past 'Ain Feshkha, and climbs the steep slope of Ras Feshkha onto the broad Buqei'a plateau of the eastern Judean wilderness (believed to be the Valley of Achor of Joshua 7:24-26). From there the path continues to rise as it winds westward through dry wadis, finally crossing the traditional Shepherds' Fields to Bethlehem. It was this very route which Ruth and Naomi, in the familiar Biblical story, would doubtless have taken between Moab and Bethlehem. David too, no doubt, explored the same route in his youth and probably sent his parents to Moab that way (I Samuel 22:3-4). Amos, who lived nearby in Tekoa, must have known the region intimately.

For almost three centuries the Bedouins of the tribe called Ta'amireh have roamed this wilderness east of Bethlehem.[4] By 1947 it was also true that the three Bedouin tribes of the area had found that the high duties imposed by the Mandate Government of Palestine on American goods — which were plentiful in independent Trans-Jordan's capital, Amman — offered a tempting opportunity for profit in their Bethlehem market place. Under cover of darkness they could ford the lower Jordan River, well out of range of the customs post at Allenby Bridge (where Butrus Sowmy's brother was a customs official), and following this shore path soon be lost in the desert fastness.[5]

It was during the early fall of 1946 that three Ta'amireh Bedouins descended with their flocks of sheep and goats to 'Ain Feshkha in search of water, forage, and warmth, as they normally do at that time of the year.[6] The two older herdsmen were Khalil Musa and his younger cousin, Jum'a Muhammed Khalil.[7] The youngest of the trio was their teen-age cousin, Muhammed Ahmed el-Hamed, whose nickname is "edh-Dhib," because, they said, his father was "fierce like a wolf."[8]

Jum'a, according to his older cousin Khalil, had a penchant for exploring caves, for he felt confident that someday he would locate one in which a cache of gold had been stored in ancient times. Often, while tending the flocks, he would explore the rocky crags nearby to satisfy his curiosity.

Sometime during the winter of 1946-1947 (the Bedouins think it was November or December, 1946), Jum'a, it was, who happened upon two holes in the side of a rock projection above the plateau where their flocks were grazing. The lower of the two holes was barely large enough "for a cat to enter," as Jum'a described it in several interviews; the one which was several feet above eye level was large enough for a slender man to enter. Jum'a threw a rock through the smaller opening and was startled by the strange sound he heard; apparently the rock shattered an earthenware jar within. Thinking there might be a cache of gold inside the cave, he summoned the two other herdsmen to show them the curious holes.[9] In the gathering darkness of evening it was too late to attempt an entrance; the next day had to be devoted to watering their flocks at 'Ain Feshkha, so they agreed to explore the cave two days later.

Shortly after sunup on the third day,[10] while his two older cousins still slept near the flocks, Muhammed edh-Dhib quietly slipped away and climbed the 100 meters from their camp up to the intriguing holes. Placing some large rocks beneath the larger opening, Muhammed was able to reach up and grasp the rock overhang above the opening and hoist himself up sufficiently to permit his legs to enter the hole. Thus he eased himself down feet first into the cave and slid to the floor on his back.[11]

As his eyes became accustomed to the dim light, he saw about ten tall jars lining the walls of the cave, according to his own description. Several of them had covers. Some of the jars had small handles which apparently were used in tying down the covers to seal the contents.[12] In addition, the Bedouins claim that there was a pile of rocks which had fallen from the ceiling, and much broken pottery on the floor of the cave. All but two of the jars proved to be empty. One was filled with reddish earth; from the other one, a jar with a cover, Muhammed pulled two bundles wrapped in cloth which he described as "greenish" in appearance.[13] A third, the largest, was a roll of leather without any wrapping. From his description and hand motions during our interview, as well as from other evidence, it seems quite probable that the larger scroll was the now-famed Isaiah Scroll (1QIs^a), and the two smaller ones, the Habakkuk Commentary (1QpHab) and the Manual of Discipline (1QS).[14] Only these three manuscripts were taken by edh-Dhib from the cave that morning.[15]

When edh-Dhib returned to his older companions and showed them the three bundles, they were angered by the fact that he had gone alone and accused him of hiding some gold from them. This betrayal of his older cousins' confidence may account for edh-Dhib's absence from subsequent events. Although edh-Dhib did go back to the cave with Jum'a and Khalil and help them remove two large jars, he seems to have had nothing further to do with the story, as he and his cousins testify.

When one of Jum'a's five sons arrived some days later, Jum'a carried the three scrolls to the Ta'amireh center southeast of

Bethlehem. The jars meanwhile were left standing outside the entrance to the cave.[16] For several weeks the manuscripts were left in a bag hanging on a tent pole.[17] It was during this period, while the manuscripts were being shown to other members of the tribe, that the uninscribed cover on the Isaiah Scroll was apparently broken off and destroyed.[18] Also it is possible that the Manual of Discipline was broken into two parts at this time, though this matter still remains a mystery.[19]

During March, 1947,[20] Jum'a and Khalil Musa took the three manuscripts and the two jars (they had in the meantime secured them from the cave) to Bethlehem where they showed them to a carpenter and antiquities dealer by the name of Judah Ibrahim 'Ijha, who promised to see if they could be sold. 'Ijha, when interviewed in the same shop (see Appendix I), where he continues to make ax and hoe handles and ladders from native woods and to deal in a few antiquities, says that he kept the scrolls for several weeks. During that time he showed them to another antiquities dealer, Faidi Salahi. The latter suspected that the documents had been stolen from a Jewish synagogue and thus warned 'Ijha against dealing with the Bedouins.[21] When, therefore, Jum'a inquired again about the manuscripts (apparently it was on Saturday, April 5, 1947),[22] 'Ijha returned them to him, explaining that they had no archeological value and that no one would buy them. The jars, however, were left in 'Ijha's shop.

Jum'a then carried the three scrolls to the market place of Bethlehem, where he chanced to meet George Isha'ya Shamoun (usually called Isha'ya, or just Sha'ya), a Syrian Orthodox Christian who frequented Bethlehem to sell *abayahs* (cloaklike outer garments) to the Bedouins. On being shown the scrolls Isha'ya offered to arrange for their sale, but Jum'a was suspicious of him. While they discussed the scrolls, Sheikh 'Ali Subh,[23] also a Ta'amireh and a friend of Jum'a, appeared; he suggested that they all go to Khalil Eskander Shahin (locally called Kando), a cobbler near Manger Square. They agreed to ask him "to guarantee George Isha'ya for £P5 to keep the scrolls." In Kando's shop, where Khalil Musa presently joined them,[24] an agreement was reached that the Bedouins should receive two-thirds of any price Kando and Isha'ya were able to get for the scrolls. Thus the Bedouins were persuaded to leave the scrolls in Kando's care.

During Holy Week (April 7-13, 1947) Isha'ya contacted St.

Mark's Syrian Orthodox Monastery in Jerusalem and was invited to bring one of the scrolls there for the Metropolitan to examine. Sometime after Holy Week Isha'ya and Kando appeared at the Monastery with a piece of the Manual of Discipline.[25] When they described the scrolls as having been "wrapped like mummies" and found in a cave by the Dead Sea, the Metropolitan decided that they might be from early Christian times and offered to buy them. Apparently Isha'ya and Kando were in no hurry, for the sale was not completed until July 19, 1947 (see below).

In the meantime, having been urged by Metropolitan Samuel and Kando, Isha'ya persuaded the Bedouins, Jum'a and Khalil Musa, to take him to the cave. According to Jum'a (see Appendix I), the three of them went together in a taxi from Jerusalem to the point where the Dead Sea road branches from the Jericho Road. From there they hiked for an hour to reach the cave. Nothing seems to have been taken from the cave on that visit, but Jum'a said that before they left Isha'ya made a cairn of rocks to mark the site. Some weeks later, Jum'a met Isha'ya and Khalil Musa in the Bethlehem market place, and they were carrying two more scrolls from the same cave. Khalil Musa, when interviewed independently,[26] agreed that he went a second time to the cave with Isha'ya but asserted that they secured *four* scrolls from under the debris on the floor of the cave at that time.[27]

These scrolls were taken to Kando, who has confirmed that *four* scrolls were brought to him by Isha'ya and Khalil before any scrolls had been sold to St. Mark's.[28] Kando kept only one of this group, however, as payment for the advance he had made to Isha'ya on expenses for the two trips to the cave.[29] Khalil Musa and Jum'a wanted to keep the other scrolls since, as Kando put it, "they were partners" in the deal. It seems quite likely that the scroll which Kando secured at that time (probably in May or June 1947) was the Syrians' "Fourth Scroll," now called the "Genesis Apocryphon" (1QapGen).[30]

According to Jum'a's statements, the three manuscripts which he and Khalil kept were then taken to a friend of Khalil's by the name of Da'ud Musallam (see Appendix I), the cousin of 'Ayub Musallam, then mayor of Bethlehem. Da'ud had a dealer friend in Jaffa by the name of Mahmud Avghani to whom he planned to show the scrolls; but when Avghani failed to appear after several days, Da'ud returned these scrolls to the Bedouins.[31] It was then, probably in June, 1947, that Jum'a and Khalil de-

cided to take these three documents to Faidi Salahi, who purchased them for £P7 ($28.35). At the same time, Salahi secured
the two jars for twenty piasters each (about 80 cents). It was this
group of manuscripts and the two jars which E. L. Sukenik later
purchased from Salahi for the Hebrew University.[32]

It was probably Saturday, July 5, 1947,[33] when Kando finally
arranged for Isha'ya to take Jum'a and Khalil,[34] with the first
group of four scrolls, to Jerusalem to St. Mark's Monastery. Metropolitan Samuel, having been apprised of their coming, waited
impatiently for their arrival. Isha'ya took the two Bedouins first
to his home in the Katamon Quarter, where he gave them lunch,
and then they went together to St. Mark's.[35] When they arrived, a
priest by the name of Bulos Gilf, knowing nothing of the negotiations, met them at the gate and was repulsed by the appearance of
the ragged Bedouins and their dirty bag with foul-smelling
scrolls inside. Despite the appeals of Isha'ya that the Metropolitan was expecting them, Father Bulos was adamant and refused
them admittance.[36]

At lunch, Father Bulos mentioned casually, and with disdain,
the appearance of the Bedouins with Isha'ya at their gate. Metropolitan Samuel hastened to the telephone to call Kando in
Bethlehem. Kando confirmed the story and added that while
Isha'ya and the Bedouins were leaving the Old City, they met a
Jewish antiquities dealer to whom the scrolls were shown. He
offered to buy them and sought directions to the cave. When he
asked the Bedouins to accompany him to his shop to get the
money, Isha'ya warned them that it was a trick to turn them over
to the government authorities, who would put them in jail.[37]
Thus they all fled back to Bethlehem, and the four scrolls were
again left in Kando's shop.[38]

Metropolitan Samuel meanwhile told Kando to "pay the
Bedouins a good price" for the scrolls whenever he could again
contact them. It was two weeks later (July 19, 1947) when Kando
saw the Bedouins again.[39] He told them of the prelate's offer and
paid them £P16 ($64.80). When Kando delivered the four scrolls
to St. Mark's Monastery, he received £P24 ($97.20), according to
his agreement with the Bedouins.[40]

Eager to learn more about the place of origin of the scrolls,
Metropolitan Samuel persuaded Isha'ya to take someone from
the Monastery to the cave. About the middle of August, Isha'ya

took a priest of St. Mark's (Father Yusif) to the cave, traveling by way of Kallia in a car. Father Yusif reported back with the same information which Isha'ya had provided, as already related in the previous chapter. The location of the scrolls in a jar in a cave by the Dead Sea, and their fragile state of preservation, strengthened the prelate's belief that the scrolls might date from early Christian times.

Meanwhile the Metropolitan had contacted a member of his community who was an assistant librarian at the Palestine Archaeological Museum, Stephan Hanna Stephan. Being an Arabist only, he had little basis for a judgment about Hebrew scrolls; but he did claim that they were worthless — certainly not as old as the Metropolitan alleged. He is reported to have said that they were "not worth a shilling."

Metropolitan Samuel then called Father S. Marmardji, a friend and teacher of Arabic at the Dominican École Biblique in Jerusalem. He examined the scrolls but seriously doubted the prelate's claim for their antiquity. A few days later — it must have been before the end of July[41] — the Metropolitan invited Marmardji to bring Father J. van der Ploeg, an Old Testament scholar who was staying at the École Biblique, to St. Mark's Monastery to examine the scrolls. Because of his interest in Syrian Orthodox history,[42] van der Ploeg had already visited St. Mark's Monastery twice several months before.

Seated in the Monastery lounge, the Dominicans were brought four scrolls on a large platter.[43] Van der Ploeg examined the largest one, which was apparently rolled with the central part exposed, and found the script difficult to read at first. Having prepared a doctoral dissertation thirteen years before on some texts of Isaiah, his eye happened upon one of them on the scroll before him. Soon he detected others. It was he, therefore, who first identified the scroll and informed the Syrians that their scroll contained the book of Isaiah.

When told that the scrolls had been found in a jar and were two thousand years old, van der Ploeg was incredulous and asked the Metropolitan to produce the jar as proof. At the Dominican School that afternoon, van der Ploeg discussed the prelate's claim for his scrolls' great antiquity with the eminent archeologist and retired professor of the École Biblique, Father L. H. Vincent.[44] The elderly Dominican scholar so impressed van der Ploeg with the possibility of forgery, through several notable examples, that he determined to await the Metropolitan's proof from the pottery. Since the latter was never produced, he left Palestine on December 11, 1947, believing that the manuscripts were probably medieval and of relatively little importance.[45]

Among the buildings owned by the Syrian Monastery near the Street of the Prophets was a clinic rented to a Jewish doctor. During the summer of 1947 the doctor died. Dr. Maurice Brown, another Jewish doctor, learned of the vacant clinic and sought to rent the property; thus he visited St. Mark's Monastery sometime that August.[46] With the rental arrangements completed, Metropolitan Samuel produced the scrolls and asked Brown's advice about their value. Having no opinion to offer, the doctor assured him that expert advice could be obtained and that he would arrange for it immediately.

Dr. Brown called the president of the Hebrew University, Judah L. Magnes, and advised him to send a Hebrew specialist to examine the scrolls. Magnes in turn communicated the request in a note to the head librarian. Two librarians arrived at St. Mark's in a few days, and the Metropolitan showed them the scrolls, explaining this time that they had been kept for many years in a library of their monastery near the Dead Sea. He asked their advice about the age of the documents, their contents, and whether the University library might consider their purchase. The librarians judged the documents to be of Samaritan origin and decided that an expert in that field should be consulted.[47]

Since the librarians spoke Hebrew to each other, their comments were not understood by the Metropolitan. To him they said only that they must consult an expert before offering any suggestions. It was at least two weeks before they called the Syrian Monastery again. Then they learned that the Metropolitan was to be away for some time.

Apparently Brown also called a Jewish antiquities dealer by the name of Sassun; for that same day, after the librarians had left, Sassun appeared at the Monastery, asking to see the documents. His suggestion was that the Metropolitan should send pieces of the scrolls to antiquities dealers in Europe and America to have them evaluated, but the Metropolitan was opposed to such an idea. Sometime before the first of October Sassun offered £P100 ($405) for the five scrolls.[48]

Late in August the Metropolitan sought counsel from Anton Kiraz concerning some complications in the prelate's personal affairs. (Kiraz had learned about the scrolls only a few weeks before.) When Kiraz revealed that he was planning to leave shortly for a vacation trip to Lebanon and Syria, Samuel urged him to delay until after the Feast of St. Mary on August 28 in order that he might accompany Kiraz. On September 5 they left Jerusalem, the Metropolitan carrying the scrolls in a small leather satchel. They entered Lebanon via the coast road at Ras en Naqura and soon were in Beirut.

Leisurely they traveled in the area for several days, visiting the Cedars of Lebanon, Tripoli, and other places. At Homs, in Syria, the Metropolitan remained with the scrolls at the Syrian Patriarchate, while Kiraz continued his vacation trip to Aleppo to visit a friend. On his return Kiraz again stopped at Homs to visit the Patriarchate; there he learned that the Metropolitan had decided to remain a few more days. Kiraz continued on to Jerusalem without him and arrived there on September 19.

His Holiness, Mar Ignatius Aphram I, Patriarch of Antioch,[49] was highly respected in the Syrian community for his learning. With deep interest he examined the scrolls, but he could not share the Metropolitan's belief in their great antiquity. He suggested they might be as much as three hundred years old but doubted any greater antiquity. He counseled Samuel, however, to seek advice from the professor of Hebrew at the American University of Beirut. The idea appealed to the Metropolitan, who proceeded to visit the University in Beirut on September 22. The professor of Hebrew, unfortunately, was on vacation. Thus the Metropolitan returned to Jerusalem on September 26[50] without obtaining any further light on the scrolls.

About the first of October, Metropolitan Samuel called Kiraz to inform him of his return and urge him to come to the Monastery at once. On arrival Kiraz found the prelate much agitated over his worsening personal affairs. Without revealing the specific cause for his dilemma, he told Kiraz about Sassun's offer of £P100 for the scrolls. Since the Metropolitan was in urgent need of funds, he asked Kiraz how much he would give for the documents. According to Kiraz, he gave the prelate £P25 and said, "Let's be partners in whatever the scrolls may bring."

The following day Kiraz relates that again he was called to

the Monastery at the behest of the troubled Metropolitan. This time he unburdened to Kiraz a story of duplicity at the hands of a friend whom he had trusted. The prelate seemed desperate. Kiraz, on hearing the tragic story, assured Metropolitan Samuel that he would solve the problem, even if he had to mortgage his home to do so. Leaving another £P50, therefore, Kiraz urged that the prelate be patient; it would take time to work out a solution to the dilemma, he counseled. Kiraz was true to his word, though it took him almost nine months to solve the problem. Thus arose Kiraz's claim to partnership with the Metropolitan in the further explorations regarding the scrolls.[51]

More eager now to learn the value of the scrolls, Metropolitan Samuel again called Stephan[52] at the Museum. He requested that Stephan bring some Hebrew grammars to St. Mark's to enable the Metropolitan to study the scrolls himself. The books taught the prelate very little, but he continued confident of the antiquity of the manuscripts.

In a few days Stephan called to say he was bringing an expert in Jewish antiquities to the Monastery. Shortly thereafter Stephan arrived with Tovia Wechsler, who was shown the scrolls and recognized the book of Isaiah among them. He also saw what he thought was a scroll of *Haftarot*.[53] Blank spaces in the text, which he seems to have interpreted as the spaces between the selected readings, influenced his decision. Apparently he was influenced also by the numerous marginal markings. The *Haftarot* scroll, he told the Metropolitan, had indications of recent usage — the blackness of ink corrections on it led primarily to this conclusion.[54] When the Metropolitan claimed great antiquity for the scrolls, therefore, he said Wechsler's reply was, "If that table [a small table in the Monastery office] were a box and you filled it full of pound notes, you couldn't even then measure the value of these scrolls if they are two thousand years old, as you say." Though intended to discourage the Metropolitan, Wechsler's remark provided the prelate with some hope for the scrolls' value.

Probably the best known of all the stories relating to the Dead Sea Scrolls is that which involved the late E. L. Sukenik, Professor of Archeology at Jerusalem's Hebrew University, when he returned from a prolonged leave of absence in the United States during 1947. Since his story has been dramatized on television and related in numerous popular books, only a sketch is necessary here.[55]

An Armenian antiquities dealer identified by Sukenik only as "Mr. X,"[56] whose shop was near the Y.M.C.A. in Jerusalem's "B" Zone, left an urgent telephoned message at the Hebrew University on Sunday, November 23, 1947, to have Sukenik call him immediately about an antiquity. That afternoon when he called the dealer, Sukenik was unable to learn the nature of the discovery; but he agreed to meet the dealer the next morning at the gate to Zone "B." There, through the barbed-wire barricade, the eminent archeologist saw a ragged fragment of leather inscribed in strange Hebrew characters. The dealer told him of its discovery by Bedouins who were seeking to sell many such pieces to their mutual friend, Faidi Salahi, an antiquities dealer in Bethlehem. When Sukenik noted a resemblance between the script on the fragment and that which he had often seen scratched on first-century ossuaries, his initial skepticism soon gave way to excited curiosity. He therefore offered to buy the fragments for the Hebrew University and urged the Armenian dealer to get more samples of them from the Bethlehem dealer.

Thursday, when at Lake Success the United Nations Assembly was approaching a final vote on the Partition of Palestine, the Jerusalem dealer again called, suggesting that Sukenik come to his shop. There he saw more leather fragments with the same kind of script. Now convinced that the fragments must be genuine and ancient, he arranged to go to Bethlehem to meet Faidi Salahi. Had it not been for the decision at Lake Success the next day to delay the final vote on Partition until Saturday, the twenty-ninth, Sukenik probably would not have been able to go. That day of respite gave Sukenik courage to believe that there would be no violence for at least another day.

To clarify this situation, it should be pointed out that, as a member of the Palestine Archaeological Advisory Board, Sukenik had a means readily available for securing the materials without risk.[57] A call to the Director of Antiquities, R. W. Hamilton, would at that time have assured a safe procedure for bringing the manuscripts and the cave under scholarly control.[58] Faidi Salahi, furthermore, as a licensed antiquities dealer, was technically required to consult the Department of Antiquities prior to any attempt to sell such materials elsewhere.[59]

Together, the Armenian dealer and Sukenik (according to the

latter's writings) made the trip to Bethlehem by bus that Saturday. In an upstairs apartment not far from the market place they met Salahi and were shown the two jars as well as the bundles of leather scrolls and fragments which Salahi had purchased from the Ta'amireh Bedouins the previous summer. Sukenik persuaded the dealer to let him take the scrolls to Jerusalem, promising that he would give his decision about purchasing them within two days through the Armenian dealer.[60]

That evening he found that two different documents were contained in the bundles. One seemed similar to the book of Psalms but was obviously not Biblical (it is now called *Hodayot* or "Songs of Thanksgiving," 1QH). The other was a description of a battle "between the Sons of Light and the Sons of Darkness" (now commonly called the "War Scroll," 1QM). As he studied the ancient script, the news of the affirmative vote for Partition was announced over the radio. Sukenik joined the Jews of Jerusalem in their paroxysms of joy, his own excitement generated as much by the manuscripts as by the United Nations news.

Despite the increasing tensions and disturbances which followed the U.N. Assembly's recommendation to partition Palestine, Sukenik succeeded on December 22 in obtaining the two jars from Bethlehem and in purchasing another scroll. The latter was apparently the poorly preserved and fragmentary copy of Isaiah (1QIs^b), the nature and contents of which were not discovered until it was opened during the summer of 1949.

Quite by accident one day in early December, Sukenik mentioned the scrolls to one of the librarians who had been sent to St. Mark's Monastery the preceding August. Immediately the librarian remembered his experience there. He left Sukenik puzzled, however, by his reference to the Syrian scrolls having been in a monastery library near the Dead Sea for many years. Sukenik sought Magnes' permission to handle future negotiations with the Syrians and forthwith set about to make the contact, but to no avail. Jerusalem was by then too sharply divided.

During December and the early part of January, 1948, Metropolitan Samuel was again in Syria. On his return he consulted Kiraz about the next steps with the manuscripts. It was then that Kiraz remembered the excavation of the tombs on his property by Sukenik of the Hebrew University; surely Sukenik could evaluate the scrolls, he suggested. It was agreed that Kiraz should pursue this approach. Wrapping the scrolls in Arabic newspapers, Kiraz took them to his home, where he wrote a somewhat vaguely worded letter to Sukenik. It took three days for the letter to arrive at a point barely a mile to the northwest.

Immediately on reading the letter, Sukenik thought of the scrolls mentioned by the University librarian and contacted Kiraz to arrange a meeting place. Kiraz suggested that they meet on February 4 in Zone "B" in the office of the Y.M.C.A. librarian, Malak Tannourji, who was also a member of the Syrian Orthodox Church. Knowing that during those days seldom was a Jew at the Y.M.C.A., Sukenik carried a few books on pretense of returning them. As he entered the building, he was relieved to notice Kiraz sitting on the terrace among a group of Arabs.

Soon Kiraz sauntered into the librarian's office, having allowed time for Sukenik to meet Tannourji. When the Syrians drew forth three of the scrolls from a desk drawer,[61] the appearance of their script immediately reminded Sukenik of the scrolls which he had already purchased.

Gradually the story of the origin of the Syrian scrolls emerged from the conversation, and Sukenik realized that it tallied with what he had already heard from his Armenian dealer friend. Assuring Kiraz that he would buy the scrolls for the Hebrew University, Sukenik requested the privilege of taking them to show President Magnes and some of his colleagues. According to Kiraz, he was offered £P100 for the documents,[62] but he replied that he would have to discuss the offer "with his partner," the Metropolitan. The three men agreed to meet again in the same place Friday morning, February 6. During the interim Sukenik copied several chapters from the Isaiah Scroll. The two other Syrian scrolls (one portion of the Manual of Discipline and the Genesis Apocryphon) remained in Tannourji's desk drawer.

Sukenik later reported that when the men again met in the same office Friday morning, the first words of Kiraz were, "What will you offer?" According to both Kiraz and Tannourji, Sukenik offered £P500 ($2,025) — £P250 for each of the partners to the scrolls. Again Mr. Kiraz demurred on the grounds that he must consult his partner. Sukenik then promised to give Kiraz an extra £P500 if he would persuade the Metropolitan to conclude the deal.[63] Another meeting was planned for the Yugoslav Consulate, according to both Kiraz and Sukenik, when Kiraz was to bring the Metropolitan, and Sukenik the president of the Hebrew University.[64]

Kiraz and the Metropolitan now realized that the scrolls must be worth a great deal; but the problem was, how much to ask? Meanwhile Tannourji counseled Kiraz to get another appraisal, reminding him of the story of the Codex Sinaiticus. He suggested that the A.S.O.R. would probably be a good place to get an opinion. Days went by while Sukenik waited impatiently for a call about the meeting at the Yugoslav Consulate. It never came.

For more than a week the Syrian scrolls remained in a paper bag at the home of Kiraz. Butrus Sowmy meanwhile had been in Lebanon for almost a month; the Metropolitan awaited his return, for apparently he valued the monk's opinion highly. On his arrival in Jerusalem about February 17, Sowmy expressed strong opposition toward the negotiations with Sukenik.[65] The suggestion that the A.S.O.R. be consulted, however, he supported. He recalled, in fact, some pleasant associations with the American School some ten years before. The Metropolitan therefore requested Kiraz to return the scrolls to the Monastery, which he did that same day. To find out who could be reached at the A.S.O.R., Sowmy called Bishop Stewart at St. George's Cathedral and was given the names of Millar Burrows and William Brownlee. He then called the A.S.O.R., and asked for Brownlee, who was away at the time (see Chapter I, n. 4).

When the Syrians decided to accept my suggestions about the best procedure for handling the scrolls, apparently they said very little to Kiraz. Toward the end of February, however, Kiraz wrote to Sukenik, saying that they had decided to wait until after the troubles were over before selling. During March and April Sukenik continued to try to contact Kiraz, calling Tannourji several times in an effort to reach him. After the episode in late March, when Kiraz offered the photographs to Sukenik (see pp. 83-84, 86), however, there were no further communications between them.

13

The Odyssey of the Scrolls

OFF THE RUNWAY at Haifa, where on April 5, 1948, we stopped for half an hour, the small plane darted out over the Bay of Acre and headed north. The pilot kept a safe distance from the coast, thus providing a breathtaking panorama of Galilee and the lofty Lebanon ranges. Sloping gently down to the narrow ribbon of cultivated coastlands with their deep undulations formed by many rivulets, the majestic peaks stretched away for endless miles. The sea below was spread like a carpet, its brilliant blue as deep as the lapis lazuli of King Tut-ankh-amen's jewels before which I had stood enthralled at the Cairo Museum.

Beyond the hills of Galilee, Mount Hermon poked its snow-capped peak above a bracelet of fluffy cumulus clouds surmounted by a deep azure sky. Swiftly the ancient cities of Tyre and Sidon passed below, and in a matter of minutes we were swooping down over the red sand and Aleppo-pine watersheds that guide the planes into the busy Beirut airport. Mount Senin, still heavy with winter's snow, rose high above the red-tiled roofs of Beirut, which sits on the Lebanon slopes as though guarding the broad entrance to St. George's Bay.

The peace and beauty of Lebanon, the cordial hospitality of two gracious missionary families who entertained me, and the sights and scenes of more Biblical history soon soothed nerves that had been shattered by the strife I had now left behind. Nahr el-Kelb (Dog River) on the famed route of the conquerors; Jebeil, ancient Byblos of the Egyptian story of Wen-Amon, and the Gebal of the Old Testament; the ski slopes of the regal Cedars of Lebanon above Tripoli; exotic Baalbek in the lush Litani Valley between the Lebanons; the bazaars of Damascus; caves and streams behind Sidon — all these brought refreshing inspiration and memorable experiences. Study of the manuscript photographs, safely stored in their leather satchel, was therefore postponed.

Somewhere in Beirut the scrolls themselves were secreted. My closest link with them was a visit one day in the home of Karim Sowmy, a cousin of Butrus Sowmy. There I met again the latter's brother, Ibrahim, and was introduced to the Syrian Metropolitan of Beirut, who was to become the Patriarch of Antioch[1] nine years later.

For almost two weeks I waited for a boat that failed to arrive, and finally boarded another headed for Marseilles. As the outline of Beirut faded into the gathering twilight, a wave of nostalgia gripped my whole being and I lingered at the stern until the last twinkling light dropped below the horizon. During the four subsequent restful days on the gently rolling S.S. *Transylvania*, a Rumanian ship crowded with refugees fleeing communist rule, I spent many hours comparing the text of the Isaiah Scroll with that of the traditional Hebrew Masoretic text.[2]

It soon became apparent that the text of the ancient scroll was substantially the same as the Masoretic text, as Albright had presaged in his letter; but small variations were numerous. The differences tended to fall into a few broad categories, by far the largest of which constituted the liberal addition of certain consonants used as vowel letters to aid pronunciation. After the fifth century B.C., when Hebrew fell into disuse as a living tongue, being supplanted by the more common Aramaic, aids for reading sacred Scripture became imperative for new generations of readers. This feature on the Isaiah Scroll seemed to add another argument for its antiquity. Already the appearance of the outside of the scroll, darkened by many hands and repaired at many points, had indicated a much-read scroll. The text, too, now presented additional evidence for its use in community worship. Its many marginal marks argued further in this direction.

A second category included the many obvious errors of the scribe. Though his script was skillfully executed, he lacked that meticulous care which was the mark of the later Masoretic scribes. Occasionally he corrected an error by inserting the proper letter above the line, or by an erasure. Other errors were left, as already noted, to be corrected by later hands.

Minor grammatical differences appeared fairly often; and variations in spelling, particularly of Biblical names, were also frequent. It was apparent that the discussion of these so-called morphological and orthographic features would occupy scholars for years to come. (See Chapter 17.)

Additions of *and*, *the*, and some prepositions, and occasionally an omission of one of these, were numerous. Important variations which would affect a translation or the meaning were few. None was startling or what might be considered a significant difference. It was obvious that some superior readings would emerge and ultimately be accepted by Biblical scholars, but certainly there would not be many.[3]

A tally of the first column, for instance, produced these results: of a total of 91 variations of all kinds from the Masoretic text, 51 are additions of vowel letters, 7 others are minor spelling variations, 13 are grammatical differences; 8 are probably errors (not including 5 corrected by the scribe); 11 are additions of articles, conjunctions, or prepositions (in addition, one *and* was omitted); and only 2 are significant word additions. Of all the 91 variations, only the 2 word additions and 2 variations in spelling would be worthy of much discussion. Though a close parallel to the later Masoretic, the text clearly reveals a scribal tradition at Qumran that was by no means slavishly literalist. Here was the first exemplar of another textual tradition of the Hebrew text of Isaiah.

On the problem of whether there was one or more authors for the original book of Isaiah, the scroll makes no contribution. It was obviously copied at least a hundred years after the text of Isaiah had reached its present structure. A much older manuscript — one at least antedating the third century B.C. — would be necessary to shed significant light on that problem. Interesting marginal markings at the beginning of Chapter 40 on Column 32 provide the only point worthy of comment in this regard. They probably served to point out a major transition in thought as similar marks do elsewhere in the manuscript. The numerous marginal marks seem to divide the book into Scripture lessons.

During his long sea voyage on a freighter, Burrows collated the entire manuscript, while I finished less than a dozen columns in the few days while crossing the Mediterranean and the Atlantic.

Arriving in London on April 25, I learned that our news release about the scrolls had been flashed around the world two weeks earlier. The next day's papers, furthermore, carried Suk-enik's release about the scrolls which he had purchased for the Hebrew University. I was amazed to learn that more scrolls had come from the same cave! When the A.S.O.R. release had appeared on April 11, I was high up in the Lebanon mountains enjoying the fellowship of skiers and the enthralling beauty of the ancient cedars. No one in Lebanon mentioned seeing the release, but at the British Museum there was an atmosphere of curiosity about the discovery. I quickly discovered that my knowledge of the background of the story was an "open sesame" to scholarly circles, but normal scholarly reserve over the startling news was immediately apparent.

In London I eagerly sought out the great manuscript expert, Sir Frederick Kenyon, whose profound writings had made a deep impression on me. When I unfolded some of the scroll story, the aged papyrologist seemed to thrill to my tale of adventure, which touched so intimately his long life of scholarly concentration. Not a Hebraist, however, he had no opinion to offer.[4] While touring Oxford and Cambridge Universities, I visited G. R. Driver of Magdalen College, Oxford, and J. L. Teicher, who was cataloguing Hebrew manuscripts in the Cambridge University Library. They pumped me with questions; but, to judge by their later writings, they did not share my convictions concerning the antiquity of the scrolls. At the Cambridge Library Teicher brought forth the original Nash Papyrus, which I examined with avid interest.

Crossing the Atlantic on the R.M.S. *Queen Elizabeth*, after the fourteen-day voyage on the lowly S.S. *Marine Carp* the previous August, was like moving from the slums to a king's palace. Reveling in the wonders of that great ship, I found concentration on manuscript study most difficult. Even the swift pace of the "Queen," however, was not enough to satisfy my impatience to be reunited with my family, still far away in California.

Early on the morning of May 15, in Las Vegas, Nevada, that longing was fulfilled. Having promised my brother to address the Community Church of nearby Boulder City the following morning, it was there my journey ended. In my sermon the next morning I could not refrain from unburdening my heart of some of the tragic scenes I had left behind in the Holy Land.

Even as I spoke, eight thousand miles away Jerusalem was embroiled in one of its worst blood-baths, despite the U.N. intention that it be internationalized. As the British forces withdrew on the morning of May 14, all bedlam let loose. A voluntary truce committee had been set up on May 13, comprising the three consuls of the United States, France, and Belgium. They strove desperately to achieve a cease-fire, which was agreed to for the morning of the sixteenth but failed to be observed. During the holocaust that followed, St. Mark's Monastery suffered severe damage, and fragments from a bursting bomb struck and killed Father Butrus Sowmy.

Two days before, Anton Kiraz had driven the Rev. John Malak and his two sisters to Beirut. Having lost his home and all but one of his cars, Kiraz was now one of the many thousands of refugees who fled with only the few possessions they could carry. Metropolitan Samuel meanwhile went to Madeba in Trans-Jordan.

The summer weeks sped by, as my attention was turned to the task of becoming oriented into a new position. The International Council of Religious Education had arranged a schedule of many speaking engagements related to my responsibilities as Representative of the Committee for the Revised Standard Version of the Bible. Lectures, addresses, special short courses, sermons, and a host of other tasks dominated my daily life. I even forgot to submit the proposed publication contract discussed with the Syrians in Jerusalem. A letter from Burrows in late May, inquiring about the arrangements I had finally been able to work out, jolted me to action. Quickly I dispatched the points agreed upon, but it was months before the A.S.O.R. could get their revised agreement through to the Metropolitan.

Unexpected complications arose, as Sukenik pressed for equal rights to publish the Syrian scrolls on the basis of an agreement he claimed to have with Kiraz. It was the first we had heard of such an agreement, though now the deeper meaning behind the Metropolitan's concerns expressed on March 19 seemed to be coming to light (see pp. 83-84). I prepared a summary of my understanding of the situation for Burrows, but it lacked the specific details needed.

In the meantime we began to prepare some preliminary articles that would give as complete as possible a picture of the discovery and what it entailed, as far as we then understood it. It was agreed that I should write an abbreviated account of the story for the *Biblical Archaeologist* (September, 1948), a publication by the A.S.O.R. for laymen; and that Burrows would follow it with a summary of the contents of the three scrolls thus far studied. For the more academic *Bulletin of the American Schools of Oriental Research*, I was asked to prepare a descriptive summary of the four scrolls in the possession of the Syrians and an analysis of the method of dating documents through paleography. For this same journal Burrows was to summarize the results of his collation of the Isaiah Scroll and Brownlee to present his tentative translation of the Habakkuk Commentary.[5] Meanwhile Sukenik published a more elaborate monograph in Hebrew as a preliminary report on two of the scrolls of the Hebrew University.[6] In it he included a transliteration of Isaiah 42 and 43, which he had copied out when the Syrians' scrolls were in his hands February 4-6, as recounted in the previous chapter.[7]

Each of the publications carried sample photographs of the texts, so that by the end of 1948 portions of each scroll, except the Hebrew University Isaiah Scroll (lQIs*b*) which had not yet been opened or identified, had been made available to scholars. With these sample photographs before them, the scholars of the world trained their guns of expected criticism upon our conclusions, and the first "battle of the scrolls" began in earnest.[8] That December Burrows, Brownlee, and I presented papers before the annual joint meeting of the Society of Biblical Literature and Exegesis, The National Association of Biblical Instructors, and the American Schools of Oriental Research, when the largest gatherings of scholars in the history of these meetings crowded into a huge lecture hall at Union Theological Seminary to hear our firsthand reports. The world of Biblical scholarship was thoroughly aroused.

All three of us were greatly handicapped by the various complications of our personal lives in trying to write our reports. Both Brownlee and I were particularly frustrated by the necessity of beginning new jobs. Brownlee not only faced his first year of college teaching at Duke University, but also was making plans to be married. My work with the I.C.R.E. kept me traveling so much that pullman cars, hotel rooms, and seemingly every place except the quiet of a private study were used for research and writing. Everywhere I went, a satchel well stocked with photographs of the various scrolls was my constant companion. The work on the paleography, at that time the only sound basis for dating the scrolls, demanded extensive library resources which could be found in only a few of the finest libraries in the country. Generally I was hundreds of miles from the nearest library resources when some strategic point demanded checking.

Every letter on the entire Habakkuk Commentary, on a dozen columns of the Isaiah Scroll, and on the columns of the Manual of Discipline was carefully examined to be certain of the standard forms used by each scribe. A chart of letter forms, which was crucial to illustrate my thesis and to establish it visually, was prepared mostly in hotel rooms and private homes where I was entertained in various communities across the United States.

About the middle of August, 1948, a letter from Metropolitan Samuel at last arrived. He was replying to my note of sympathy which had been sent through a Beirut address as soon as I learned of the tragic death of Father Sowmy. The first truce which had been successfully negotiated by the newly appointed United Nations mediator, Count Folke Bernadotte, lasted only from June 11 to July 9. The resumption of hostilities on July 9 produced thousands of additional refugees who were flooding into Trans-Jordan and other Arab countries. The pitiful plight of the refugees touched the Palestinian religious leaders deeply, and superhuman efforts were put forth to cope with the heartrending situation. A neatly contrived plan of ours to bring tourists to a museum featuring the scrolls at St. Mark's Monastery was now obsolete. The Monastery was badly damaged, and thousands of Syrian Orthodox Christians were suffering. The Metropolitan therefore was thinking of the scrolls in terms of ameliorating the situation to some degree. Already the Patriarch had suggested he visit their communicants in America, at which time he had planned to bring the Fourth Scroll for scientific treatment. Now it was imperative that he come to seek help in a larger way. In his second letter, which reached me late in September, he wrote:

> As you know our Convent in Jerusalem is partly damaged and we lost all our income and my people were obliged to escape from the Calamity leaving everything, house, furniture and even their clothes and are dispersed in the surrounding countries and as the

hard times of Winter are coming they need everything. Lately I visited them and I found that 3000 of them are in immediate need of help. To help them is practical and real Christianity.

Feeling the situation intimately, both Burrows and I saw the plans of the Metropolitan as a hopeful means of aiding many suffering refugees. Thus, we encouraged him to come to America with the scrolls. We offered to do what we could to expedite a sale. He sought my help to finance his trip, but I was in no position to offer such extensive assistance; my intermittent efforts to arouse interest in the plight of the Arabs had met with paltry success.

We began to consider how we might be able to assist toward a sale of the scrolls. In the light of Sukenik's claim to equal rights, a major obstacle stood in the way. Cautiously I raised the matter in a letter to Metropolitan Samuel, who was then in the Patriarchate in Homs. His handwritten reply, dated September 14, 1948, contained a firm denial of the claim.

Meanwhile Ovid Sellers, then Dean and Professor of Old Testament at McCormick Theological Seminary in Chicago, was able during the first truce to reach Jerusalem on July 7 to assume the duties of Director of the A.S.O.R. Together we had discussed the scroll story at length before his departure; but the chaotic situation which followed two days after his arrival in Jerusalem, with the end of the first truce, left no opportunity for him to pursue negotiations. Mere survival was the predominant concern. He gave yeoman service under most trying and dangerous conditions. Joining forces with other foreign religious leaders, he sought to elicit aid from America for the thousands of Arab refugees.

Early in September, Metropolitan Samuel visted Sellers and showed him some newly acquired scroll fragments which were carried in a flat tin box. Shortly thereafter Sellers was seriously injured when the plane in which he was riding from Beirut to Jerusalem was shot down by a fighter plane over the Sea of Galilee. For weeks he was hospitalized.

Despite the war and such tragedies, curiosity about the scroll discovery was increasing throughout the Near East. Not until November was peace restored to Jerusalem. In January restrictions on travel were relaxed sufficiently to revive hopes for a visit to the cave. When Sellers was finally able to visit St. Mark's Monastery, he learned that the Metropolitan had already left[9] and that Father Bulos was in charge. He reminded them of their promise to cooperate with the A.S.O.R. in visiting the cave, and was introduced to George Isha'ya, who demanded an advance of £P75 ($303.75) and other exorbitant requirements to take anyone to the cave. Negotiations with the Monastery therefore ceased; the cave had to be rediscovered.

Already, in December, 1948, Belgian Captain Philippe Lippens, an observer for the United Nations who was housed at the King David Hotel in Israeli Jerusalem, was thinking about how the manuscript cave might be reached. When transferred to the Arab side of Jerusalem, he visited the A.S.O.R., St. Mark's Monastery, and the École Biblique to gain what information he could. Father Roland de Vaux, Director of the École Biblique, showed him a few published articles which had recently reached their library. A vague reference in my article about the location of the cave and the story of our failure to reach it fired Lippens' enthusiasm. On January 24, 1949, he succeeded in obtaining an interview with Major General Lash, the British Commander of the 3rd Brigade of the Arab Legion at Ramallah. General Lash called Brigadier Ashton, his archeological advisor, who in turn contacted G. L. Harding, Chief Inspector of Antiquities, in Amman, Jordan. Harding confirmed the importance of the cave project. Thus, General Lash dispatched Brigadier Ashton with two Bedouins and Captain Akkash el-Zebn to search the area mentioned in my article.

On January 28 Captain Akkash el-Zebn spotted a strange-colored disturbance of the earth high up on the cliff; it looked a little like the results of an excavation. On closer examination it proved to be what they were seeking. A guard was posted, and Harding was called. Though dubious at first, Harding soon found evidence to associate the cave with the manuscript discovery. He began at once to arrange for the excavation.

A lengthy tour of addresses kept me in Southern California during January, 1949. Among other things forwarded to me from my office about the middle of the month was a note from Metropolitan Samuel written in longhand on the back of one of his calling cards. Dated January 6, from Alexandria, Egypt, the brief note said that he would arrive in New York on January 28 aboard the S.S. *Excalibur* and asked that I meet him at the dock. My scheduled tour would not end until February 1 in St. Paul, Minnesota. Burrows therefore made plans to meet the boat, neither of us knowing that a reception committee of some twenty-five Syrian Orthodox communicants was being organized at the same time in West New York. I satisfied myself with an *ahlan wa-sahlan* (Arabic words of welcome) cablegram to the boat, a letter to be delivered at the dock, and a promise to visit the Metropolitan on February 4 in Jersey City.

On the twenty-eighth the S.S. *Excalibur* wallowed in heavy seas not far from New York (while in Jordan Captain Akkash el-Zebn was climbing up to rediscover the manuscript cave). Unable to remain to see the delayed boat dock on the afternoon of the twenty-ninth, Burrows too wrote his *ahlan wa-sahlan* in a letter to be delivered to the Metropolitan by the chairman of the reception committee, and returned to New Haven.

On February 4 I found my way to the Hotel Plaza in Jersey City to greet the Metropolitan. It was a happy reunion in the midst of a host of Syrian Orthodox people who surrounded him. Not knowing how much his people knew about the scrolls, I waited for him to initiate the subject. Little was said until most of the friends had left; then, in the presence of only two Syrian laymen, opportunity was given for me to ask some of the myriad questions I had listed.

An engagement his friends had planned for the evening prevented any lengthy discussion. Having registered at the same hotel, I spent the evening in my room, recording the results of the interview. About 10:30 the telephone rang, and Metropolitan Samuel asked if I would come to his suite — at last he was alone. For over two hours we sat discussing the problem of how to raise funds to aid the refugees. We agreed to draft an appeal to be printed and sent to members of his church in this country. Then, for sentimental reasons, I asked if I might see the scrolls again. From a closet he drew forth a shining new leather satchel, from which I tenderly lifted out the Isaiah Scroll. Opening the precious document to Column 32, I read aloud the familiar words of Isaiah 40:1-8, which conclude, "The grass withers, the flower fades; but the word of our God shall stand for ever" (RSV).

14

The Mystery of the Daniel Fragments

DURING the long train trip from the Pacific Coast to New Jersey, intense expectancy had dominated my mind. Eagerly I sought to examine some new scrolls which, according to his letter, the Metropolitan had purchased during the previous summer.[1] Then there were the new fragments, carried by the prelate in a metal cigarette box, which had been shown to Ovid Sellers in Jerusalem the previous September. It was with difficulty, therefore, that I restrained my keen anticipation when, on arrival, I found Metropolitan Samuel surrounded by many Syrians in the hotel suite.

When only an attorney and a cousin of the late Butrus Sowmy remained, the Metropolitan did not seem hesitant about discussing the manuscripts; apparently these men knew about the documents. Presently from the closet he drew forth two sizable bundles and handed them to me. Hopefully I unwrapped the protective paper only to discover within two large rolls of shiny white parchment, as new as last June's college diploma. Though smaller than most similar scrolls I had seen, the first column of each revealed in an elegant script the familiar opening Hebrew words of the book of Genesis. They were quite modern Torah scrolls, not even as early as the huge Torah scroll I had seen in the St. Mark's Monastery library (see p. 54). Without hesitation I asserted that these scrolls would not even deserve the designation of "antiquities."

Next he handed me a flat tin cigarette box which fit Sellers' description. Gently lifting the cover, I found a layer of cotton under which lay fragments of familiar dark-brown, ragged-edged leather. Hardly a letter of script was immediately visible, but the appearance and faint odor emitted immediately associated the group with the cave scrolls. This matted mass of leather fragments, and under it a sizable piece of papyrus plus several smaller inscribed leather pieces, recalled at once the description Sellers had given of some fragments he had seen (see p. 118). These must be the same ones, I concluded.

The largest of the group, measuring 3½ x 2¾ inches overall, was a folded mass of at least three different kinds of leather welded together at one corner by an area of disintegration which had reached the gelatinized stage. Separation of the fragments, it was apparent, would be difficult because of this gluey, fused section. On top was a loose piece which had become folded over the rest like a cover. Pulling it gently back, I discovered a somewhat flowing script which appeared to be semi-cursive. Letters were run together, but not intentionally connected by ligatures (1QDan^b). There was some similarity to the script of the Manual of Discipline, it seemed at first glance.

Adhering to the right side of the mass, and lying on top of each other, were several smaller fragments of a very thin, light-tan leather inscribed in an exquisitely fine hand. Though more perfectly executed, the script reminded me of the insertion on Column 28 of the Isaiah Scroll. Several fragments from this same scroll could be clearly seen projecting in layers beneath the upper one, probably parts from other turns of the same scroll. Three other fragments with the same beautiful script were lying loose in the box (1Q34^{bis}).

On the back of the mass was still another kind of leather, considerably lighter, though mottled, but folded so that nothing of its script could be seen. The whole mass gave the appearance of two scrolls which had been lying atop each other and deliberately squashed under someone's foot in ancient times.

Also in the box was a coarse piece of leather with very irregular edges, partly broken from disintegration and partly from having been eaten by insects. It measured about 2 by 2½ inches overall. Only a few crude letters had been preserved on its surface (1Q19^{bis}).

The most unusual fragment, however, was a piece of papyrus about an inch wide by 2 inches long, a vertical piece broken from a column which had been inscribed in large, coarse Hebrew characters. Some of the letters had partially flaked away. Not a single word was complete (1Q70^{bis}). Hebrew papyri have been rare among manuscript discoveries, and thus it called for very careful study.

Several small fragments in the box seemed to belong with those in the matted mass, to judge by their texture, color, and script. Six uninscribed fragments, some with pieces of cloth attached, looked like what had been described in the early reports as "pitch," supposedly used to seal the jars in the cave. It was clear, however, that these were actually pieces of fused leather from the outer disintegrated crust of some of the scrolls. Through the many centuries of exposure in the cave, even in the extremely dry climate of that wilderness area, the outer turns of leather had become reduced to a gluey, amber-colored mass. When dry, this crust would crack easily and fall away unless handled with great care. Under humid conditions it would bend like plastic or hard rubber.

While I studied the fragments, the Metropolitan related the story of their origin. In view of the fact that we had been unable to get to the cave the previous spring, during the fall he had decided to send "one of his men"[2] to the cave to see whether it still remained in the same condition as when Father Yusif visited it in August, 1947. The Jews had left the region, having destroyed the Potash Works and the hotel at Kallia, thus allowing for easy access to the cave. He went on to say that these fragments were picked up along with a large piece of cloth at that time. Otherwise the cave was in the same condition as it had been the previous year. Even one complete jar was still there.[3] Why the jar was not removed, the Metropolitan was unable to explain. (But see Chapter 12, n. 32.)

From my many questions about the early history of the scrolls, the idea of publishing the story arose. Assuring the Metropolitan that such an article would probably be appreciated by the *Biblical Archaeologist* editor, I set about to gather notes toward that end. He requested that I compose the article, then let him review and correct it until we were certain it represented the most accurate account possible. Urging him to think the whole story through carefully, I warned that such an article was bound to receive very critical scrutiny by scholars.

For over an hour later that night, when we were alone, I questioned him about various details of the story, jotting down copious notes in which I included every name he mentioned. When the name of Anton Kiraz arose, I asked casually how he came into the story. The prelate mentioned Sukenik's excavation on Kiraz's property in Talpioth and the fact that Sukenik, knowing that Kiraz was a Syrian, had written to him, requesting to see the Syrian scrolls. It was in January, while Butrus Sowmy was in Syria, that he had decided to let Kiraz show the scrolls to Sukenik for his evaluation, he continued. He did not give permission, he emphasized, for the scrolls to be left with Sukenik for several days.

Of primary concern to the prelate, however, was the drafting of a statement to be printed and circulated to his people as a means of raising funds for the many Syrian refugees. After discussing its proposed contents at great length, I agreed to draft a suitable statement the next morning.

A typewriter was delivered to my room in the hotel at 8:30, but the Metropolitan insisted that I join him at breakfast before starting to work. Taking advantage of our privacy, again I pressed him with more questions. He seemed somewhat irritated by my incessant queries about dates and chronological relationships of events, but I insisted that these were essential to establish the record. After breakfast, I first typed all the notes about the scrolls. A rough draft of the fund-raising statement had been barely completed when the Metropolitan called to invite me to join some of his friends at lunch.

After lunch his people gave us another opportunity to be alone, but again most of the time had to be spent in further discussion of the statement. Occasionally it was possible to interject a question which had arisen that morning while I typed the notes about the scrolls. When I left that afternoon, therefore, it was with considerable confidence that the essential accuracy of the story about the discovery of the scrolls had been recorded.

Another series of speaking engagements took me to the Pacific Northwest during late February and early March. The following weeks were crowded as I attempted to prepare a first draft of the proposed article on the Metropolitan's story. In addition, the article on the paleography of the St. Mark's scrolls for the *Bulletin of the A.S.O.R.*, and an accompanying chart, were already overdue in Baltimore, Maryland. Taking advantage of the long train rides and the isolation and quiet of numerous hotel rooms between engagements, I gradually assembled the materials. The draft of the Metropolitan's article, containing many blank spaces for names and details to be filled in, was finally dispatched for his review prior to our next meeting.

In the meantime word reached me in Oregon that Sukenik had arrived in New York and was seeking an interview. Having planned a second visit with the Metropolitan for the afternoon of March 22, I suggested to Sukenik that we meet in New York that morning at the headquarters of the American Friends of the Hebrew University, where he was staying.

Eager to hear his side of the story, I listened carefully as Sukenik related his experiences. His statements revealed the clarity and precision of the great scholar that he was. The interview proceeded very pleasantly until he began to make strong claims regarding the disposition of the Syrian scrolls, which he asserted belonged to the State of Israel. With mounting agitation he insisted that the scrolls were a part of Jewish heritage. He was then preparing a document, he revealed, to circulate to all libraries and universities which might consider purchasing the scrolls. In it he was warning them that such a purchase would be illegal and subject to the antiquities laws, which could be invoked to return the scrolls to the country of their origin. Despite the somewhat heated conclusion to our interview, I departed with additional valuable information and proceeded at once to record it in detail. To unravel the story back of the discovery had become for me a vital concern.

On the New Jersey side of the Hudson River that afternoon, I found Metropolitan Samuel well prepared and eager to discuss his story for the *Biblical Archaeologist*. Much revision of the first draft was necessary, for he had given each event considerable thought, he asserted, and found evidence to provide a more accurate picture. Paragraph by paragraph we went over the draft, rewriting much of it, particularly at the beginning and the end. It was then that a number of changes, destined to complicate our problems in the future, were introduced.

Believing it unwise to reveal my interview with Sukenik that morning, I failed to challenge the Metropolitan's claim that the scrolls were shown to him late in February, 1948. Samuel's evidence — that he offered instead to Sukenik the photographs which I had prepared in the meantime — seemed valid. Thus I agreed to his revision without debate. The article seemed fairly consistent with the facts we had been able to check up to that time.

In the meantime Carl Kraeling, then president of the A.S.O.R., was moving ahead with arrangements for unrolling the "Fourth Scroll" (1QapGen), a fragment of which I had deciphered the previous December. From my transcription of its few incomplete lines, Albright had concluded that the scroll was related to the apocryphal book of Enoch. Soon this tentative identification began to appear in news releases.

Arranging to take the month of April, 1949, away from my office, I planned to assist in the unrolling process. With high hopes of success at last in this long-awaited adventure, I drove with my family and the necessary photographic equipment to New Haven. There the Metropolitan met with us to discuss the procedure. Our plans to do the work at Yale University had, in the meantime, collapsed. Immediately Kraeling had suggested that we contact authorities at the Metropolitan Museum of Art in New York. Technical experts there agreed to examine the scroll and consider undertaking the task. We persuaded the prelate to take the scroll there the next day.

Arriving on the morning of April 6 at the New York Museum ahead of the Syrian prelate, I discussed with the two technical experts the nature of the problem, on the basis of photographs. When the Metropolitan arrived with the scroll an hour later, the interview therefore took relatively little time. Already the conclusion had been reached that we should seek the services of Rutherford J. Gettens, who was then associated with the Fogg Museum at Harvard. We were advised, however, that a special box should be prepared to preserve the scroll more adequately.

That afternoon, while we were guests of the priest of the Assyrian Orthodox Church of West New York, the Metropolitan secured the Isaiah Scroll from the bank vault in which it was being kept, in order that I might add a tiny fragment containing portions of five letters which had not been properly located in Jerusalem. It belonged in the gap in Column 6. This meant rephotographing the column, though it was already too late to get it into our publication. At the same time, I rephotographed several of the final columns which had been done in Jerusalem on the poorer sheets of portrait film.[4] Although I should have liked to have done many more, the circumstances permitted only a few exposures.

In view of the delay in the "Fourth Scroll" plans, it was decided that I should take the box of fragments and the scroll to New Haven for further analysis and study while negotiations were proceeding with the Fogg Museum. Thus, I carried the documents to New Haven that night.

To expedite the process, Kraeling arranged for the use of a laboratory at the Yale Gallery of Fine Arts. On closer examination of the fragments, it became apparent that they offered few obstacles to adequate treatment for photographing. While studying them the previous February, I had cleaned the loose ones and mounted them between lantern-slide cover-glasses for protection. These were therefore ready to photograph at once. With my photo equipment mounted on the table nearby, I then began a careful study of the matted mass of leather. Gently unfolding to one side the loose piece on top, I laid a sheet of glass over the whole exposed surface to record its initial appearance on both sides. A check of some Aramaic words on this piece quickly led to Daniel 3:22-25 as its text. New zest was thus added to the delicate task.

Nine layers of leather could be detected along the edges of the total mass, though three were obviously folded pieces, indicating that at least six different fragments from three different scrolls might emerge from the total. The upper edges of the mass showed no signs of adhering, and almost at once the fourth and fifth layers fell from their position. They comprised a small folded piece of thin, light-tan leather (1⅜ x 2¼ inches). Though already cracked along the line of its fold, the piece opened up easily, revealing a script that was the same as that on the fragments beneath which it had lain. Physically, it seemed unrelated to any of the adjacent fragments; but I called it unit "d," and immediately mounted and photographed it with three other loose fragments.

A fine crack at the lower right of the first layer on the mass indicated on examination that it could be removed quite easily by gently working down from the top. As this fragment separated from the gelatinized area, unfortunately the first two letters of the word for "man" remained with the next level, where they appeared on the subsequent photograph. Just before photographing this first layer, I noticed that one of the already mounted loose pieces joined perfectly with it, completing three words along an original fold. Thus, the two were joined and mounted together and photographed as unit "a," measuring 1½ x 2 inches.

Another of the loose fragments immediately associated itself with the exposed second layer, producing a sizable fragment (2½ x 2 inches) with seven lines of text (unit "b"). Again a crack separated this layer from the disintegrated leather at the lower corner; its removal was equally simple. With this operation, however, the two letters from layer one still adhering at the lower right crumbled away. As this fragment was removed, a small, narrow, uninscribed fragment, totally unrelated to any of the other fragments in texture and color, fell from beneath; it had been completely hidden from view.

Still another of the loose fragments matched along a fold at its right edge with the third layer on the mass, forming unit "c" (2 x 3¼ inches), which again was immediately photographed. This third layer was already cracked down its middle and showed signs of crumbling in several places. Since it adhered tightly to the back of the fragment which lay beneath, I made no attempt to separate them; the danger of loss to either or both was too great.

The sixth layer (layers four and five had slipped out already, as mentioned above) was of a different kind of leather and seemed to have been folded over in ancient times on top of the seventh layer. Disintegration along the entire lower part of this fragment made separation very difficult; with gentle prodding, however, it finally came loose without any loss. The script on this sixth layer was identical with that on the seventh. The piece was badly blackened with age, but its script was dimly readable. Soon it was identified as a part of the same column of text, containing portions of Daniel 3:27-30. This scroll is now called 1QDan^b.

With the sixth layer removed, the remainder of the largest fragment was revealed. Now parts of Daniel 3:22-31 (3:22 — 4:1 in English) had appeared on two fragments. Since it had impressed me at first as revealing a script somewhat similar to the Manual of Discipline (1QS), I tentatively thought of the fragments as belonging to the middle of the first century B.C. Although the text contributed nothing new, its significance among Biblical manuscripts was immediately apparent. *Here was a fragment written barely a hundred years after the original composition of the book of Daniel!*[5] Since my first study of the fragments, however, I have come to believe that a mid-first-century A.D. date of origin is more likely. Even at that, these fragments may be unique among Old Testament manuscripts in point of proximity to the date of original composition.[6]

Only the folded leather adhering to the back of the large Daniel fragment (layers eight and nine) now remained unopened. At first the two layers appeared to be so firmly pressed against each other that I wondered if they might have been completely fused. After some moments of careful probing of the edges at almost every point, suddenly these layers literally burst apart. Almost immediately I noticed the expression, ". . . and Daniel said unto . . . ," in a beautifully-formed script, as black as though it had been inscribed but a few days before. The appearance of the script reminded me of a printed page, it was so elegantly executed. The fine leather on which it was written had been carefully ruled, probably with a reed, and the letters formed with utmost precision. Although they bore an impression of modernity, closer examination left no doubt that they belonged to the same paleographic tradition as the rest of the scrolls from the cave.[7] This fragment is now designated 1QDan[a].

On the right half of the fragment appeared portions of Daniel 1:10-16 from the upper lefthand corner of a column, while at the left half were parts of Daniel 2:4-6 from the upper righthand corner of the adjacent column. A paragraph indentation appeared on the fourth line of the left portion, and all that followed on the fragment was in Aramaic. It is in the middle of Daniel 2:4 that the Biblical book shifts from Hebrew to Aramaic, the latter continuing through Chapter Seven. Fortunately, this interesting feature of the book has been preserved on such an early fragment.[8]

The main question posed by these two sections from Daniel was whether or not they belonged to the same scroll. The fact that the Songs of Thanksgiving Scroll (1QH) was prepared by two quite different hands argued immediately for a similar phenomenon for the Daniel Scroll. It now seems paleographically probable that both parts come from shortly before the demise of the Community in A.D. 68.

The nature of these fragments and their relation to each other creates the impression that they were deliberately torn from a scroll in ancient times and crumpled together with destructive intent. Could it have been that this scroll of Daniel came into the hands of some Roman soldier who gave it this treatment, only to have the pieces picked up by a devout member of the community and cast into the cave to avoid further desecration? Only theories can explain the strange form in which these fragments were found. These were not the only scrolls from the cave, however, which indicated such ruthless treatment in the ancient past. Sections of the Hebrew University Songs Scroll (1QH) appeared to have suffered similar abuse, as well as their scroll of Isaiah (1QIs^b).

Gradually during the subsequent months, as I found time to translate the other fragments from my photographs, the relation of units "a," "b," and "c," with their closely written lines, became apparent. They all belonged together, forming a strip of inscribed leather about 2 inches wide and 8 inches long. They formed sections from two columns of a Hebrew prayer scroll. One prayer ended, ". . . from generation to generation, blessed be our Lord who has caused us to rejoice." Another began, "A prayer for the Day of Atonement: Remember, O Lord . . . ." Another contrasts the fate of the wicked with the blessings of the righteous. But most important in the text are the words, "Thou hast chosen for thyself a people in the time of thy pleasure, for thou hast remembered thy covenant . . . . Thou didst . . . separate them for thyself as holy from all the peoples, and thou didst renew thy covenant for them in a vision of glory . . . ." The writer of this manuscript believed himself to belong to a people of the New Covenant![9] This scroll is now designated 1QPrayers (1Q34).

Other fragments from the cigarette box gradually found their places among these two scrolls, leaving unidentified only the piece of papyrus, a ragged piece of coarse leather with crude writing (it later proved to be a fragment of "The Book of Noah" [1Q19]; see p. 149), and a few uninscribed pieces of disintegrated leather adhering to some cloth. All the fragments were carefully mounted between glass and photographed in both black and white and color films. Although a few letters were lost from one fragment of the prayer scroll during the separation process, they were preserved in the photographs.[10]

The next few days in New Haven were spent on the "Fourth Scroll." Soon a sturdy wooden box replaced the inadequate cardboard one I had made in Jerusalem. Study of the scroll revealed that above and below the place where I had removed the fragment while in Jerusalem, additional loosening of the leather had occurred on the soft side of the scroll. Along the edges of the brittle, badly disintegrated side, slight additional cracking had occurred.[11] Without damage to the rest of the scroll, it was soon apparent that, with patience, considerably more of the softer part could be removed. Most of one day was spent gently probing the edges along the cracks until finally a large fragment, measuring 4¾ x 8½ inches, came loose.[12] Gradually it flattened enough to mount between glass and photograph.

More than half of each of twenty-six lines of Aramaic text from this scroll were now available for study. Since the ink used for this manuscript had apparently been metallic, the lines of script were badly disintegrated. With this large number of lines, however, gradually more and more words could be deciphered.

Some weeks later, Burrows pointed on my transcription to the combination of letters *lmk*. "Is that the name Lamech?" he asked. I had been trying to read it as a verb. Toward the end of the same line were the letters *bt'nws*, which I thought might mean "daughter of Enosh." Since it all seemed one word, however, the name "Betenosh" seemed also probable. A check in R. H. Charles' huge volumes, *Apocrypha and Pseudepigrapha*, led to Jubilees 4:28, where Betenos is the name of the wife of Lamech; they were the parents of Noah. Soon the whole line became clear: "Then I, Lamech, hastened and went to Bitenosh, my wife. . . ." Since the name Lamech occurred once again with the first-person pronoun, we began to call the document the Book of Lamech, for such a writing was mentioned in an early Greek source.

Albright's suggestion that the smaller fragment was related to the Enoch literature was now further confirmed. At least this part of the manuscript seemed to be an elaboration of the story of the birth of Noah, as developed from the book of Genesis in the Noah portions of the Enoch literature (chapters 106-107). There, however, Enoch speaks in the first person. The possibility that this scroll might have been one of the sources from which the book of Enoch developed seemed also to be indicated.[13]

In the midst of all these efforts toward the handling and publication of the scrolls and fragments, our major project was the preparation of the first A.S.O.R. Dead Sea Scroll volume. Edited by Burrows, with assistance from Brownlee and myself, it was to contain introductory information along with full-sized facsimile photographs of the Isaiah Scroll and the Habakkuk Commentary. To speed its completion for the scholarly world, the usual critical discussions found in such publications were omitted. Some months previously, I had begun the process of producing the necessary enlarged prints of each column from the negatives made in Jerusalem. The large negatives, however, posed a problem for my equipment. Only one half of each column could be enlarged at a time; the two halves, therefore, had to be spliced together.[14] While in New Haven I imposed upon the kindness of a commercial photographer friend, who permitted me to use his laboratory and equipment to complete the full-sized prints for our publication.

Contacts with the Fogg Museum proved encouraging, and arrangements were soon made for the Metropolitan to meet there with Gettens. Since the Syrian prelate was then in Rhode Island, it fell to me again to carry the "Lamech Scroll" to Cambridge, Massachusetts on the afternoon of April 13. Arriving at the Fogg Museum well ahead of the Metropolitan the next morning, I discussed the scroll problems privately with Gettens. Although he exhibited much enthusiasm for the delicate task, his previous commitments unfortunately would not permit undertaking it short of several months.

By the time the Metropolitan arrived, most of the discussion was completed, and there was left merely the formality of obtaining the prelate's permission to leave the document in Gettens' care. We were confident now that at last the proper procedure had been established and the process of opening the rest of the scroll would be only a matter of scheduling.

The weeks sped by as I tried, in the midst of my other duties, to include the writing of a detailed report on the fragments for the A.S.O.R., while seeing several articles through to publication.

Late in May, 1949, the belated April issue of the *Bulletin of the A.S.O.R.* appeared. In it was an article by Ovid Sellers, reporting the rediscovery and excavation of the cave by the Dead Sea the previous February. There I read the words: "The operation was complicated by previous clandestine excavators, who last November dug up the surface of the cave to a depth of several inches in vain hopes that the Bedouins had missed some scrolls. . . . The identity of two who conducted the unauthorized excavation is known. . . ."[15] The background of the fragments on which I had been working suddenly took on new light.

Immediately I wrote to the Syrian prelate, outlining Sellers' report and suggesting that, in view of the circumstances under which these fragments had been secured, he should expect them to be claimed by Jordan. Since Sellers had seen at least some of them prior to November,[16] I assumed they must have been picked up before the clandestine excavation; but the connection with the latter seemed too close to allow any claim to ownership, I reasoned. In a letter dated June 10, 1949, the Metropolitan replied that the fragments had been secured in 1947 and requested that nothing about them be said or published.[17] Meanwhile, however, the belated May, 1949, issue of the *Biblical Archaeologist*, which included the Metropolitan's own article along with an editorial report about the fragments, had just been mailed. The scholarly world would know about the existence and the nature of the fragments within a matter of days.

Correspondence flew between the A.S.O.R., myself, and Metropolitan Samuel. He telephoned me from Detroit and made a trip to my home in Des Plaines, Illinois, to discuss the issue. Meanwhile I hastened to complete the work of assembling, mounting, photographing, and studying the fragments.

It seemed to me that only one procedure was proper — the fragments must be immediately reported and offered for return to Jordan. The prelate requested that I draft for him an appropriate letter to send to the Jordanian Department of Antiquities, which I did on July 16. Copies of a full report, which included my step-by-step photographs, were sent to the A.S.O.R. and to the Jordanian authorities in late July. On December 3 I delivered the mounted fragments to the Metropolitan in New Jersey. The A.S.O.R. meanwhile decided to delay publication until the fragments were returned to Jordan or until Jordan's Department of Antiquities granted permission. The latter was given early in 1950, but the fragments were not returned.

Silence descended upon the matter, as other problems took precedence. The A.S.O.R. understandably continued to hesitate about publication. A transliteration and French translation, made from the photographs sent to Jordan, appeared in 1955 in the official publication of the Cave I materials;[18] but the mystery of the disposition of the fragments continued.

In an interview with Metropolitan Samuel on August 19, 1962, and in subsequent letters dated November 10 and December 19, he again stated that the fragments were secured in 1947 and that he considered them his property.[19] There the matter stood for several years.

Determined that these fragments must be published, I was

grateful for an invitation from the editor of *Revue de Qumran* suggesting that I submit an article that would include natural-sized reproductions of the fragments. The article was dispatched early in 1965 and appeared that Fall.[20]

A new dimension to the story was added when, in 1966, Samuel's autobiography was published. At the very end an appendix appeared with very poor reproductions of these same fragments.[21] The illustrations revealed that all of them except the papyrus fragment had seriously deteriorated. It was distressing to see large sections of the Daniel and Prayer Scroll fragments completely eroded away. Some areas that I had hoped with more scientific treatment might yield some additional letters were lost forever. Having just returned from Jerusalem, where I had observed the deterioration of the great Isaiah "A" Scroll, then on exhibit in the newly opened "Shrine of the Book," I had become especially sensitive to the problem of preserving scroll materials.[22]

During the summer of 1970 the American Bible Society exhibited Samuel's fragments in their New York headquarters beside color reproductions which I supplied. When I compared the originals with my photographs taken in 1949, I was appalled to see how much disintegration of the leather had taken place in so short a time. Apparently the high humidity of New Jersey and probably some bacterial action were responsible. The story of these peripatetic fragments from Qumran, therefore, may end with their complete demise. Fortunately they had been published from the 1949 photographs which revealed their former state of preservation.

The beautiful script of the Daniel "A" fragments soon proved to be of special importance. Closer study convinced me that they represented the latest of the scripts I had seen from Qumran. But how late was the question. During a brief sojourn at Harvard Divinity School in the Spring of 1968, I happened upon Yadin's preliminary report of the excavations at Masada. Among the illustrations appeared a small section from a scroll which he called "Songs of the Sabbath Sacrifices" and which he claimed was from Qumran. The script of the five words in the illustration immediately struck me as very similar to the Daniel "A" fragments. Here was the clue that might establish the *terminus ad quem* for all the Qumran scrolls — the terminal point in history for the Qumran scripts. The reasoning seemed simple: If 1QDan[a] was among the last manuscripts produced at Qumran before its destruction in A.D. 68, and if the same scribe had copied the Songs of the Sabbath Sacrifices document found in the debris left by the Roman destruction of Masada in A.D. 73, not the slightest doubt would remain that the period of Qumran writing ended at that time.

Immediately I set about to gather the evidence, which was presented as a paper at the Society of Biblical Literature meetings the following December and published some months later.[23] By then it seemed certain that the Daniel "A" fragments established clearly the fact that all the Qumran scrolls had been copied before A.D. 68-70. Our paleographic process for dating the manuscripts had therefore been vindicated.

15

Failure as a Salesman

THOSE OF US who lived in the midst of those tragic last months of the British Mandate of Palestine continued to be deeply concerned about Partition's injustice to the native Palestinian Arabs. All of us had written numerous letters and articles describing our personal experiences and insights, in the vain hope of stemming the flood of political propaganda that had engulfed the United States.

To unburden his concerns, Burrows departed from his usual scholarly pursuits and wrote a little book entitled *Palestine Is Our Business* (1949). My own thoughts were published in our Methodist periodical *The Christian Advocate* ("Viewing Palestine from the Inside," April 15, 1948, pp. 4-6, 31). Several hundred dollars were provided for Syrian Orthodox Christian refugees with profits made from the sale of scroll photographs.

Along with these direct expressions of our concern, we assumed that efforts toward the sale of the scrolls could produce more significant results toward the relief of suffering. Several major obstacles, however, stood in the way of a successful sale.

In the first place, not long after the Metropolitan arrived in the United States, a rumor began to circulate that he was claiming a value of one million dollars for the scrolls. Potential donors, having a distaste for the Oriental bargaining custom, shied away from such a fantastic figure. Through two widely separated experts in rare books, W. F. Albright and I had appraisals made of the Syrian scrolls. The estimates ranged from $150,000 to about

$250,000 for the four scrolls, in the light of all the current factors. Both appraisals were communicated to the Metropolitan, who offered no comment other than an expressed desire for our assistance. Repeatedly he called upon me to draft letters and statements.

A second problem arose almost immediately upon the appearance of the first preliminary publications. Our appraisal of the antiquity of the scrolls was vigorously challenged in scholarly circles, as we had expected. Until 1952 the number and influence of negative pens seemed almost to outweigh those which came to our defense. If the scrolls were medieval, as some of these antagonists proposed, their value could barely exceed a few thousand dollars. Would-be purchasers therefore could be expected to await a resolution of this major obstacle. One scholar published a vigorous attack against the Isaiah Scroll, in view of certain technical details which he interpreted as rendering the manuscript virtually worthless to Biblical studies, regardless of its age. Much printer's ink was expended from 1950 to 1952 over these fine points.[1]

Probably the most knotty problem was the tangle which arose in 1949 over the Syrian prelate's ability to deliver a clear title to the scrolls. After Trans-Jordan and the West Bank of Palestine were joined on December 1, 1948, to form the Hashemite Kingdom of the Jordan, jurisdiction of the cave area by the Dead Sea came under that country's Department of Antiquities. Almost immediately, G. L. Harding, Director of Antiquities for Jordan, sought to control not only further cave explorations but also the circulation of already discovered scrolls and fragments.

Queries were also raised concerning the observance of the antiquities laws in connection with the original find. Early in 1949 Sellers communicated Harding's concern to me, and I immediately prepared a full report about the dealings the previous spring with the Syrians and the Mandate Department of Antiquities (see pp. 59-60, 70, 72, 76-77). That report, unfortunately, failed to reach Jerusalem. Without having a proper understanding of the situation, therefore, Harding published in a leading British archeological journal a harsh condemnation of all those who originally dealt with the scrolls.[2]

Meanwhile Sukenik's statement about invoking the antiquities laws to force a return of the Syrian scrolls to Palestine (see p. 125) was circulated widely. An aura of possible illegality thus surrounded these documents. Libraries and potential donors were wary.

To complicate the problem of title, several compatriots of the Metropolitan voiced strong claims to partnership with him in the ownership of the scrolls. Having learned that he was asking a million dollars for the documents, both Kando and Isha'ya put forth a claim, based on the fact that they had guided the Bedouins to St. Mark's Monastery and that the Syrian prelate had "promised to remember them with a gift" when the scrolls were sold.[3]

A more serious and persistent claim to partnership was that of Anton Kiraz (see pp. 105, 108-110), whose connection with the scrolls was first made known through Sukenik's writings. Having lost most of what he owned as a result of Partition in 1948, Kiraz suffered the plight of many refugees. Early in 1949, a serious illness added to his predicament. Finally he was sent to a sanitarium in Beirut, where the high cost of his convalescence soon reduced him to a state of virtual poverty. In the midst of his despair and illness, he naturally resorted to his hope for assistance from the sale of the scrolls. When he read the Metropolitan's published account about the scrolls, in which Kiraz's claim was categorically denied, he sought the help of an attorney, who advised a lawsuit.

None of these obstacles, it seemed to me, was insurmountable. Having received reliable guidance in the matter of price, I urged Metropolitan Samuel to establish a reasonable price as a basis for negotiation. In numerous discussions with potential purchasers, I always stated the figure of $250,000 as the probable top price, even though the Syrian prelate gave me no specific confirmation of his willingness to sell at that price.

Although on the basis of paleography my confidence in the antiquity of the documents remained unshaken throughout the intense debate which arose among scholars, that problem could only be handled through the ponderous process of scholarly research and publication. At first, paleography was our only reasonably reliable method of dating the scrolls; the early disputes therefore centered mostly around that approach. In February, 1949, however, the rediscovery of the cave produced the long-awaited pottery and other archeological evidence. Significant weight was then added to our arguments, even suggesting that our conclusions were somewhat conservative.[4] Late in 1950 results from the application of the "Carbon-14" age-determination test applied to some of the linen cloth found in the cave proved most timely. This test provided a "mean date" of A.D. 33 for the cave deposit. The margin of error of plus or minus 200 years, however, left a degree of uncertainty about the value of that evidence.[5] By 1952 only a few scholars had not conceded the substantial accuracy of our initial dating proposals.[6]

The problem of title plagued us most. During July, 1949, at the request of the Metropolitan I drafted a letter for him to send to the Director of Antiquities for Jordan, in which the Daniel and other fragments were reported and a request for clearance of his title to the four scrolls was made. Apparently the letter failed to arrive, and a second one was sent in late December. Finally an answer was received by the Metropolitan in late January, 1950, in which certain conditions were articulated for clearance of title. On reading a copy of the reply, I was personally convinced that clearance of title with the Jordanian government could be achieved. The conditions seemed both reasonable and not too difficult to meet. I urged the Metropolitan to begin immediately to carry them out.[7]

The claim to partnership by certain Syrians in Jordan proved elusive and troublesome. That of Kando and Isha'ya offered no serious obstacle, but the testimony of Kiraz seemed to carry some evidence to support it. During his serious illness in the summer of 1949, he appealed to me for help. Having no firm basis for judgment, I could only express my sympathy to him and explain the problem that a lawsuit against Samuel would create. To secure aid for himself and other suffering Syrian Orthodox Christians, I pointed out, a sale of the scrolls was imperative; but a lawsuit over title would obstruct any sale. As a gesture of sympathy with him in his plight, some relief assistance was sent to him from funds raised by the Metropolitan. The threatened lawsuit was averted.

Meanwhile a mystery figure, a Czechoslovakian refugee in Jerusalem, entered the picture as a protagonist for Kiraz. Long, involved, and difficult-to-read letters began to pour in from him; he claimed to have concrete evidence in support of Kiraz and was preparing to publish a book on the whole story. When he sent a photograph of several pages from the book, it was immediately apparent that, if published, it could only serve to hurt the whole

Taw	'Ayin	Samekh	Mem (final)	Mem (medial)	Kaph	He	'Aleph
T	'	S	M	M	K	H	'

Taw	'Ayin	Samekh	Mem (final)	Mem (medial)	Kaph	He	'Aleph	
תת						תדד	יצע	1.
תתך	עע			מהמ מ	גהא	אדאא	אא	2.
תתן	עי		תספ	גגבב	גהי	צא	אצ	3.
תת	עע	חמ	בבך	מג	גצ	הד	אא	4.
תת	עע	מב	טט	מב	עע	חד	אא	5.
תתן	עעי	ממי	ךמד	בב	גב	חהד	אא	6.
תתן	עעי	סס	מם	כל	בב	חה	אא	7.
תתע	עע		מטט	מע	בב	חה	אא	8.
ת	עעי	סס	ף	בבנ	כ	חהד	אאצ	9.
תתע	עעי		טסף	מב	גגנ	חחה	אאצ	10.
ת	ע	ס	ם	מ	כ	ה	א	11.

J.C.T.

DATING THE DEAD SEA SCROLLS BY PALEOGRAPHY

This chart illustrates how paleography provided the clue to the dating of the first Qumran scrolls. Seven representative letters are shown (with medial and final forms of the "M") from each of eleven different manuscripts dating from about 410 B.C. to A.D. 895. In most cases two examples of each letter are supplied to show the slight variations of each scribe. A study of each letter from lines 1-11 reveals an evolvement of the basic form in the direction of the stabilized forms at the bottom. Note how lines 9-11, which cover about A.D. 75 to 895, reveal very little change during over 800 years, representing the very careful work of the Masoretic scribes.

The manuscripts represented here are: 1. Leather letter V from Arsham about 410 B.C.; 2. Edfu (Egypt) papyrus document from 3rd century B.C.; 3. Nash papyrus from Egypt about 2nd century B.C.; 4. Qumran Cave I Isaiah "a" scroll; 5. "Rule of the Community" (1QS); 6. "Habakkuk Commentary" (1QpHab); 7. 1QDaniel "a" scroll (latest of the Qumran scripts); 8. "Songs of the Sabbath Sacrifices" scroll from Masada (must have been copied prior to A.D. 73); 9. Psalms scroll from Nahal Hever, about A.D. 75-100; 10. fragments of Exodus from Wadi Murabba'at, about A.D. 125; and 11. the Ben Asher "Cairo Codex" dated A.D. 895.

This chart was prepared by cutting each letter directly from photographs of these documents and pasting them in position. The paste-up was then xeroxed to provide the copy used for the line-cut. Each letter, therefore, is a separate photograph of the original scribe's work.

Note that the final form of the "M" does not appear until late in the 3rd century B.C. Examples of the *samekh* ("S") are lacking from documents 3, 8, and 10, unfortunately.

cause and do no one any good. After investigation of the circumstances, through those who were close to the man, I refused to cooperate in his endeavor to get the book published and impressed upon him the damage such a publication would bring to all parties concerned. When I sought assistance for him in his own physical plight through other channels, he abandoned his plans, so far as I know.[8]

Confident that all these obstacles could be surmounted in the face of a firm bid from a prospective donor, I continued to press various leads toward a possible sale. Our first hope had been that Yale University would be able to secure a donor, but recent purchases of the Boswell papers and the Bay Psalm Book had tapped their potential resources to the limit. The J. Pierpont Morgan Library in New York expressed keen interest, but the fanfare over the problem of title at that time soon cooled their ardor.

Our thoughts then turned to the Library of Congress, and an exhibit of the scrolls in October, 1949, opened up a new approach. During the exhibit I discussed the prospects with the head librarian, who made it quite clear that the million-dollar claim had closed the door to their potential donors. My assurances that a figure nearer $250,000 would very likely solve the problem brought no change in the picture.

Another exhibit of the scrolls at the Walters Art Gallery in Baltimore the following month opened new contacts; but the same obstacle appeared, and again potential donors lost interest. Additional exhibits followed during 1950 at Duke University and the Oriental Institute of the University of Chicago. Although huge crowds formed long lines to view the famed scrolls at each exhibit, potential donors failed to appear.

All my efforts toward a sale of the scrolls ceased on October 15, 1950, for six months. Through an agreement between the International Council of Religious Education and the A.S.O.R., a leave of absence was arranged to enable me to pursue my paleographic studies uninterrupted. For the first three months I attempted to exhaust the University of Chicago libraries of every resource relating to early Hebrew inscriptions and manuscripts, as well as those in Aramaic and other closely related languages. Much time also was spent at home, developing a new technique for preparing paleographic charts by means of photographs to avoid "the human element" which some scholars were claiming was falsifying our evidence. Using unretouched photographs from which selected letters were clipped and pasted to the chart, all freehand drawing of letter forms was eliminated. When rephotographed with a high-contrast copy film, a perfect chart resulted.[9]

Fellowship stipends from the A.S.O.R. and the American Philosophical Society enabled me to spend the last three months of my leave in England scouring the libraries of the British Museum and of Oxford and Cambridge Universities. Several thousand Hebrew and Aramaic manuscript fragments were examined, primarily to see if any could be found which might show similarity of script to that on the Dead Sea Scrolls and thereby challenge my former conclusions. At Cambridge University Library alone, more than two thousand fragments from the famed Cairo Genizah collection were systematically examined.[10] There, also, I spent several days examining under a magnifying glass every letter of the Nash Papyrus and took copious notes on my observations. Special photographs were secured of many of the documents for use in a master chart already being developed.

Everywhere Elizabeth and I went, we were most cordially received. Visits with dozens of Hebrew scholars produced immeasurable values in both information and friendships. Several days spent in the home of the eminent Hebraist, Paul Kahle, in Charlbury, near Oxford, proved an education in itself, despite his skepticism regarding paleography as a means of dating Hebrew manuscripts. The assistance of David Diringer at Cambridge was equally helpful. Another highlight of the experience was an interlude of several days in Paris at the Louvre Museum, where I examined a number of ancient Hebrew inscriptions. André Parrot, Director of the Near Eastern Section, graciously arranged a reception one evening, where we met many of the leading savants of Paris. Another fine evening was spent in the home of A. Dupont-Sommer, who was even then becoming a controversial figure in the interpretation of the scrolls. With a satchel loaded with photographs and abundant notes, and more convinced than ever about the validity of paleography as a means of dating ancient Hebrew manuscripts (as well as the accuracy of my dating of the Dead Sea Scrolls), we sailed for home in April, 1951.

Metropolitan Samuel was growing impatient. The long delay over the sale of the scrolls, together with the complexities involved in attempting to clear the problem of title and negotiate the arrangements for the opening of the "Lamech Scroll," gradually brought our relations with the prelate to a breaking point. Suddenly he withdrew the "Lamech Scroll" (1QapGen) from the Fogg Museum and refused any further cooperation, declaring that his agreement with the A.S.O.R. had expired. Technically the agreement had expired, if figured from April 3, 1948, when we had worked out the details in Jerusalem.

Burrows, during an exhibit of the scrolls at the Art Museum in Worcester, Massachusetts (October, 1951), attempted to ameliorate the situation. While on a trip to New York two months later, I spent an evening with the Metropolitan to discuss the whole problem, and we seemed to part with a much better understanding. A letter received a few weeks later, however, indicated that the situation had not improved, as I had hoped. A break with the Metropolitan seemed inevitable for both the A.S.O.R. and myself.

Fortunately, the first A.S.O.R. volume *The Dead Sea Scrolls of St. Mark's Monastery*, Vol. I, which included full-sized reproductions of the Isaiah and Habakkuk Scrolls, had appeared in March, 1950. A similar publication of the Manual of Discipline had been pressed to completion by Burrows early in 1951. The scholarly world therefore had access to the three main documents.

Meanwhile, on November 30, 1951, the Metropolitan placed the scrolls under a trust agreement, leaving financial matters relating to them in the hands of the chairman of the trustees.[11] This move impressed me as a good one to inspire confidence in his intentions with regard to the disposition of funds which might accrue from the sale of the scrolls.

Continuing to believe that a successful sale of the scrolls would relieve all the tensions, I eagerly seized every opportunity to discuss the documents with potential donors. Dozens of detailed letters were written. The nature of my lecturing schedules throughout the United States provided numerous contacts with interested persons; given the slightest opening, I related the story in detail. Invariably the problems of price and title plagued the discussions, but always I emphasized my conviction that both could be solved once a sizable sum was assured.

On one occasion, when I visited Midland, Michigan, the Dow Chemical Company arranged for a discussion with some of their technical experts on the problem of preservation of the scrolls. New channels of interest there at first seemed promising. This contact, too, proved fruitless.

In March, 1953, an invitation to lecture in Dallas, Texas, before a large group of prominent businessmen appeared to open a most promising door toward success. Carefully planned by a number of influential and keenly interested religious leaders, educators, and businessmen, the event seemed to set the stage for some real progress. One enthusiastic officer of a large company generously provided my round-trip plane fare to support the program. An illustrated address, designed to arouse enthusiasm for the scrolls, was presented in a large home to the select audience. Private conversations with several key leaders followed, and I returned to Chicago full of hope.

Not many days later, Norman M. Yonan arrived in Dallas with what has been claimed to be a fourth- or fifth-century A.D. Syriac New Testament. Having the document with him, he was able to arouse interest in it immediately; but in the course of those negotiations he learned about the interest in the Dead Sea Scrolls. Yonan, apparently influenced strongly by Sukenik's circulated statement, injected serious doubt about title into the minds of those interested. On learning of this unfortunate turn of events, I outlined in detail how the problem of title could be solved, but to no avail. The hope vanished.

A considerable prospect list had been gradually compiled, and I wrote copiously to every name on it. Much interest was expressed at every contact, but each trail disappeared into a hazy blur. Periodic attempts to learn what progress the Metropolitan was making brought only silence, so I continued hopeful that a sale might be made that would solve all the problems shrouding the story of the Syrians' scrolls.

During the fall of 1953[12] an idea was born that appeared to offer the finest possible disposition of the four scrolls. It was a by-product of a project on which I was working for the Religious Activities Committee of the United States Junior Chamber of Commerce.

A book entitled *Cradle of Our Faith* was being planned to enunciate the new religious emphasis added to the "Jaycee" Creed — "We believe that faith in God gives meaning and purpose to human life." Two men who were keenly interested in the book piloted me in their war-surplus, remodeled "Twin Cessna" plane to Baltimore one day for an interview with Albright concerning the project. Passing over the first range of the Shenandoah Mountains in western Virginia, we entered a heavy bank of clouds. Dropping beneath the overcast, the pilot followed a valley northeast, seeking a break over the next ridge. None appeared. He climbed above the overcast, hoping to get into Harrisburg — again only clouds. Minutes seemed like hours. Suddenly, through a hole in the clouds, some green fields appeared below. The pilot plunged the plane earthward as the co-pilot spotted a yellow airport wind-sock beside a large grassy meadow. Circling the unidentified landing strip, our pilot skillfully set the plane down lightly on the grassy field and taxied toward the deserted fieldhouse and hangar. Not a soul appeared, but beside a gateway to the field a large sign said, "Welcome to Gettysburg." With his location known, the pilot wanted to take off again and head on into Baltimore on instruments. Firmly I said, "We are staying in Gettysburg tonight."

With our appointment postponed by telephone, we relaxed in a small hotel room while I shared the story of the Dead Sea Scrolls with my friends. Their enthusiasm mounted with each episode. An idea began to emerge that night that could tie our project to the sale of the scrolls. By the time the book was ready for release the next fall, therefore, we had agreed upon a plan to present to the International Junior Chamber of Commerce, which would be meeting for its Ninth Congress in Mexico City the last week in October, 1954.

The book was interfaith and international in scope, and the International Jaycees embraced almost every country of the world. We proposed to the Congress that the book be accepted as an international project with the understanding that all profits from sales would be used to build a fund to purchase the four Dead Sea Scrolls, which in turn would become an international project. Title to the scrolls would be placed in the Palestine Archaeological Museum and arrangements made through the International Jaycees to conduct exhibits of the scrolls around the world, after which the documents would continue to reside in Jerusalem, Jordan. The money paid for the scrolls, we suggested, would go to rebuild the Syrian Orthodox Monastery in Jerusalem and to support other educational and rehabilitation projects there. Thus we hoped a double benefit could accrue from the project.

For almost a week we discussed our idea with the international leaders in caucus rooms, lobbies, and halls of the Del Prado Hotel in Mexico City. It was only exploratory, we knew, but the interest and enthusiasm exhibited by men from many corners of the world gave us assurance that the project could succeed.

With renewed confidence I returned home ready to lay the plan before the trustees of the scrolls. Lying on my office desk was a letter from Burrows; its words hit me like a dash of cold water — the scrolls had been sold!

Mystery surrounded the sale, but the fact of it seemed certain. A letter to the Metropolitan seeking confirmation brought no reply. Again I wrote, outlining the plan we had so carefully prepared — again silence. On February 13, 1955, the details were finally revealed by the Prime Minister of Israel at a news conference in Jerusalem. Yigael Yadin, son of the late Eliezer Sukenik, had secretly secured the scrolls for the State of Israel through the help of Samuel Gottesman of New York, and had sent them to the Hebrew University in Jerusalem.[13] The sale had been consummated on July 1, 1954, at a price of $250,000, the highest estimate our advisors had claimed could be expected.[14] Another battle of the scrolls was ended. Sukenik had won, posthumously. I had lost.

16

Further Adventures of Discovery

THUS FAR the discoveries in Cave I, which the Bedouin shepherd boy first entered during the winter of 1946-1947, have dominated these chapters. By 1952, however, other adventures in the Judean desert — which were destined to dwarf those related to that first cave — occupied the attention of scholars and public alike. For the reader who has not followed closely these oft-repeated stories, a brief summary of these later adventures seems warranted here. Furthermore, before any attempt is made to evaluate what has been discovered, more of the evidence needs to be reviewed.

With the rediscovery of the first cave early in 1949, a meticulous excavation of the debris left by the Bedouins and the Syrians was carried out by a group of archeologists from February 15 to March 5. Fragments of some fifty tall, cylindrical jars, and almost an equal number of bowl covers, were recovered. It took several months of tedious work in the Palestine Archaeological Museum to reconstruct a few of them to their original shapes. Four small oil lamps, three bowls, a cooking pot, a pitcher, two forehead phylacteries,[1] parts of four arm phylacteries, a wooden comb, some pieces of wood, and an abundance of linen cloth constituted the artifacts recovered. Hundreds of fragments of inscribed leather, indicating the presence of at least seventy manuscripts at one time in the cave, were sifted from the debris. Several pieces belonging to seven of the scrolls and larger fragments previously found by the Bedouins and Syrians clearly related the cave to the original discovery.[2]

From among many tiny bits of leather, scholars were gradually able to identify portions of Biblical scrolls of Genesis, Exodus, Leviticus (written in archaic Hebrew script), Deuteronomy (two different scrolls), Judges, Samuel, Psalms (three scrolls), and Ezekiel. Adding these to the two already-described scrolls of Isaiah and Daniel (possibly two scrolls), a total of fifteen different Biblical manuscripts were represented in the first cave.

At least fifty-five non-Biblical scrolls are therefore indicated by the rest of the leather (and some papyrus) fragments. Among these, "commentaries"[3] of Micah, Zephaniah, and the Psalms were also identified. Adding the famed Habakkuk Commentary, four manuscripts of this type are known from that cave. Other documents represented among the fragments included phylactery scrolls (one containing the Decalogue in Deuteronomy 5:1-22), the Book of Jubilees (six fragments), the "Book of Noah" (Enoch 6-10, 106 — twenty-one fragments), the "Testament of Levi," "Sayings of Moses," a book of "Mysteries," some hymns and other liturgical scrolls, and several unknown apocryphal works. From all these it is clear that the cave once contained a considerable library of varied religious literature.

During the spring of 1949 Yusif Saad, then the indefatigable secretary of the Palestine Archaeological Museum, was hard on the trail of the Bedouins and their Bethlehem agent, Kando, who had kept discreetly in the background. Saad's chance meeting one day with a woman who lived across the street from St. Mark's Monastery uncovered the fact that her husband, Jabra, had participated in the Syrian clandestine excavation during November, 1948.[4] Jabra, when shown the materials secured during the official excavation, and with the help of some generous "bakshish," identified the cave beyond any question of a doubt. (He recovered his cigarette roller from among the ancient finds spread on tables in the Museum!) Finally he revealed the name of the Bethlehem cobbler, Kando; and Saad set off for Bethlehem by donkey via the tortuous and circuitous road through the Judean widerness. The story of Saad's efforts to make the acquaintance of Kando, and finally (in 1950) to secure the mass of fragments which the cobbler and his associates had dug from the cave, reads like a Sherlock Holmes detective adventure.[5] It was then that fragments of the Hebrew University Isaiah Scroll (1QIs^b), some from the "Genesis Apocryphon" (1Q20, now 1QapGen), several large pieces (including two almost-complete columns) from the Manual of Discipline (1QS), and some fragments of a scroll of Deuteronomy (1QDeut^b)[6] were secured for the Department of Antiquities, but only after payment of the large sum of £P1,000 ($2,800).[7]

During the long period while Saad was seeking out Kando, this Bethlehem merchant (according to John Allegro) seems to have become fearful and buried a number of large pieces of scrolls on his Bethlehem property. When he went to retrieve them later, the moisture of the soil had reduced them to lumps of worthless glue.[8] How many manuscripts and fragments were lost through this fatal error can only be surmised. Probably it was the remainder of the materials secured during the November, 1948, "excavation."

During the official excavation of Cave I, the small ruin called Khirbet Qumran, lying on a prominence of the marly plateau barely half a mile to the south where it ends abruptly at the Wadi Qumran, was examined briefly. Some nearby tombs also were excavated, but the archeologists drew the tentative conclusion that the *khirbeh* ("ruin" in Arabic) had no relation to the cave. The ruin appeared to be the remains of a Roman military outpost abandoned about the end of the first century A.D. Further excavation there seemed unwarranted. For more than two years, therefore, the focus of attention was turned on the scholarly battle which raged in the United States and Europe over the authenticity and antiquity of the scrolls.

Mounting pressure from scholars who sought further archeological evidence finally refocused interest on the *khirbeh*. Late in 1951 (November 24 to December 12), the first of six seasons of meticulous examination of the area of occupation was undertaken by G. L. Harding and Father R. de Vaux. Their excavation had not proceeded very far into the southwest corner of the main building when coins and pottery began to link the site to the same period of history and events represented by the cave. One jar in particular, found sunk in the floor of one room, was the same shape and size as those found in the cave. Some indications pointed toward a sectarian religious center, perhaps of the Essenes, who had already been suggested as related to the scrolls. Archeological enthusiasm mounted.

In the meantime, however, the Ta'amireh Bedouins had been actively searching for new caves, and during October, 1951, appeared in Jerusalem with some fragments from a new source. Mystery surrounded the discovery, though authorities were led to a cave out in the Judean wilderness. Twice the area was visited, but prospects of more scrolls and a fruitful excavation seemed dim; excavation was not deemed advisable.

Hardly had the excavation at the *khirbeh* begun, when Kando offered Father de Vaux a sizable group of leather and papyrus fragments for purchase. With patience and adroitness, de Vaux pursued negotiations directly with the Bedouins until finally, on January 21, 1952, an expedition was begun among the precipitous cliffs of the Wadi Murabba'at, almost twelve miles south of Khirbet Qumran.[9] Four huge caves produced a vast amount of valuable manuscript and archeological data related not to Qumran, however, but mostly to the second Jewish revolt of A.D. 132-135, under Bar Kokhba ("Son of a Star"). A new door to manuscript discoveries in the Holy Land had been opened.[10]

With the scholars momentarily absent from the Qumran area, the indefatigable Bedouins resumed their search for caves there. During February Cave II (2Q), just south of the first cave, produced some scroll fragments. Parts of seventeen Biblical scrolls were recovered, plus numerous non-Biblical pieces, a total of 187 fragments. It was now apparent that Cave I was no isolated cache from ancient times.

An expedition was needed to stem the clandestine Bedouin diggings. From March 10 to 29, seven scholars and two dozen Ta'amireh Bedouins, who were pressed into their employ, scoured close to 275 caves and crevices along a five-mile stretch of cliffs north and south of Wadi Qumran in search of the precious bits of inscribed leather. Twenty-six caves produced characteristic Qumran pottery sherds, but only one contained manuscript fragments. This one, Cave III (3Q), discovered on March 14, turned up the strangest document of all — a copper scroll (in two sections) which added mystery and a treasure hunt to the already fantastic story. Fifty-nine inscribed leather fragments were recovered, representing seven scrolls (four Biblical), a commentary on the first verse of Isaiah being the only one of significance.

The approaching heat of summer brought peace and silence once more to the Judean desert. July, 1952, however, found the Bedouins again in Jerusalem with more manuscript fragments, the source of which remained undisclosed (see pp. 153, 156). Apparently from somewhere south of Wadi Murabba'at, these documents, which included a Greek text of the Minor Prophets, were also related to the second Jewish revolt and not to the Qumran materials.

Shortly thereafter other manuscripts were brought in by the Ta'amireh tribesmen. This time they included Greek New Testament papyri and some early Arabic documents. Already some scholars had begun to link early Christianity to the Qumran community, and the first reports of the finding of New Testament manuscripts near Qumran added confusion to the story. It was soon apparent, however, that these manuscripts had no relation to the Qumran materials, for they dated from the fifth to the eighth centuries A.D. They were from the ruins of a Byzantine (Christian) monastery at Khirbet Mird, the site of the ancient Maccabean fortress of Hyrcania, five miles west of Qumran. (For an earlier similar discovery, see Appendix II, "1937.")

A new wave of excitement began in September, 1952, when the Bedouins came upon Cave IV (4Q), a few hundred feet southwest of Khirbet Qumran and separated from it by a deep ravine which cuts north into the terrace from Wadi Qumran. On a prominence overlooking Wadi Qumran, Cave IV was dug in ancient times into the face of the eroded terrace. From a deep hole on the west side of the cave, thousands of leather and papyrus fragments were exhumed. Fortunately, the archeologists discovered the new dig before all the fabulous cache had been emptied by clandestine diggers; fragments from a hundred manuscripts were thus recovered under controlled conditions during a systematic excavation there from September 22 to 29. Thousands of dollars had to be raised, however, and several years were to elapse before scholars would be able to recover the great number of fragments looted by the Bedouins.[11]

It is estimated that some 40,000 fragments came from Cave IV alone. An international team of scholars — two from America, two from England, two from France, one from Poland, and one from Germany — was selected to tackle the arduous task of cleaning, assembling, and analyzing them. The work of assembling the myriad fragments was not completed until the summer of 1960.[12] Almost 400 different manuscripts were found to be represented, about 125 of which were Biblical. The scroll story thus took on gargantuan proportions, and another new chapter began. Publication of this vast assembly of manuscript fragments will occupy many years and many volumes. A small portion of the fragments have been published in scattered articles.[13]

During the excavation of Cave IV another cave a few yards to the north was noticed and proved to contain about 250 decomposed inscribed fragments from which about two dozen documents have been reconstructed, including seven Biblical manuscripts. Fairly sizable parts of a scroll of the "New Jerusalem," a phylactery, and some bits of a scroll of the "Damascus Document" were among the non-Biblical scrolls represented. Cave V (5Q), like Cave IV, had been cut into the side of the marly terrace in ancient times and, like many of the caves along the cliffs, may have been used as living quarters by members of the community. One suggestion is that the caves cut into the terrace were originally made for use as tombs, perhaps in the eighth or seventh century B.C. Another possibility is that they were cut by community members as an additional source for clay used in the manufacture of pottery, large quantities of which were made in the pottery center.

About the same time, Bedouins located Cave VI (6Q), this one in the face of the rocky cliff close by the north side of Wadi Qumran. Only fifty-seven fragments of leather were recovered from it, but 718 papyrus pieces were gathered — a most unusual proportion of papyrus for a Qumran cave. Although at least six Biblical books are represented among these finds, the most interesting feature is a group of five first-century A.D. leather fragments from a copy of the "Damascus Document" (6Q15). First discovered in the famous Cairo Genizah in 1897, this document is similar in contents to the "Manual of Discipline" (1QS); but its reference to a sojourn in Damascus continues to arouse considerable debate.

After all the excitement of 1952, with its five Qumran cave discoveries (plus the excavation of four Wadi Murabba'at caves and another somewhere farther south), the scholars returned to the meticulous task of excavating what was now clearly the community center from which the Qumran scrolls had come. The long second and third seasons of work (February 9 — April 24, 1953, and February 13 — April 14, 1954) confirmed beyond any doubt the nature of the community center. The general outlines of the main building (100' x 120') and its adjacent assembly room (15' x 73') with a pantry to the southwest, the pottery-manufacturing center to the southeast, the east wall, and the elaborate water system of cisterns and channels were exposed. Most significant during the second season was the discovery of the remains of a "scriptorium," a second-floor room in which a long, plaster-covered table and bench, a wash basin, and three inkwells indicated that manuscripts had been copied there. The only inscribed evidence was an ostracon (an inscribed potsherd) from a nearby first-century B.C. "dump." On the ostracon the Hebrew alphabet had been copied in a hand that suggested a schoolboy practicing his lesson. Its value to paleography was immediately apparent, despite the crude script.

Numerous coins made possible a reconstruction of the history of the community, which was established about 135-125 B.C. (Period Ia), was expanded about 100 B.C. (Period Ib), and was abandoned in 31 B.C. after severe destruction, apparently caused by an earthquake. It was restored about 4 B.C. (Period II) along lines similar to those of Period Ib, and continued to flourish until its violent overthrow by the Romans, about A.D. 68, during the first Jewish revolt. (See pp. 162-163, 195 for outlines of the community's history.)

A fourth season of excavation (February 2 to April 6, 1955) concentrated on the western quarter of the community center and revealed the complex beginning of the water conduit and cistern system with its sluice gates at the northwest corner of a large courtyard northwest of the main building. Further evidences of the daily activities of the community center were also uncovered in this area. In the midst of this season, a new series of caves was discovered by the excavators along the edges of the Qumran terrace on which the *khirbeh* lay. Caves VII-X (7Q-10Q), though mostly collapsed and eroded away along with the many manuscripts they probably once contained, produced only seven identifiable scrolls among 126 fragments, plus some inscribed pottery.[14] Meanwhile the Bedouins discovered another obscure cave in Wadi Murabba'at, not far from those excavated in 1952. There they came upon an almost complete, but badly disintegrated Hebrew scroll of the Minor Prophets from the second century A.D. It was the only manuscript found in that cave.

During the fifth season of excavation at Qumran (February 18 to March 28, 1956) the final clearing of the entire community center was accomplished, revealing all that could be recovered from the ancient ruins. In addition, eighteen of the more than one thousand tombs in the cemetery directly east of the center, beyond its outer wall, were excavated. Each grave was identical to the others, dug in an "L" shape (a vertical shaft with projection at the bottom, in which the body was laid and sealed off with stones), always oriented north and south. They were humble burials, without artifacts. Two other cemeteries were located, one farther north and another farther south from the center. Some evidences of what appeared to be related buildings near 'Ain Feshkha, a mile and a half to the south, were also uncovered.

During January, 1956, once again the Bedouins came upon a cave, this time about a mile north of the community center, not far from Cave III. This one (Cave XI, 11Q) took ingenuity to locate and superhuman effort to open, for the face of the cliff above had collapsed over the cave's entrance. Apparently it was discovered from a very small opening from which bats were seen to emerge. Tons of rock had to be removed to expose the cave. Once it had been opened, however, the discovery was amazing: two well-preserved manuscripts and large portions of five others made this discovery as significant as that of Cave I. For a long time lack of funds stood between these scrolls and the scholarly world avidly waiting to study them. Endowment funds of the Palestine Archaeological Museum were sacrificed to recover the scrolls from the Bedouins, until finally all the documents were safely locked in the Museum vault.

In the meantime, only tempting, sketchy descriptions of a few of the manuscripts were released. A scroll of Leviticus in archaic Hebrew, an extensive, well-preserved Psalms scroll (11QPs^a), a very fragmentary scroll of Ezekiel, an Aramaic translation (Targum) of the book of Job, and an apocryphal scroll about the "New Jerusalem" were announced as being among these significant finds. During the summer of 1956 curiosity heightened with the opening of the two copper scrolls from Cave III, and the discovery that they contained a list of fabulous treasures stored in remote and vaguely identified places.[15]

A sixth and final season of digging in the Qumran area was conducted from January 25 to March 21, 1958, in the area just north of 'Ain Feshkha, where soundings in 1956 had indicated related buildings were to be found. A significant irrigation system was traced, and farm buildings were exposed. Here stables (or drying sheds?), toolsheds, and what appeared to be channels and basins for preparing leather for its various uses completed the story of the daily life of the Qumran community.[16]

But adventures with manuscripts in the Holy Land were not yet ended. From a rumor in Israel that Bedouins had found manuscript fragments in a cave in 1952 in the Nahal Se'elim (Wadi Seiyal) area north of Masada, the Israelis were spurred into a systematic search of that treacherous mountain and desert region which lies west of the Dead Sea, from En Gedi south to Masada. For two weeks beginning March 23, 1960, teams of scholars and students explored the rugged terrain which provided refuge for the Jews' last determined stand against the Romans in A.D. 135. In the Nahal Hever, about three miles south of En Gedi, the team under Yigael Yadin met with amazing success. There, in a cave high up on the sheer cliff, fifteen papyrus letters in a goatskin bag were unearthed, along with several baskets of skeletal remains which punctuated the grim end of the Bar Kokhba revolt in A.D. 135.

Further explorations in the same cave during March, 1961, uncovered a still larger collection of papyrus documents, some thirty-five dated business documents (A.D. 88-132) relating to the affairs of families in and near En Gedi. These were written in Aramaic, Nabataean, and Greek. Another leather bag contained five manuscripts, of which three were in Hebrew and relate to Bar Kokhba's lease of some property in En Gedi. Thus it is called the "Cave of Letters." [17]

On the opposite (south) cliff of Nahal Hever was another large cave (VIII) in which several fragments of the Greek Scroll of the Minor Prophets were discovered by Y. Aharoni, thus solving the mystery of the location of the "unidentified cave" (see p. 151). But Cave VIII is called the "Cave of Horror" from the multitude of human skeletons it contained, another evidence of the tragic end of the Bar-Kokhba revolt. [18]

Meanwhile negotiations in Jerusalem continued in order to release the scrolls from Cave XI for study and publication. A generous gift received by the A.S.O.R. from Elizabeth Hay Bechtel of San Francisco was used to secure the rights to publish the Psalms Scroll. During November 10-20, 1961, J. A. Sanders, then at Colgate-Rochester Divinity School, to whom the scroll was entrusted, opened and began to study this well-preserved scroll. The beautifully inscribed document is more than half the length of the famed Isaiah Scroll, or about thirteen feet long (fifteen feet with its nine fragments). It contains some thirty-seven Psalms, plus eight "non-canonical compositions" which have elicited much discussion. The fact that Psalms 151 and 154-155, previously found only in Greek (the Septuagint), Old Latin, and Syriac versions of the Psalms, appear in Hebrew in this manuscript is of itself most significant. A large fragment of the same scroll came into the hands of Yigael Yadin in October, 1960, and added four more Psalms to the preserved total. This second-best-preserved Biblical manuscript from Qumran has the distinction of having been copied during the ministry of Jesus, or very shortly thereafter, in a skillful "Herodian" script.[19]

Attempts about the same time to open the badly disintegrated Ezekiel Scroll (11QEzek) from the same cave unfortunately proved disappointing to Brownlee, who had been assigned to study it. Only a few lines of text could be obtained from the entire document.[20]

Two Dutch scholars, J. van der Ploeg and A. J. van der Woude, secured rights to publish several other Cave XI documents, among which were two partial columns of a scroll of Melchizedek (11QMelch), an Aramaic Targum of Job (11QtgJob), and a scroll of apocryphal Psalms (11QapPs).[21]

Despite the diligence of authorities and the search by scholars, the Judean wilderness west of the Dead Sea may not yet have yielded up all its manuscript secrets from the ancient past. One of the problems now is to sift rumor from fact, and forgery from authentic document. During 1960 it was reported that the Ta'amireh Bedouins had discovered still another manuscript cave. When I interviewed some of these Bedouins during the summer of 1962, they hinted broadly about a new cave discovery recently made near Nablus; but they produced no sound evidence of it, as they had promised. Many manuscript fragments were shown to me, but they all proved to be either forgeries or modern Hebrew manuscripts which had been treated to appear ancient.

Indeed the Bedouins had discovered another cave, as was revealed a few months later, this time about sixteen miles north of Khirbet Qumran. While their flocks were grazing southeast of Nablus, they happened upon a tremendous cave complex in the Wadi ed-Daliyeh in a most rugged and treacherous terrain. There, in a huge cave called Mughâret 'Abu Shinjeh, fragments of some forty Samaritan papyrus business documents were recovered from among hundreds of human skeletons and personal artifacts, all clearly dating from the fourth century B.C.! It soon became apparent that the cave had been the refuge of the Samaritan leaders when Alexander the Great attacked Samaria on his return trip from Egypt in 331 B.C. The grim evidence revealed that the Samaritans had been trapped and massacred, or perhaps suffocated.[22] But another footnote to ancient Biblical history had been added from the discovery.

During the winter of 1963-64 Professor Yadin's excavation of Herod's fortress at Masada, thirty miles south of Qumran, yielded ninety ostraca, a fragmentary scroll of Psalms (81-85), five chapters of a first-century B.C. Hebrew scroll of Ecclesiasticus, and a sectarian liturgical scroll, plus some other papyrus fragments. Most of them appeared in a stratum clearly related to the Jewish Zealots' suicidal last stand against the Roman legions in A.D. 73. The sectarian scroll contains "Songs of the Sabbath Sacrifices" (MasSirSabb) identical to some Qumran Cave IV documents, and is the first Qumran document found outside the Khirbet Qumran area.[23] For me it provided the clue for dating the end of Qumran scribal activity, as noted above. (See pp. 134-135.)

During the turbulent succeeding years, the Dead Sea Scrolls became more embroiled in the political conflicts of the Middle East. Just as negotiations in the West Bank of Jordan were proceeding to release the largest of all the scrolls (probably from Cave XI) for treatment and publication, the "Six-Day War" of June, 1967, descended upon Jerusalem. The day after the capture of East Jerusalem by the Israelis, the scroll was also captured, resulting in a long controversy over its ownership. Kando sued for the Ta'amireh and his rights according to Jordanian agreements and, in 1969, was finally paid reparations of $100,000.

Meanwhile the scroll had been opened and Yadin was engaged in its analysis, promising publication within a few years. From his preliminary report released early in 1968,[24] the world of Biblical scholarship was again aroused by the scope and dimension of what the scroll apparently revealed. The longest of all the Qumran scrolls, with over twenty-eight feet of very thin leather and sixty-six columns of 70 per cent preserved text, it was called the "Temple Scroll" (11QTemple) because of its detailed description of the Temple believed by its author to be the "inspired" instructions David gave to Solomon, according to I Chronicles 28:11-19.[25] The importance of the scroll cannot be overemphasized, and its publication is awaited with keen anticipation.[26]

A few months later a Jerusalem antiquities dealer offered

Yadin a complete head-*tefillin* (see footnote 1) with its four tiny "slips" of Torah quotations still folded and tied in their leather capsule. The first complete example to be discovered from such an early time, it has provided new insights into that ancient custom which was based on a literal interpretation of Deuteronomy 6:8.[27]

During the road building project along the west shore of the Dead Sea south from 'Ain Feshkha to 'En Gedi, in 1970, evidences were discovered of an ancient site near 'Ain Ghuweir, nine miles south of Khirbet Qumran. P. Bar-Adon excavated the site and discovered a Qumran-like building, 64 by 140 feet, and artifacts which suggested a limited occupation relating to Qumran Period II (A.D. 1-68). Half a mile to the north is a cemetery which revealed graves similar to those at Qumran. In twenty of the graves were found skeletons of twelve men, seven women, and one child, indicating that an Essene family center was nearby.[28]

In the meantime publication of the official Jordanian series of Cave IV and Cave XI manuscripts has suffered repeated delays, partly because of the direct political complications, but also as a result of the reticence of scholars to publish in the face of the confused political situation. Just how much delay has resulted from scholars' determination to wrest the last bit of evidence from their privately controlled fragments, we may never learn. Jordan had nationalized the Palestine Archaeological Museum in the fall of 1966, thus removing it from the control of its international independent Board of Trustees. As a result, after the Six-Day War, the vast collection of Qumran fragments in the Museum Scrollery became a part of "occupied territory" with all the political confusion that implies. Despite repeated promises that more volumes of the *Discoveries in the Judaean Desert* series would appear, at this writing only two Cave IV volumes (the *Pesharim* documents and the Enoch materials) and one more Cave XI volume (the Aramaic Targum of Job) have appeared.[29] Others are promised for the near future, assuming they successfully surmount the obstacles.

A major breakthrough of the obstacles, however, was accomplished in 1974, when photographs of all the unpublished Biblical scrolls and fragments (there are known to be 179 Biblical manuscripts from the eleven Qumran caves) were delivered to the Committee for the Revised Standard Version of the Bible. That

Committee has been hard at work analyzing and evaluating all the Biblical evidence in preparation for the new edition of the RSV to be issued in 1982, which will mark a significant step forward in Bible translation.[30]

So the amazing story of the Dead Sea Scrolls continues to unfold.

17

Putting the Pieces Together

DESPITE the delay in publication of the many volumes of Qumran manuscript fragments, it can be asserted that the academic values emerging from the discoveries in the Judean Desert by the Dead Sea are already enormous. More than any other archeological discovery, the Qumran materials have enabled the student of the Bible literally to walk into Biblical history at that crucial time which separates the Old Testament from the New — that pivot point in time that saw the rise of sectarian Judaism and the birth of Christianity. We are now able from the excavations at Khirbet Qumran and the hundreds of manuscripts from the eleven caves to sit where the people of Qumran sat, to see what they saw, to think as they thought and even to feel as they felt. We have gained insights into Judaism and its internal struggles that are invaluable, whether our objective is better to understand sectarian Judaism or the religious ethos in which Christianity was born.

Light on Sectarian Judaism

Through the past quarter of a century scholars have sought to identify the Qumran covenanters with every known ancient sectarian movement within Judaism: Pharisees, Sadducees, Zealots, Ebionite Christians, and even the medieval Karaites. That era has now passed. With very few exceptions, consensus has focused the discovery on the Essenes, whose descriptions by the ancient writers Josephus, Pliny, and Philo coincide with the vast majority of the evidence from Khirbet Qumran and its manuscript caves.

Early in the second century B.C. a group of pietistic Jews called Hasidim ("the pious ones") arose to resist the inroads of Hellenism imposed upon them by the Syrian Antiochid rulers who, in 198 B.C., had wrested Palestine from the Ptolemaic Egyptian rulers after the battle of Paneas near the foot of Mt. Hermon. The Jewish resistance movement, under the aggressive leadership of Judas Maccabeus and at first supported by the Hasidim, in 165 B.C. succeeded in driving the Greeks out of a small area around Jerusalem and setting up an independent Jewish state, which gradually expanded until most of Palestine came under Jewish control. Barely a generation later the descendants of the Hasidim became disenchanted with the religious and political developments within the new Jewish state. They saw their orthodox faith being threatened as the sacred Torah, the festival observances, and the Temple rituals were violated by the religious leaders who yielded to Hellenistic and unorthodox influences. The "last straw" seems to have been when Simon Maccabeus assumed the high priesthood and legally transferred the official line of the highest religious authority from the historic Zadokite family to the Hasmoneans in 142 B.C. With this corruption of the faith they felt compelled to believe that God was about to bring an end to decadent world history and usher in a new age of divine rule.

Inspired apparently by the apocalyptic book of Daniel, of which eight fragmentary scrolls have been recovered from the caves, and under the leadership of one who is referred to only as the "Teacher of Righteousness," who they believed was endowed by God with the ultimate meaning and interpretation of Scripture, a small band of these pietists migrated into the Wilderness of Judea about 135 B.C. The Teacher believed that they had been chosen by God to be the new Israel and literally to fulfill Isaiah 40:3 by going into the wilderness to keep Torah with perfection and thus prepare the way for God's new age. In their "Rule of the Community" (1QS) we read:

> And when these things occur for the community in Israel, according to these ordinances they shall be separated from the midst of the habitation of unrighteous men in order to go into the wilderness, there to prepare the way of the LORD, just as it is written, "In the wilderness prepare the way of the LORD. Make straight in the desert a highway for our God" (Isaiah 40:3). That

[refers] to the pursuit of Torah [the Law or teachings] which he [God] commanded by the hand of Moses to do according to all that has been revealed from time to time according to that which the prophets revealed through His holy spirit. [1QS VIII:12-16]

They chose a site on a plateau beneath the precipitous cliffs near the northwest shore of the Dead Sea, eight miles south of Jericho, where some remains of an eighth-century B.C. military outpost, probably one of Uzziah's "towers in the wilderness" (II Chronicles 26:10), provided a foundation for their center. Perhaps they were influenced in their choice by the fact that these ruins were within view of the traditional site of Mt. Nebo and the Valley of Shittim northeast of the Dead Sea. Living in the shadow of Mt. Nebo, where they believed Moses had written the Torah many centuries earlier (Deuteronomy 31:9, 12), they were daily reminded of their call to "renew the Covenant" of Torah (1QPrayers II:6). In many ways their documents reveal that the early history of Israel was a prototype of their experiences in end time and the age to come.

Except perhaps for twenty-five or thirty years after the earthquake of 31 B.C., which severely damaged their center, the community continued to live out Torah by an austere life in that wilderness isolation for over two hundred years (c. 135 B.C. — A.D. 68). When Vespasian's Roman legions invaded Palestine to put down the first Jewish revolt (A.D. 66-73), probably shortly after the capture of Jericho in the spring of A.D. 68, the community was dispersed and disappeared from history. Thus ended the Qumran eschatological experiment.[1]

The great bulk of the literature recovered from the eleven Qumran caves, almost four hundred documents out of a total of about six hundred, casts a flood of light upon sectarian Judaism in that turbulent period. The community rule books, including the "Damascus Document," provide firsthand, detailed information about the practices of the Essene sect. Many documents expand on their intensely eschatological concepts, like the War Scroll (1QM) with its detailed account of the ordering of the forty years of battles that would precede God's new age, and the Melchizedek Scroll (11QMelch). Other documents add much to what was already known about such books as Jubilees, the Testaments of the Patriarchs, and Enoch, now found for the first time in their original Hebrew. It is conceivable that the new evidence will prove that some of these books were composed at Qumran. At least a dozen other documents, called *pesharim* ("interpretations"), reveal clearly the community's method of handling Scripture. But these documents also reveal bits of historical information, often couched in veiled language, thereby enlarging our knowledge of the intertestamental period. These many new manuscripts will become an important addition to that rapidly expanding religious literature from late Bible times called "pseudepigraphic literature," that which was not canonized by either Jews or Christians. It should be pointed out that, having been rejected by early Judaism and Christianity because of their sectarian origin, such documents can hardly be expected to gain canonical status now.

Recovering the Old Testament Text

Anyone who was privileged to visit the "Scrollery" in the Palestine Archaeological Museum (now called the Rockefeller Museum) in East Jerusalem, during those years when the international team of eight scholars labored untold hours to assemble close to four hundred partial manuscripts from some forty thousand fragments of fragile leather, could only stand in amazement at the prodigious task they faced. Having been involved with the repair and assembling of a few of the Cave I scrolls, I can say with profound empathy that those who care about the Bible to any degree owe those scholars an inestimable debt of gratitude for their skills, patience, wisdom, and endurance exercised in this incredible accomplishment. To clean, straighten, and separate the myriad fragments; then to sort, identify, and piece them together, sometimes with only the barest available clues, tested their human capacities and learning to the limit. The long delay in the publication of their monumental efforts is regrettable. They deserve at least the reward of seeing the results of their labors in print.

The fact that Biblical Hebrew manuscripts copied before the tenth century A.D. have at last been discovered in the land of the Bible's birth is of itself of greatest importance. One hundred and seventy-nine Old Testament manuscripts, including every book except Esther (many of them very fragmentary, to be sure), have now been recovered from eleven Qumran caves. Among these are thirty scrolls of Psalms, twenty-five scrolls of Deuteronomy, nineteen scrolls of Isaiah, fifteen of Genesis and Exodus, eight each of Leviticus, the Book of the Twelve (the Minor Prophets), and Daniel, and six or fewer of all the others. For Chronicles only a small fragment has been found.[2]

The documents range in date of copying from about 275 B.C. (a blackened fragment of Exodus, 4QEx^f) to about A.D. 65 (a Daniel fragment, 1QDan^a, in an elegant script). Many, therefore, are more than a thousand years older than previously known Biblical texts in Hebrew. In addition, there are the many second century A.D. fragments found in the caves of Wadi Murabba'at, Nahal Se'elim, Nahal Hever, and in a casemate room atop Masada (most of these are non-Biblical), not to mention Samaritan and Christian documents from Wadi ed-Daliyeh and Khirbet Mird. A whole new horizon for Old Testament textual studies has thus been provided for those with the patience and skills to study them.

From the lay Bible reader's perspective, we should add at once that scholars have not expected to find any startling alterations of the traditional (Masoretic) Old Testament text to be necessary from what has come to light. Some surprises have appeared, such as the seven extra-canonical Psalms (11QPs^a) and the shorter form of Jeremiah (already known from the Septuagint). Long before 1948 scholars had assumed that the basic Hebrew text of the Old Testament had reached essentially its present form well before 100 B.C. and was carefully copied ever since, especially after the efforts of Rabbi Akiba and the Council of Jamnia to stabilize the Hebrew Scriptures at the end of the first century A.D. The textual contributions from the Qumran scrolls, in fact, will probably seem insignificant to most lay people; but to Biblical scholars every manuscript that corrects a word or even a letter of the text is an important step toward the dream of recovering texts of Scripture as near to the autograph originals as possible.

It should be added here, however, that the great antiquity of the Qumran scrolls does not guarantee the textual superiority of any particular manuscript. Each point of difference from the traditional text must be weighed carefully, and many variant readings may be rejected on sound academic grounds. Others will continue to be disputed. It can be expected that many differing analyses will appear during the decades to come before the textual values of these scrolls will have been exhausted. Already the number of publications on the subject is enormous.

At the present stage of the analysis, nevertheless, it can be asserted that the scrolls from the Judean wilderness have provided scholars with a major breakthrough into the complex pre-history of the standard (Masoretic) Hebrew text of the Old Testament. While New Testament scholars have been at work for a century with several "families" of Greek texts from the almost five thousand ancient and medieval New Testament manuscripts that have become available, Old Testament scholars have had only one Hebrew text tradition with which to work — the Masoretic — and only from late medieval copies at that. Thus Old Testament scholars have had to be satisfied with studies of the Samaritan, Greek Septuagint (LXX), Syriac, Coptic, Latin, and other early versions (or translations) in an attempt to penetrate toward the original autographs. Except for a few LXX Greek papyrus fragments of Deuteronomy and some very late medieval Samaritan texts, almost all early manuscripts of these versions have been copies done by Christian scribes since the second century A.D.

Now suddenly we have four more textual traditions of sizable parts of the Hebrew Scriptures that were in existence well *before* Christians began disputing with Jews over the meaning of their Scriptures in relation to Jesus. These different traditions, or "families," might be listed as follows: (1) proto-Masoretic text types, such as the Isaiah "B" text (1QIs^b); (2) local Palestinian texts, like the great Isaiah "A" Scroll (1QIs^a) and the Leviticus Scroll from Cave XI (11QLev); (3) texts which represent the Hebrew used for the Greek Septuagint, which was developed in Egypt (from Palestinian texts), such as the extensive Cave IV Samuel manuscript (4QSam^a), as well as pieces of Joshua, Kings, and Jeremiah from the same cave; and (4) some Pentateuch texts which might be called proto-Samaritan texts, such as those of Exodus (4QExod^a) and Numbers (4QNum^b). If we add the fourth-century B.C. non-Biblical documents from Wadi ed-Daliyeh, our knowledge of Samaritan history is indeed enlarged significantly.

Frank M. Cross, who will publish most of the Cave IV Biblical fragments (as well as the Wadi ed-Daliyeh Samaritan documents), summarizes the textual achievements from these materials in the following significant statement:

> The recovery of nearly a hundred biblical scrolls from Cave IV came, therefore, as incredibly good fortune. Here at last was

material for sampling the textual types extant in virtually every book of the Old Testament. Here was a substantial basis for the establishment of the archaic, pre-Masoretic history of the Hebrew Bible. Moreover, thanks to the Murabba'ât texts which extend the series from Qumrân down into the second century A.D., we have direct evidence for the first time as to just what happened to the text in the crucial era before, during, and after the time when the official text was fixed.[3]

One thing is clear: there was no fixed textual tradition at Qumran despite the sect's zealous devotion to Scripture. The men of Qumran were by no means literalists, even though they had strong convictions concerning the ultimate meaning of Scripture, convictions which they had received from their beloved Teacher. They worked with the Biblical texts freely and apparently engaged in expanding and harmonizing as they copied or interpreted texts. They were not slavish copyists — and they often made errors. A word of caution, therefore, needs to be given here concerning generalizing from the evidence. Textual criticism, commonly called "lower criticism" among scholars, is exceedingly complicated; and the lay reader should be warned against using the expression that "the Scrolls have proved the Bible." Such a generalization is certainly not warranted from the myriad variant readings found in this great variety of texts gathered from the caves. If, however, the expression is used to refer to the basic message of the Bible, then it might apply in a broad sense. But there is certainly no room for its application to the expression "Biblical inerrancy," or "plenary, verbal inspiration of Scripture," as far as the details of the text are concerned. Such a view is now forced to retreat to hypothetical, non-existent original autographs, as many conservatives seem to have done since the discovery of the scrolls.

Another caution needs to be issued to those who hold to the priority of the Greek Septuagint text, which was usually quoted by the ancient New Testament writers. Just because the Hebrew prototype of the Septuagint has appeared for several historical books and even a scroll of Jeremiah, one should not generalize this evidence to mean that the Septuagint therefore represents a more accurate text for all the Old Testament. The variety of text types at Qumran is far too great to allow such a hasty conclusion. That Septuagint studies have been greatly aided by these discoveries, however, there is no doubt.

A pertinent illustration of the need for caution might be that, despite the fact that nineteen scrolls of Isaiah have come from the caves, there is not a single bit of evidence to suggest that any Hebrew text of Isaiah 7:14 ever included the word for "virgin," though it is found in Greek LXX copies made by Christians. The oldest Isaiah text (1QIs*a*) clearly shows *ha'almah* in a context that related to a historical event of 735 B.C. and carried the obvious reference to a particular "young woman" who was *then* pregnant and "about to bear a child." The shift of interpretation to give the passage Messianic connotations must, therefore, have happened either in the first-century B.C. Septuagint translation in Egypt (for which we still do not have any Jewish manuscript evidence) or in the first century A.D. within Christian circles.

Despite the rigidity of their orthodox convictions, the men of Qumran were by no means simplistic biblicists who handled Scripture in a way to suggest belief in verbal inerrancy.

Dating Hebrew Manuscripts

One contribution of the scrolls discovery that has developed certainty during the years since 1948 is Hebrew paleography. In the beginning it proved to be the one tool that provided the necessary clues to point toward the antiquity of the documents, but it was severely challenged. The validity of the methodology has now been confirmed. The paleographer needs evidences from many scribal hands to date documents of unknown date, and the "many" were lacking in 1948; but the few clues were sufficient to point the way while other scientific techniques were being sought and finally did help to confirm the first conclusions. Now Hebrew-Aramaic paleography has been promoted to the level of a respectable science. What were thin threads of inscriptional and manuscript materials in 1948 have now been woven into a sizable fabric by the thousands of fragments spread over such a broad, yet crucial period of history — about 375 B.C. to A.D. 135. Many types of script used by the scribes of that period have been recovered (more than five hundred hands have been identified from the Qumran materials alone), some datable within narrow limits, even to the very year, as in the Wadi ed-Daliyeh and Bar Kokhba documents which include date formulae.

Thanks to that first clue provided by the tiny Nash Papyrus (see Chapter 2), the Jewish scripts can now be classified with precision into fourth century B.C. (dated documents from Wadi ed-Daliyeh), third century (4QExod^f and 4QSam^b), early and late Hasmonean (150-50 B.C.), early and late Herodian (50 B.C. — A.D. 65), and late first century to early second century A.D. (70-135) or first and second Jewish revolt types. Within these periods appear formal book hands, semi-cursive, and cursive scripts, which further classify the types and will enable future paleographers to date with fair precision any new discovery that might appear in the area.

The Language Jesus Spoke

The fact that numerous Aramaic manuscripts, some of them quite extensive (such as the "Genesis Apocryphon" from 1Q and the Targum of Job from 11Q), have been gathered from this great horde is especially significant for the linguistic background for New Testament studies. It is a happy coincidence that at least some of these documents can be dated paleographically to the very lifetime of Jesus, whose native language they represent. Several of these documents, written in literary Aramaic, may bring us close to the colloquial tongue that indeed makes the first-century Palestinian scene come alive. That this closer touch with the language of Jesus can in any way shed light on what has been transmitted to us only in Greek translation in the New Testament may, however, remain a futile hope since Jesus did not write anything himself.

Joseph A. Fitzmyer, a meticulous Scrolls researcher, refers to the "new corpus of Qumran Aramaic" as "a subdivision of Palestinian Aramaic," and then adds: "But in the *Genesis Apocryphon* we have a substantial literary text, whose Aramaic is best described as a transitional type between the Biblical Aramaic of Daniel and that of the Palestinian Targums or Christian Palestinian Aramaic." Thus he calls it "Middle Aramaic."[4] It is much too early to predict what values may emerge in this area of research, which has been greatly stimulated by the discovery.

Interpreting the Biblical Text

The freedom with which the Biblical text was handled at Qumran, as witnessed by the great Isaiah Scroll, the Aramaic Genesis Apocryphon with its expansion of patriarchal stories, the many *pesharim* documents interpreting the prophetic writings, and the "Temple Scroll" which is the boldest of all, should force us to reconsider our own methods of handling Scripture. If one wishes to glean the lessons the scrolls teach, the study of hermeneutics, or the art of interpreting Scripture, is imperative. The Qumran story is the prototype of a plethora of Christian sectarian movements today, each of which has emerged from its special way of handling Scripture, and each claiming divine authority for its scriptural pronouncements. We must take a long, hard look at what the Qumran documents demonstrate regarding hermeneutics, so clearly presented especially in the *pesharim* documents. The process could prove to be an enlightening experience for polarized Christians.

Space permits only a sketchy statement here.[5] Essentially the Qumran method revolved around what the late Nels Ferré was wont to call "the isness of the was"; that is, what is happening is what the ancient writers were predicting. For the Qumran Teacher history was telescoped into the present and provided a blueprint for what he believed was about to happen. For instance, when Habakkuk wrote about the "Chaldeans" (Habakkuk 1:6), the Teacher did not read the name as a powerful people living in seventh-century B.C. Mesopotamia and causing a problem for the Hebrews, but rather he interpreted it as the Romans confounding the lives of his Jewish compatriots four or five centuries later (1QpHab II:12). Thus each sentence, line, or phrase of Habakkuk 1-2 is given a direct parallel to some experience known to the Teacher. By this method the "lion" in Nahum 2:11b becomes "Demetrius, the king of Greece" (4QpNah I:2). Every preacher, of course, does this same kind of juxtaposing as he seeks to make Scripture relevant for his congregation, as he strives to make the Word the "living Word." The problem arises when the process becomes *eisegesis* rather than *exegesis*. Does he read the present back *into* the author's words and give it divine authority, or does he seek to draw *from* the author's words lessons for the spiritual needs of the present? The former method often misses or distorts the Biblical message and purpose. The latter lets the Word speak from the words, thus providing the living Word.

A comparison of the Teacher's hermeneutical method with that used by the writers of the New Testament reveals a close similarity, but with quite a different outcome. A striking example is Habakkuk 2:4b. In 1QpHab VIII:1, which interprets Habakkuk's famous words, "but the righteous shall live by his faith" (or "faithfulness," RSV), the Qumran Teacher says, ". . . This concerns all those who do Torah [the Law] in the house of Judah, whom God will deliver from the house of judgment because of their suffering and because of their faith in the Teacher of Righteousness." Paul, on the other hand, gives quite the opposite interpretation in Romans 1:17 and Galatians 3:11, which the RSV has translated, "He who through faith is righteous shall live" (based on Paul's use of the LXX). Devotion to "doing the Law," which was central for the men of Qumran, is thus supplanted by the primary exercise of faith for Christians. Both interpretations were given divine authority but are quite unequal in meaning, although the *pesher* expression "faith in the Teacher of Righteousness" points somewhat toward Paul's approach. Who was right, or is it possible that both were wrong because of a wrong method of interpretation? Perhaps both should have started with precisely what Habakkuk intended, by seeing his message in its context. In that case the emphasis would have been placed on faithfulness to God, and anything beyond that would then become a testimony of faith, rather than a doctrinal assertion. Both could then be right. This is a method that starts with being honest with Scripture, striving to be faithful to its intent and thus letting the faith of the writer speak to the reader's faith. Such a method, though admittedly more difficult, more assuredly opens the door for God to speak through Scripture in more than one way.

Had the writer of Matthew followed this latter hermeneutical method, for instance, he would not have related Hosea 11:1b, "and out of Egypt I have called my son," to a trip that the Holy Family may or may not have taken to Egypt (Matthew 2:15). He could thus have spared many generations of serious-minded Christians a troublesome passage that does more to confound the community of faith than to sustain it.

In an indirect way, therefore, the Qumran documents support what sound historical Biblical criticism has been seeking to promote for over a hundred years.

Qumran and Canonical Scripture

The men of Qumran, like most Jews, were "people of the Book" to such an extent that most of their lives focused wholly on Scripture. It is difficult to define what constituted canonical Scripture for Judaism during the first centuries B.C. and A.D. Torah, of course, was primary; and the historical and writing prophets, as well as the book of Psalms, seem clearly to have been considered authoritative for all Jews, to judge by the reference in Luke 24:44 where these same three categories are listed. The evidence from Qumran, however, makes it quite clear that what we might call canonical Scripture was far more extensive, though Esther is quite conspicuous by its absence. At Qumran all the Old Testament accepted by the Jews as canonical (except Esther), plus at least Ben Sirach (Ecclesiasticus) and Tobit from the traditional Apocrypha, plus numerous writings generally called "Pseudepigrapha" (Jubilees, the Testaments of the Patriarchs, Enoch, the New Jerusalem, and a host of other documents), seem to have been given authoritative, or canonical, acceptance. Their Bible was indeed "open-ended." These documents from the men of Qumran were no mere musings of desert mystics; they were compositions infused with the Word of God by which they shaped their lives and daily expectations.

The *pesharim* documents which give the interpretations of the words of the prophets have all the appearance of authoritative books, while the Temple Scroll is unique among them all. Nothing like the latter has been seen before from Jewish history. The longest of all the Qumran scrolls, it has all the appearance of a deliberately produced canonical book at its outset. In it, we are told, are laws concerning ceremonial purity, laws for four sacred festivals, instructions for building the Temple, and regulations relating to the royal bodyguard and mobilization of the army in times of national danger. Written in the first person, it reads as though God is the author. The sacred divine name is written in the same script as in other canonical books.[6]

Yigael Yadin considers it a Qumran attempt to supply missing Torah, such as would be expected from I Chronicles 28:19, where David is mentioned as having written down the instructions for Solomon to follow in building the Temple. There we read: "All this he made clear by the writing from the hand of the LORD concerning it . . . ." What could be more Torah than that? Yet no such document has been known before. Yadin assures us that the document, on the basis of its language, must stem from the first century B.C., which points directly to Qumran as its source. This is something quite new in the history of canon, for always before canonical books endured a long sifting process before they gained such a status. But the men of Qumran, convinced that they had the final word from God, wrote with a conviction of authority.[7]

Once again the evidence from the Qumran documents is such that it should force concerned students of the Bible to take a new and careful look at the history of the Biblical canon. Books that deal with how the Bible came to be must be rewritten. More attention must be paid to the human decision-making process that has always been implied in the story of the Bible but now comes forcefully to light in such a way as to demand new answers to the vital question, How does God work in history? Our definitions of such phrases as "the Bible as the inspired Word of God," or "the Bible as revealed Word," or "the prophetic Word," must be re-examined. The manuscripts from Qumran, especially the Temple Scroll, provide fresh new resources for such discussions. They have added significantly to Biblical theology. They are calling for new answers to old theological questions which have plagued the Christian Church since its inception.

What Happened to the Men of Qumran?

Many academic questions arise from this discovery for which no answers have come forth from spade or scroll, but perhaps the most intriguing one is what happened to the two hundred or more men of Qumran in the spring or summer of A.D. 68 when Vespasian's army destroyed their headquarters by the Dead Sea. Although evidence of violence and military destruction was uncovered by the spades of the excavators, no human skeletons were found in the ruins. Perhaps some who met their end during the attack were given a simple burial in the neatly ordered cemetery east of the Qumran center where evidences of over a thousand graves can still be seen. But one wonders how that might have been achieved in the heat of battle. We are left with the conclusion that at least the majority of the people must have fled at the onset of the Roman attack. When the Messiahs of Aaron and David, along with the hosts of heaven, did not arrive as the men of Qumran had been taught to expect on that day when the "Sons of Light" would engage in battle with the "Sons of Darkness," the faith of the men of Qumran was sorely tested. Their reaction must have been similar to that experienced by the disciples of Jesus on that fateful night in the Garden of Gethsemane. Being unarmed and defenseless, what else could they do but flee? Where would they go?

Two possible routes of escape would immediately be suggested to anyone caught in the dilemma of the men of Qumran. They could go south, deep into the Wilderness of Judea; or under cover of darkness they could slip across the Jordan River near where it enters the Dead Sea and go north to the Decapolis, where the gentile cities would provide them a refuge. A third possibility might have been that, being without a means of defense, they merely surrendered to the advancing Romans. The latter option, however, leaves little room to explain the evidences of destruction and especially the violent abuse apparent on some of the manuscripts. Violence was certainly involved when Qumran fell to the Romans.

One piece of evidence from the excavations at Masada, thirty miles south of Qumran, suggests that at least some of the men of Qumran decided to join the Zealots who led the revolt against Rome in A.D. 66. Fragments of a scroll of "Songs of the Sabbath Sacrifices," written in a script almost identical to that of the scribe who copied one of the Daniel scrolls from Cave I (1Q-Dan[a]), were found atop Masada. It is clearly a manuscript from Qumran and a direct link with the Essenes. At least some men of Qumran must have been at Masada at the time of its capture in A.D. 73.

It would seem more reasonable, however, that the basically peaceful men of Qumran might have responded to the loss of their community center in a way similar to that of the Jerusalem Christians. If Eusebius' account of the flight of the Christians to Pella on the east side of the Jordan Valley in the Decapolis is historically accurate, it would suggest that there was the place and time where Christians and Essenes might have met. With their apocalyptic visions eclipsed, the faith of the men of Qumran would have been dashed. They were certainly depressed, providing ideal candidates for preachers of the Christian Gospel. At least some Essenes, it is reasonable to suppose, became Christians.

The word battle of the late fifties over the relation of the scrolls to Christianity has largely subsided.[8] It needs to be remembered that nothing has been found in the Qumran caves or at Khirbet Qumran itself that can be called genuinely Christian. Though the whole historical lives of both John the Baptist and

Jesus, it is now clearly established, were contemporary with the second period of the occupation at Khirbet Qumran, no artifact nor any manuscript so far discovered and reported reveals any direct contact between these religious movements.[9] What have been claimed as evidences of contact are merely literary and ideological parallels and similarities. Furthermore, the fallacy of *argumentum ad ignorantiam* (arguing from the absence of information to the contrary) has loomed large in many of the published theories, such as the one which claims that Jesus must have spent his early life at Qumran.

Scholars have identified many literary parallels to Qumran literature in the New Testament, and it seems not unlikely that Essene Christians may have influenced some Christian writings composed after A.D. 68. Other literary parallels would be expected from their common heritage in Judaism and Old Testament literature.

One thing is certain: the voices of the dedicated men of Qumran were silenced about A.D. 70 and the words from their pens almost completely erased from the pages of history. Except for a few minor contacts through some discoveries from their scroll caves, it was to be almost 1900 years before the world would hear again about that exciting adventure in sectarian Judaism during a most crucial period in religious history.

That adventure reveals numerous lessons for us to ponder today. In essence these lessons confirm the validity and methods of sound Biblical scholarship as practiced for almost two centuries. They do not make our hermeneutical task easier, to be sure, for they demand an honest, responsible, and disciplined sorting out process of what is human and what is divinely inspired in the faith testimonies from ancient times. I for one believe, however, that the results build and strengthen the foundations for vital faith today.

18

Spiritual Gleanings From Qumran

HIGH UP ON the precipitous cliff that dominates the Qumran plateau to the west, I climbed to a rocky ledge one Sunday afternoon (May 4, 1958) to gain a panoramic perspective of the Essene community center. At last, the dream of many years had been fulfilled; before me lay the scene of the drama of the Dead Sea Scrolls, the source of my own adventures.

Like a great cathedral, the scene provided an appropriate setting for a unique experience of worship. My rocky ledge was the back "pew" of the balcony. Below, perhaps 100 feet and stretching some 300 yards to the east, the marly plateau formed the great nave. Deep undulations cut into the plateau from the Wadi Qumran at the right, simulating the pews of the imaginary nave. Remains of an ancient water conduit followed the sloping plateau at the left, like an aisle beside the pews. The terrace, where ruins of the ancient community center lay exposed by the spades of the excavators, formed a natural sanctuary dominated by the altar, the focal point of most Christian churches. Symbolizing commitment and sacrifice, the excavated remains of the Qumran community fulfilled the function of the altar in the church of my imagination. The deep azure of the Dead Sea, and the purple-tinted cliffs of ancient Moab beyond, provided the reredos and dossal curtain to complete the ecclesiastical setting.

It was a service of silence. Not a cricket could be heard, nor the song of a bird or the whirr of its wings; not a breeze stirred among the crags. The sun's glare bore down with irritating intensity upon the placid scene, having already blighted the few tufts of grass which had managed to emerge from the sparse soil in rocky crevices during the brief rainy season long past. Here was consummate desert isolation in Palestine's "Great Rift," the lowest point on the surface of the earth — a veritable inferno of heat nine months of the year. Frequented for centuries only by Bedouins, until one of them accidentally happened upon that certain cave a half mile to the north of where I sat, this barren waste was now a focal point of world attention.

The sermon was a deep, silent meditation with the usual three or four emphases. The first, as might be expected, was a personal reminiscence. Fifteen miles to the west, across the rugged Wilderness of Judea, the Israelis were celebrating the tenth anniversary of the formation of their state; but I was enjoying my own tenth anniversary in peaceful solitude. Exactly ten years before, I had traveled across Europe clutching a satchel full of photographs and negatives that would make possible the publication of three of the now-famed Dead Sea Scrolls. The thrill of those weeks immediately preceding that homeward journey flashed momentarily through my mind. It had been a privilege to be the first American to examine, evaluate, and photograph the oldest Biblical documents yet discovered, and to bring them to the attention of the world. The whole panorama of events which the Qumran site had unfolded during those ten years crowded together to dominate my thinking.

A second phase of meditation soon overshadowed the joy of pure reminiscence, as provocative academic questions arose, like some of those reviewed in the previous chapter. But from my rocky "pew" high above Khirbet Qumran, several religious questions seemed even more important: What is this drama recovered from the past trying to tell us? What does it mean for our faith?

Into that barren wilderness, and inspired by their devout, dedicated teacher, went a small band of religious enthusiasts who believed that they were the "Sons of Light" chosen to "prepare the way of the LORD" (Isaiah 40:3). Human history was nearing its dénouement, they sincerely believed; time was running out. The "Sons of Darkness" (all unbelievers), who were thought to be under the demonic power of Belial, were destined to destruction. The final struggle between truth and falsehood, right and wrong, purity and perversity (subsumed under the terms "light" and "darkness"), was upon them, and end time was near.

There on the wilderness plateau by the Dead Sea, the men of

Qumran led austere, disciplined, dedicated lives under a most rigorous, semi-monastic organization. Frequent lustrations, sacred meals, and solemn assemblies marked their daily routine; nor did they shy away from hard work and menial tasks to meet daily needs in their isolated community center. Every act and duty seems to have been a sacred act in fulfillment of their divinely appointed mission. Apparently they spent the nights in tents on the plateau or in caves among the cliffs. Reading, copying, and meditating upon Scripture occupied much of their time. Anyone who sought to join the community was placed under the most severe testing and disciplined preparation for at least two years.[1]

The men of Qumran carried out their religious activities in daily anticipation of the final drama of history in which they would play an important part. After the appearance of the Messiah (or Messiahs), there was to be a forty-year holy war between the Sons of Light and the Sons of Darkness. The victory of the Sons of Light, however, was a foregone conclusion, they believed, for the hosts of heaven would assure it, as their War Scroll makes vividly clear (1QM, XII). Their faith was focused on the God of history who acts to carry out his will, which had been revealed to their teacher in a "glorious vision" (1QPrayers, col. II, line 6).

A Lesson about Apocalyptic Literature

But the grim evidence from the excavations at Qumran is that in the summer of A.D. 68 the community was ruthlessly destroyed at the hands of pagan Romans of the 10th Legion under Vespasian. The Sons of Darkness, destined for destruction, were victorious over the Sons of Light! Perhaps a most important lesson from the scrolls and the community, therefore, for the late twentieth century focuses on this historic fact. For once again, the voices of sectarian religious groups are proclaiming the near approach of the "Day of the LORD" and that final "battle of Armageddon." They quote freely from Ezekiel, Zechariah, Daniel, and especially the "Little Apocalypse" (Mark 13, Matthew 24, and Luke 21) and the Revelation of John. A sober reflection on the story of the Qumran community, therefore, can be most instructive.

In that story has now been revealed the full extent of religious dedication to just such ancient apocalyptic literature. In fact, the community added copiously to that literature. We can follow the course of their experiences for over 200 years while they tested the validity of this prime element of their faith. Furthermore, we can see clearly the frustration of their expectations in the destruction of their community center and the dispersion of their members.

What has been tested by various religious groups and failed numerous times during the past two centuries was thoroughly tested almost 2000 years ago. Is not the test of the more than 1900 elapsed years enough time to require at least a reconsideration and re-evaluation of this oft-recurring apocalyptic point of view? At least the message from the scrolls is clear that apocalyptic literature from ancient times should be re-examined as to its origin and purpose. Such an examination will show that this literature invariably appeared during periods of persecution and supreme testing of religious faith and loyalty. Furthermore, the ancient documents reveal that their authors had no intention of providing blueprints for the far distant future. The relevance of this genre of literature must first be seen in terms of the immediate future from the writer's perspective. Nine times in the book of Revelation (1:1, 3; 10:6; 12:12; 22:6, 7, 10, 12, and 20) John of Patmos emphasized the imminent future with such phrases as "what must soon take place," "the time is near," or "the time is short," which countless readers have failed to take seriously.[2] Such words would not have been used by the writer except to imply the same kind of immediacy that the men of Qumran daily felt. Mark's Gospel quotes Jesus as saying, "Truly, I say to you, there are some standing here who will not taste death before they see the Kingdom of God come with power," which indicates clearly that Jesus shared this sense of nearness of the new age with others in the first century A.D.[3]

The Qumran experience drives us back to a serious look at the total Biblical message in relation to apocalyptic literature. Genesis 1-11 is the prologue that prepares the reader for the central message of the Bible which begins with the story of Abraham in chapter 12. The prologue recounts the ancient Hebrew concept of how God's good creation became corrupted, leading to divine anger and destruction by means of a flood (Gen. 6:9 — 9:17). After the flood Noah built an altar to worship the God who had saved him and his family (Gen. 8:20), and the words that follow should be carefully noted:

And when the LORD smelled the pleasing odor, the LORD said in his heart, "I will *never again curse the ground* because of man, for the imagination of man's heart is evil from his youth; neither will I *ever again destroy every living creature* as I have done. While the earth remains, seedtime and harvest, cold and heat, summer and winter, day and night, *shall not cease.*" (Gen. 8:21-22;[4] emphases added)

In other words, the writer is saying that God made a commitment "never again" to use the method of destruction to solve the problem of human rebellion against his creative purposes. In Gen. 9:11-15 this commitment is sealed with a "covenant" signified by the rainbow. Anyone who takes the words of the Bible seriously should be especially alert to the fact that God rejected destruction as a method of dealing with human depravity. What follows in Genesis 10 and 11 is a quick summary of the descendants of Noah, thus completing another cycle of human growth and resultant corruption. The story moves swiftly toward God's new plan for coping with people who rebel against his will. Again a righteous person is singled out, this time Abraham, the ancestor of the Hebrew people; and the body of the Biblical message begins.

The new master plan of God is gradually revealed as the story of Abraham and his descendants unfolds over the next seven or eight centuries (Gen. 12 through II Samuel). The method is to redeem people and nations or turn them around (the key Hebrew word is *shûbh*, "return," as so often used by the later prophets), or to change the nature of human beings and society. The prologue concept of destroy-and-start-over is thus abandoned as contrary to God's nature.[5]

Despite the danger of oversimplifying the Biblical message and overgeneralizing the Dead Sea Scrolls, it seems to me that what has been discovered at Qumran points clearly to the need to recover the Bible's basic theme. From Genesis 12 in the Old Testament through the third epistle of John in the New Testament, God's redeeming acts provide the thread that binds the whole Bible together (with many digressions along the way, to be sure). The apocalyptic books of Jude and Revelation might be considered a fitting symbolic epilogue, a metaphorical use of such literature to point toward "the new heaven and the new earth" (Rev. 21:1-7) which the Biblical drama seeks to bring forth.

Historically, however, apocalyptic literature appeared as a digression in response to human cries of desperation, first in the midst of the Exile (6th century B.C.), and then reappearing in subsequent periods of crisis which tested human faith and religious loyalties to the breaking point. The presence of this literature in the Bible (it appears in roughly 65 out of a total of almost 900 chapters, or less than 7½ per cent of the Bible) is incidental to the predominant theme of God's acts to redeem and redirect civilization toward his ultimate purpose (compare Isa. 55:6-11). By focusing on that literature as providing a blueprint for God's future plans, any religious group is destined to disillusionment, just as happened to the Qumran community.[6]

Lessons from Differences

It is difficult in the pages of history to find better examples of people who strove so diligently for perfection of moral character and religious devotion. From the limited standpoint of human perspective, at Qumran, it would seem, were people upon whom God should have looked with utmost favor. If devotion to the law, a particular interpretation of Scripture, purity in thought and deed, piety, personal denial, and rigid discipline were major prerequisites for divine favor and nurture, certainly the Qumran community should have continued to thrive.

But that community died; its voice was silenced, its manuscripts were hidden in caves, gradually to disintegrate with the passing centuries and the ravages of animals and insects. Not until a stone casually tossed into a hole in the side of a cliff aroused a Bedouin shepherd's curiosity 1900 years later were the remnants of their manuscript treasures brought to light. Except for a few allusions by some early Greek and Latin historians to the Essenes, whom this community seems to represent, the vision of the men of Qumran was swept from the stage of history.

The problem out-Jobs the book of Job, whose inimitable dialogue became canonized in the Bible and has thus survived the centuries without interruption, and whose turbulent drama and theophany (Job 42) thus continue to be shared with many who have found solace in its words. To the religiously sensitive observer, the natural question is, why this serious injustice to the devout men of Qumran?

Anyone who may be concerned about the possibility that this

manuscript discovery may undermine the foundations of Christianity needs only to remember these simple facts: the Qumran community died; Christianity lives. But a more important question is, Why did the Qumran community die, while Christianity lives? The answer seems to lie in the inadequacy of that ancient community's theological foundation — the narrow focus of their faith, with its intensely eschatological orientation. Their faith was not broad enough to embrace the possibility of suffering and defeat. It is not the similarities between the Qumran sect and Christianity, therefore, upon which we should dwell, but rather the differences, if we would gain the lessons this discovery teaches. Despite the hazards of oversimplification, the following contrasts might be pointed out by way of elucidation:

1. The Qumran community was an intensely separatistic sect; they rigidly avoided the "Sons of Darkness," contact with whom meant defilement and impurity. In the "Rule of the Community" the expression "to be separated from all unrighteous men" (or "men of error") appears repeatedly (1QS V:1, 2, 10; VIII:13, etc.).

Jesus, however, is reported to have moved deliberately among those whom Jews, in derision, termed "tax collectors and sinners." When criticized, his reply was, "Those who are well have no need of a physician, but those who are sick; I came not to call the righteous, but sinners" (Mark 2:17; Matthew 9:12-13; Luke 5:31-32). Jesus and the Apostles considered association with others essential to preaching the gospel, the "good news."

Both the Qumran sect and Christianity may be said to have drawn inspiration from the fortieth chapter of Isaiah — but from different verses. For the men of Qumran it was verse 3: "In the wilderness prepare the way of the Lord, make straight in the desert a highway for our God"; thus they moved away from secular society. For Jesus, verse 9 provided his emphasis: "Get you up to a high mountain, O Zion, herald of good tidings; lift up your voice with strength, O Jerusalem, herald of good tidings. . . ." Christians carried the "good tidings" to all people.

2. The Qumran community was esoteric. Its members were sworn to secrecy about its teachings. Many of its documents were written in obscure and cryptic language, for only the initiated were intended to know the hidden meaning. Translation of many of the documents is exceedingly difficult because of this deliberate use of veiled language. Several manuscripts from Cave IV are

reported to contain a completely cryptic, esoteric language. Some, however, have been deciphered. In the "Rule of the Community" the member is admonished "to conceal [keep secret] the counsel of the Torah among unrighteous men" (1QS IX:17).

What a contrast their attitude was to that of Jesus, who "called to him the twelve, and began to send them out two by two, and gave them authority over the unclean spirits. ∴ . So they went out and preached that men should repent" (Mark 6:7, 12)!

3. The Qumran community lived its isolated life in the wilderness, waiting for God to act — the Kingdom was yet to come but always near. We have already drawn a lesson from their intensely apocalyptic outlook. Another illustration of their focus can be drawn from the Habakkuk *Pesher's* comment on Habakkuk 1:12-13a:

> The word means that God will not destroy his people by the hand of the nations, but by the hand of his elect God will execute the judgment of all nations and by their chastisement all the wicked among his people will be punished. (1QpHab V:3-5)

Jesus and the early Christians firmly believed that God was already acting to redeem; the Kingdom was already beginning to be felt. Jesus came preaching that "The time is fulfilled, and the kingdom of God is at hand; repent, and believe in the gospel" (Mark 1:15). To the Pharisees he said, ". . . behold, the kingdom of God is in the midst of you" (Luke 17:21). Although Christianity, too, began with an apocalyptic emphasis very similar to that of the Qumran sect, it contained the spiritual basis for a gradual shift to an ongoing redemptive fellowship (compare, for instance, the book of Revelation with the Gospel of John). God was counting on redeemed persons to act and to change the world.

4. The Qumran community lived an ascetic life, rigidly disciplined to fulfill literally the commands of the Torah. Emphasis was placed on the preservation of their purity and avoidance of anything which might make them ceremonially unclean. Thus they focused their spirit inwardly, keeping themselves constantly under critical self-examination in the light of their careful observance of Torah. Repeated admonitions to perfection appear in the manuscripts, such as:

> . . . to cleanse their minds by the truth of the statutes of God, and

to direct their energy according to the integrity of his ways . . . not to deviate at all from any of the words of God in their times [of worship?]; not to advance or delay the times of any of their appointed festivals; nor to swerve from his true statutes, to go either right or left. (1QS I:12-15)

Christians shared the spirit outwardly, giving purity a qualitative rather than ceremonial emphasis. Jesus said, "Hear and understand: not what goes into the mouth defiles a man, but what comes out of the mouth, this defiles a man. . . . For out of the heart come evil thoughts, murder, adultery, fornication, theft, false witness, slander" (Matthew 15:10-11, 19). To Jesus, God's commandments dealt with those qualities which bind persons in fellowship. In a similar vein is the important Christian thought: ". . . Whoever loses his life for my sake and the gospel's will save it" (Mark 8:35).

5. The Qumran community was priest-centered. The head priest and the "Sons of Aaron" held the positions of highest authority, even above that of the "Messiah of Israel"! In the "Rule of the Congregation" occurs the statement:

> This is the session of the men of renown [literally, "the Name"] invited to the feast for the council of the community, when God begets the Messiah [to be] with them. The priest shall come at the head of the whole congregation of Israel, and all the fathers of the Sons of Aaron, the priests, invited [?] to the feast of the men of renown. They shall sit before him, each according to his rank. Next shall come the Messiah of Israel [the Davidic Messiah?], and before him shall sit the heads of the thousands of Israel, each according to his rank. . . . And when they meet for the common table or to drink the wine . . . no one shall put forth his hand on the first [portion] of the bread or the wine before the priest . . . . (1QSa II:11-15, 17-19)

Christianity began as a lay movement without any formal organization; neither Jesus nor his disciples had any priestly background. The only prerequisite for joining the fellowship was common spiritual concerns. Organization came only with expansion and as problems of the spiritual fellowship demanded it.

6. The Qumran community was rigidly organized, with a strict hierarchy of position for each member. In the "Rule of the Community," for instance, the order is clearly elucidated:

> First in order to pass over shall be the priests, according to their spirits, one after the other. Then the Levites shall pass over after them. Third in order to pass over shall be all the people,

each after the other by thousands and hundreds and fifties and tens. Thus every man of Israel will know his position in the community of God for the eternal council. And none shall be lowered from his position and none shall be raised above his allotted place; for all of them shall be in true community. (1QS II:19-24)

In the passage quoted from the "Rule of the Congregation" (in "5" above), the rigidity of the order seems to be projected even into the Messianic age.

Christianity began as a fellowship (*koinonía*) of believers. Jesus was opposed to hierarchy, as the Gospels articulate so forcefully:

> And they came to Capernaum; and when he was in the house he asked them, "What were you discussing on the way?" But they were silent; for on the way they had discussed with one another who was the greatest. And he sat down and called the twelve; and he said to them, "If any one would be first, he must be last of all and servant of all." (Mark 9:33-35)

After the Resurrection the fellowship was loosely organized around the leadership of the Apostles; only later and very gradually did a hierarchy develop. Certain parallels in structure have been pointed out between the Qumran order and that of primitive Christianity, to be sure; but the Spirit and teachings of Jesus were clearly foreign to a rigid hierarchy.

7. To the Qumran community Scripture was central, and the accuracy of its inspired teacher's interpretation of it was unquestioned. The vast manuscript horde, with about a dozen *pesharim* or interpretations, and frequent references therein are testimonies to their belief in the authority of the written Word. In the Habakkuk Commentary (*pesher*), the source of their faith in interpreted Scripture is made clear:

> Now God told Habakkuk to write what would happen to the last generation, but the consummation of the end he did not make known to him. And when it says "In order that he who reads in it may run" [Hab. 2:2], that refers to the Right Teacher, to whom God made known all the secrets of the words of his servants the prophets. (1QpHab VII:1-5)

Jesus, though thoroughly familiar with Scripture and strongly influenced by it, emphasized its spirit rather than its words. His was no esoteric interpretation of hidden meanings; it was the obvious intent of the message of Scripture that he made transparent. His "You have heard that it was said. . . . But I say to you" (Matthew 5:21-44) implied not so much a new teaching as a shift from the stress on written words to the spirit of the message of Scripture as a whole. In the writings of Paul this contrast becomes striking: ". . . the written code kills, but the Spirit gives life" (II Corinthians 3:6).

8. The Qumran community divided the world into light and darkness, and saw the two in mortal conflict. Each member was instructed "to love all the sons of light, each according to his lot in the counsel of God, and to hate all the sons of darkness, each according to his guilt under the vengeance of God" (1QS I:9-11;[7] see also the doctrine of the two spirits described in 1QS III:17 — IV:26).

Christians, however, were admonished to carry light into the dark world, proclaiming God's redeeming love to the sons of darkness. In its prologue, John's Gospel announces, "The light shines in the darkness, and the darkness has not overcome it . . . . The true light that enlightens every man was coming into the world" (John 1:5, 9). The words of Jesus were unequivocal: "But I say to you, Love your enemies and pray for those who persecute you . . ." (Matthew 5:44).

The vitality of the Qumran organization and faith, though sufficient to perpetuate the community for almost 200 years, was apparently inadequate to survive the final cataclysmic destruction meted out by the "Sons of Darkness," the Romans. Such a reversal of their belief concerning the end of the age was too severe a blow to their neatly ordered faith, and it was shattered.[8] The vitality of Christians, on the other hand, sustained by a dynamic faith focused on God (whom they found revealed in the living presence of the resurrected Christ), could not be destroyed by the most heinous connivings of Roman persecutors. Instead of an order of prescribed rules, Christians possessed a faith which brought the very Spirit of God into their daily lives.

One is reminded of the response of Jesus to those Pharisees who engaged him in a dialogue concerning ceremonial purity: "Well did Isaiah prophesy of you hypocrites, as it is written, 'This people honors me with their lips, but their heart is far from me; in vain do they worship me, teaching as doctrines the precepts of men.'[9] You leave the commandment of God and hold fast the tradition of men" (Mark 7:6-8).

A faith centered in the "traditions of men" will die, but a faith that unleashes in humanity the Spirit of God cannot be destroyed.

Historic Christianity was clearly not "a child of the Qumran sect" and certainly was no mere "episode in the history of Judaism," as some interpreters of the scrolls have claimed. That Christianity stood closer in its origin to the Qumran sect — in its structure, outlook, ideology, and even its spirit — than it did to normative Judaism of the first century, is apparent. Sectarian Judaism offered the kind of environment — with its enthusiasm, its dedication, its prophetic zeal, its sense of urgency concerning the end of the age, its devotion to the prophetic as well as the legal literature of the past — in the midst of which a movement such as that of the Galilean Carpenter would more naturally be nurtured. Thus one would expect to find literary, ideological, even some ecclesiastical similarities between Christianity and the Qumran sect. But these are not the essentials which have made Christianity the dynamic religion that it is.

When one is confronted by the rediscovered Qumran community (even the virtuous and inspired "Right Teacher"), their devotion to the order is impressive; their discipline is admirable; the rigors of their environment in the wilderness, where they went to prepare the way of the Lord, are amazing. One may even share some of the apocalyptic hopes that underlay their chosen way and praise their love for each other. Rather than being moved to dedication, or endowed with a new spirit, however, one is conscious of a story out of history, a community that died. It seems remote, detached, a narrowly focused temporal faith — not a living reality that surges with contemporary relevance. It is "back there." In that ancient community, dynamic faith was secondary to the authority of rightly interpreted Scripture and the strict disciplines of the order.

On the other hand, when one is confronted by Jesus and the Christian gospel, even today, he is moved and disturbed; his faith is inspired, and if not spiritually transformed, he is at least deeply challenged. Thus Jesus has continued to live, ever renewed, ever renewing. It is the Person, not Scriptures nor an order, who has continued to unleash the Spirit in the world and sustain vitality within the Christian movement. Thus Christians continue to proclaim that Jesus Christ is Lord.[10]

APPENDICES

APPENDIX I

Interview With Ta'amireh Bedouins

During the fall of 1961, Anton Kiraz, with the help of 'Ayub Musallam, then the Mayor of Bethlehem, arranged for a lengthy interview with Muhammed edh-Dhib and Jum'a Muhammed, his older cousin, two of the three Bedouins who happened upon the first scroll cave. Sixty-three questions were sent to Kiraz to address to the Bedouins, and he arranged with great difficulty to tape-record the entire interview. Mr. J. F. Docmac, Headmaster of the Lutheran Elementary School in Bethlehem, translated the answers of the Bedouins during the recording. The tape is now in my possession, and its contents have been analyzed and incorporated, with other interview results, in Chapter Twelve. I am indebted to Drs. B. E. Clarity and S. D. Goitein for their careful checking of the recorded answers of the Bedouins.

The evening before they tape-recorded the interview (November 24, 1961), Kiraz and Docmac composed the following account from stories related by the two Bedouins under oath according to oriental custom (of necessity, I have edited their English a little to remove some of the more obvious infelicities):

> While Muhammed edh-Dhib and Jum'a Muhammed, his cousin, were tending their sheep on the hills of Khirbet Qumran near the Dead Sea one day during November, 1946,[1] Jum'a noticed a hole among the rocks. It was hardly big enough for a cat to enter. Jum'a threw a stone in to see how deep the hole was, and to his astonishment a peculiar sound was heard within. He also noticed a larger hole a little higher above the other one, and it was large enough for a man to enter. He told his cousin edh-Dhib

about the holes; but neither of them dared to enter the larger hole, for it was late in the afternoon. The sun was setting and darkness came. So they postponed their adventure until later.

Three days later, shortly after sunrise, edh-Dhib ventured into the hole and fell into a cave. There he saw about ten jars around him on both sides of the cave. Some of them had covers on top and some were without covers. Some ruins in the center of the cave, consisting of stones and earth which had fallen from the ceiling, showed broken jars beneath.

From one of the jars he removed the cover and found in it three scrolls, two of which were covered with cloth. The third had no covering. The scrolls presented a greenish appearance. He also noticed a wooden pole in the cave, about three inches in diameter. Removing the scrolls, he took them to his cousin Jum'a, who was tending the sheep about 100 meters away.

Together they went back to the cave where they searched again and broke a jar full of red earth. They removed two complete jars with covers from the cave. Each jar and each cover had three handles. The three manuscripts and two jars remained with them in the wilderness for about eight days.

When Jum'a's son came to his father, Jum'a left him with the sheep and went back home to the Ta'amireh camp, taking the scrolls and jars with him. There he hung the scrolls on a tent pole. About a month later he took them to Bethlehem to try to sell them to some merchant.

First he took them to a merchant by the name of Ibrahim 'Ijha, an oriental carpenter who also dealt in antiquities. They agreed to leave the scrolls and jars with 'Ijha for some time so he could find out what value they might have. They remained with 'Ijha for about a month, after which Jum'a returned to inquire what had happened. 'Ijha told Jum'a that no one would buy such things. Jum'a therefore took the scrolls again, but left the jars with 'Ijha.

By chance Jum'a met George Isha'ya, a peddler who sold cloaks to the Ta'amireh Bedouins. Isha'ya saw the scrolls which Jum'a had and asked him to leave them with him to show to some antiquity merchants to find out their true value. Jum'a, however, did not trust George, but rather decided to go to a relative named Sheikh 'Ali Subh in Bethlehem.

'Ali Subh took Jum'a to Kando, who guaranteed to look after the scrolls, and in case they were of any value and were sold, he promised two-thirds of the price to Jum'a. Jum'a agreed and left the scrolls with Kando and George Isha'ya but they did not sell them. When, about a month later, Jum'a inquired again, he was advised to take the scrolls to St. Mark's Monastery to show them to the Metropolitan.

Together with a relative named Khalil Musa, and George Isha'ya, Jum'a started with the scrolls for Jerusalem. Isha'ya took the two men first to his home in the Katamon Quarter of Jerusalem, where he offered them lunch. Afterwards he took them to see the Metropolitan at St. Mark's.

In the Monastery they were received by Bulos Gilf, a monk, who would not let them in, but sent them away, telling them that the scrolls they had brought were of no value whatever.

They all returned to Bethlehem to Kando's shop, where the scrolls were again left with Kando. When Jum'a returned later, he was told by Kando that the sum of £P24 ($97.20) had been offered for them. Jum'a agreed to this and received, according to their previous agreement, £16 ($64.80).

Sometime later, George Isha'ya requested that Jum'a lead him to the cave where the scrolls had been discovered. Thus, George Isha'ya, Jum'a, and Khalil Musa went together in a taxi from Jerusalem to the crossroad of Jericho-Dead Sea. From there they went on foot for an hour until they reached the cave. As they were leaving, Isha'ya placed some stone markers to help him find his way to the cave again. Later Jum'a met Isha'ya and Khalil Musa in Bethlehem, and they had two more scrolls. They had left these scrolls with Da'ud Musallam for a time, but Jum'a told them to show the two scrolls to Faidi Salahi, another antiquity dealer in Bethlehem. Faidi Salahi bought these two scrolls for £P7 ($28.35).

Although there are some details given in the taped interview by Muhammed edh-Dhib and Jum'a Muhammed which are not in the above statement (and likewise there are some details in the above statement which are not in the taped interview), nevertheless there are no discrepancies between the two.

After completing the interview and the sworn statement with the Bedouins, Kiraz visited Ibrahim 'Ijha, a carpenter in Bethlehem. From his statements Kiraz compiled the following account and sent it to me in a letter dated December 10, 1961:

> Jum'a Muhammed and Khalil Musa, some fourteen years before, brought three scrolls and two jars with conical covers to him. They remained in his shop for about twenty days, during which time he showed them to Faidi Salahi. Salahi suspected that the scrolls might not be ancient but were stolen from a Jewish synagogue. He claimed they had no archeological value. Thus 'Ijha was not encouraged to buy the scrolls and thus gave them back to Jum'a when he returned.

These accounts have the merit that they tally in several important points with the official statement prepared by G. L. Harding in 1953 (published in 1955), but they seemed irreconcilable at several points with the first accounts given in 1949 and 1952. The earlier accounts had also been based on direct contacts with the same Bedouins and had the advantage of being nearer the actual events. Numerous questions were therefore sent to Kiraz, who continued to seek answers from subsequent interviews and report them to me. He found several other persons who could confirm much of the story from personal contacts.

On July 29, 1962, and again on August 10, 1962, I met the Bedouins and these other persons and double-checked their stories, with Kiraz and Docmac acting as interpreters. The following persons were thus interviewed: Muhammed edh-Dhib, Jum'a Muhammed, Khalil Musa (the three Bedouins who happened upon Cave I), Ibrahim 'Ijha, Sheikh 'Ali Subh, Sheikh 'Abu Salim (leader of the Ta'amirehs), Jalil Elias 'Abu Sabha (neighbor of Da'ud Musallam), and Mrs. Roginah Marzurqa (witness to Faidi Salahi's dealings with E. L. Sukenik). These interviews have enabled me to construct in Chapter 12 what is very probably the correct story of the discovery.

APPENDIX II

Outline of the Dead Sea Scroll Story

I. HISTORY OF QUMRAN COMMUNITY CENTER

c. 875 – 750 B.C.	Jehoshaphat and/or Uzziah establish military outpost, apparently called 'Ir Hammelach ("City of Salt"), with round cistern (Joshua 15:62; II Chronicles 17:12; 26:10).
587 B.C.	'Ir Hammelach destroyed by Babylonians.
c. 135 B.C.	Community center established on site of 'Ir Hammelach by group of pious, sectarian Jews, probably Essenes (Period Ia). Main building about 90 x 190 feet.
c. 100 B.C.	Community center greatly enlarged to accommodate more members (Period Ib). Main building about 124 feet square.
c. 40 – 31 B.C.	Community center abandoned. Evidence of burning (by Parthians?) and earthquake (in 31 B.C.?) found in excavation.
c. 4 B.C.	Community center restored much as before (Period II).
A.D. 68	Final destruction of community center by Romans during first Jewish revolt.
c. A.D. 70 – 90	Roman military outpost established on remains of community center, using mostly main building area.

| c. A.D. 132 – 135 | Brief occupation of center during second Jewish revolt under Bar Kokhba; no formal building. |

II. MANUSCRIPT DISCOVERIES IN THE HOLY LAND

c. A.D. 220	Origen refers to some manuscripts discovered "at Jericho in a jar" which he used for his "Hexapla" text. (Also mentioned by Eusebius and Jerome in the fourth century.)
c. A.D. 800	Timotheus, Nestorian Patriarch of Seleucia, inquires about manuscripts found "in a cave near Jericho" which apparently formed basis of Karaite Jewish reform movement.
A.D. 900 – 1000	Al-Qirqisani, a Karaite Jewish historian, refers to a sect of "Magharians" (based on the Arabic word for "cave"), so called "because their books were found in a cave."

*   *   *   *   *

1937	Discovery of papyrus documents by American Colt Expedition at 'Auja el-Hafir (Byzantine Monastery of Nessana) in the Negeb. They included two fragmentary codices of John's Gospel and one of the letters of Paul from the seventh or eighth century. (Compare Khirbet Mird papyri.)
1946, November – December (or possibly January – February, 1947)	Ta'amireh Bedouins (Muhammed edh-Dhib, Jum'a Muhammed and Khalil Musa) happen upon Cave I near Khirbet Qumran and discover three manuscripts in a covered jar. They remove these and two complete jars with covers.
1947, March	Jum'a Muhammed and Khalil Musa offer the three scrolls to Ibrahim 'Ijha, a carpenter and antiquities dealer in Bethlehem. He keeps them for several weeks, but does not offer to buy them.

April	Scrolls taken to Khalil Eskander (Kando) in Bethlehem. George Isha'ya informs St. Mark's Monastery in Jerusalem about them. Metropolitan Samuel seeks to buy them.
May or June	Ta'amireh Bedouins take Isha'ya to cave. Later Isha'ya and Khalil Musa secure four scrolls, three of which they sell to Faidi Salahi, another Bethlehem antiquities dealer. The fourth scroll is kept by Kando (1QapGen).
July 5 (probably)	Four scrolls taken to Syrian Monastery by Jum'a Muhammed, George Isha'ya, and Khalil Musa. Turned away at the gate, they return the scrolls to Kando's shop.
July 19 (probably)	Kando purchases scrolls from Bedouins and sells them to St. Mark's Monastery for £P 24 ($97.20).
July (late)	Father Marmardji of École Biblique consulted by Syrians about scrolls. He takes Father van der Ploeg to Monastery to see them. Isaiah Scroll first identified, but considered medieval.
August	Isha'ya takes Father Yusif from Syrian Monastery to visit Cave I. Metropolitan Samuel consults several others about scrolls, including two librarians sent from Hebrew University.
September	Anton Kiraz takes Metropolitan Samuel to Homs, Syria, where scrolls are shown to Syrian Patriarch.
October 1 – 3	Metropolitan Samuel and Kiraz agree to become partners to the scrolls in return for Kiraz's financial assistance.
October	Tovia Wechsler examines scrolls and considers them to be late and of little value.
November 23	Armenian antiquities dealer in Jerusalem contacts E. L. Sukenik at Hebrew University about scrolls in hands of Faidi Salahi.
November 29	Sukenik buys two scrolls (and some frag-

	ments — 1QM and 1QH) from Faidi Salahi in Bethlehem.
December 22	Sukenik secures another scroll (1QIs^b?) and two jars from Faidi Salahi.
1948, February 4 – 6	Sukenik borrows St. Mark's scrolls for examination and offers to buy them.
February 18	Butrus Sowmy, monk at St. Mark's, calls the A.S.O.R. to get information about scrolls.
February 19	Syrian scrolls examined by J. C. Trever at A.S.O.R. He is told they had been in Monastery for forty years. Antiquity of scrolls suspected.
February 20	Trever visits St. Mark's Monastery to pursue examination of the scrolls and to secure permission to photograph them. Antiquity confirmed.
February 21	Isaiah (1QIs^a) and Habakkuk (1QpHab) Scrolls repaired and photographed at A.S.O.R.
February 22	Manual of Discipline (1QS) assembled from two scrolls, repaired and photographed.
February 27	Trever consults Director of Antiquities about scrolls, seeking film for further photographing. William Brownlee identifies the "Habakkuk Commentary" (1QpHab).
February 28	Millar Burrows, Director of A.S.O.R., returns from Baghdad and learns about scrolls.
March 5	Syrians reveal to Trever the true story about their purchase of the scrolls in 1947.
March 6 – 11	Isaiah and Habakkuk Scrolls rephotographed for publication.
March 12 (?)	Arrangements made with Department of Antiquities to visit Cave I with Syrians.
March 15	W. F. Albright's letter affirming antiquity of scrolls arrives in Jerusalem.
March 18	Importance of scrolls revealed by A.S.O.R.

	to Metropolitan Samuel through prepared news release.
March 20	Discussion at Haram esh-Sharif with sheikh from Nebi Musa about plans to visit cave.
March 23	Plans to visit cave abandoned after discovery that Jewish Haganah control region near cave.
March 25	Butrus Sowmy takes Syrian scrolls to Beirut for safekeeping.
April 3	Agreement worked out between Trever and Syrians for A.S.O.R. publication of their scrolls.
April 11	First news release appears in newspapers around the world.
April 26	Sukenik releases news about manuscripts at the Hebrew University.
May 15	End of British Mandate of Palestine and beginning of battle for the Old City of Jerusalem. Butrus Sowmy killed during battle.
August (?)	Apparently during second truce Isha'ya visits cave again and secures Daniel and Prayer Scroll fragments and a few others, which are turned over to St. Mark's.
September	First published articles on scrolls, with photographs, appear from A.S.O.R. and Hebrew University.
November	Isha'ya, Kando, and others "excavate" cave and secure many more fragments.
1949, January	O. R. Sellers and Yusif Saad seek to locate cave. Isha'ya demands payment, and negotiations cease.
January 24	Captain Philippe Lippens elicits aid from Arab Legion to relocate cave.
January 28	Captain Akkash el-Zebn rediscovers cave near Khirbet Qumran.
January 29	Syrian Metropolitan arrives in the United States with four scrolls and fragments.

February 4	Trever meets Metropolitan in New Jersey to begin arrangements for unrolling "Fourth Scroll" (1QapGen) and examine newly discovered fragments.
February 15 – March 5	Cave I (1Q) excavated. Fragments of about seventy scrolls recovered, and pieces of fifty pottery jars and covers.
April 7 – 9	The Metropolitan's fragments separated, mounted, photographed, and identified as parts of Daniel and, later, a Scroll of Prayers.
April 10	Large fragment removed from "Fourth Scroll" and later tentatively identified as "Lamech Document" (1QapGen).
April 14	"Lamech Scroll" taken to Fogg Museum at Harvard to prepare for opening.
Summer	Hebrew University Isaiah Scroll (1QIs^b) unrolled and identified.
October	St. Mark's scrolls exhibited at Library of Congress.
November	St. Mark's scrolls exhibited at Walters Art Gallery, Baltimore.
1950, February	St. Mark's scrolls exhibited at Duke University.
March	First A.S.O.R. volume containing facsimiles of 1QIs^a and 1QpHab appears.
Spring	Yusif Saad succeeds in purchasing the remainder of the Cave I fragments (1QSa, 1QSb) from Kando for Palestine Archaeological Museum.
Fall	"Carbon-14" Age-Determination test applied to some cloth from Cave I. Date of A.D. 33 ± 200 years determined. Published in January, 1951. Later changed to 24 B.C. ± 200 years.
November	St. Mark's scrolls exhibited at Oriental Institute of University of Chicago.
1951, Spring	"Manual of Discipline" (1QS) published by A.S.O.R.

Summer	Metropolitan Samuel withdraws "Lamech Scroll" from Fogg Museum and refuses to allow further work on it.
October	St. Mark's scrolls exhibited at Art Museum, Worcester, Massachusetts.
October	Ta'amireh Bedouins discover manuscripts in caves at Wadi Murabba'at. Two fragments of inscribed leather offered for sale in Jerusalem.
November 3	Dr. Awni Dajani, Inspector of Antiquities, and members of A.S.O.R. explore new caves claimed to be source of new fragments. Results uncertain.
November 24 – December 12	First season of excavation at Khirbet Qumran in which connections with Cave I begin to appear.
November (late)	Many manuscripts from Wadi Murabba'at offered by Kando to École Biblique in Jerusalem.
1952, January 21 – March 3	Four Wadi Murabba'at caves located and excavated under direction of Harding and de Vaux.
February	Ta'amireh Bedouins discover Qumran Cave II (2Q) close by 1Q.
March 10 – 29	Systematic exploration of the Qumran area; about 275 caves and crevices excavated by scholars with help of Ta'amireh Bedouins.
March 14	Cave III (3Q), with "Copper Scroll" and a few dozen leather scroll fragments, discovered by expedition.
July – August	Manuscripts from unidentified cave (Nahal Hever) brought by Ta'amireh Bedouins to Jerusalem. Greek text of Minor Prophets from second century A.D. among them.
Summer	Byzantine and early Arabic manuscripts (including some Greek New Testament manuscripts) discovered by Bedouins at Khirbet Mird, five miles west of Qumran.

Early September	Ta'amireh Bedouins discover Cave IV (4Q) in terrace adjacent to Khirbet Qumran.
September 22 – 29	Excavation of 4Q in which fragments of about 100 manuscripts were recovered. About 40,000 fragments ultimately recovered from this cave, including parts of almost 400 different manuscripts, about 125 of which are Biblical. International team of eight scholars chosen to assemble and study the fragments for publication.
September	Cave V (5Q) discovered a short distance to north of 4Q by excavators working on 4Q.
September	Bedouins discover Cave VI (6Q) on cliff by Wadi Qumran. Mostly papyrus fragments recovered, plus five "Damascus Document" fragments on leather.
1953, February 9 – April 4	Second season of excavation at Khirbet Qumran. Further light shed on structure of main building. Site clearly related to scroll caves and recognized as esoteric religious center.
February – May	Belgian scholars excavate Khirbet Mird.
1954, February 15 – April 15	Third campaign at Khirbet Qumran. Community meeting room, pantry, and pottery workshop cleared.
July 1	St. Mark's scrolls purchased in New York by Y. Yadin for State of Israel for $250,000 and sent to the Hebrew University in Jerusalem.
1955, February 2 – April 6	Fourth campaign at Khirbet Qumran; western quarter opened and water storage system uncovered. Caves VII-X (7Q, 8Q, 9Q, 10Q) discovered by archeologists in terrace around Khirbet Qumran. Very few manuscript fragments recovered.
March	Hebrew scroll of Minor Prophets (from second century A.D.) discovered by Ta'amireh Bedouins in fifth Wadi Murabba'at cave (5MurXII).
Spring	Publication of materials from Cave I in D. Barthélemy and J. T. Milik, *Discoveries in*

the Judaean Desert I: Qumran Cave I.

Publication of *The Dead Sea Scrolls of the Hebrew University* by E. L. Sukenik (posthumously completed by N. Avigad and others).

1956, January	Ta'amireh Bedouins discover and "excavate" Cave XI (11Q), one mile north of Khirbet Qumran — at least seven extensive manuscripts recovered.
February 7	Announcement of unrolling and decipherment of "Fourth Scroll," named "Genesis Apocryphon" (1QapGen).
February 18 – March 28	Fifth and final season of excavation at Khirbet Qumran. Eighteen more tombs in nearby cemetery explored. Another cemetery to south, one to north, and remains of buildings near 'Ain Feshkha explored.
June 1	Contents of "Copper Scroll" from 3Q revealed to be a list of deposits of fabulous treasure. Scroll cut into strips at Manchester University, England.
Fall	Publication of major parts of 1QapGen in N. Avigad and Y. Yadin, *A Genesis Apocryphon, A Scroll from the Wilderness of Judaea.*
1958, January 25 – March 21	Sixth season of excavation in Qumran area. Farm installation north of 'Ain Feshkha excavated. Basins for treating leather believed found.
Spring	Scroll fragments from cave near En Gedi in Israel discovered by Bedouins and brought to attention of Israelis.
1960, Spring	John Allegro conducts soundings at various sites in Jordan to attempt to uncover treasure deposits mentioned in "Copper Scroll." His transcription of that scroll appears in *The Treasure of the Copper Scroll* (New York, Doubleday).
March 23 – April 6	Israeli expedition to En Gedi region. "Cave of Letters" in Nahal Hever (Wadi Habra), with remains from Bar Kokhba revolt, dis-

	covered. Fragments of Psalms and fifteen papyrus letters in Hebrew, Aramaic, and Greek recovered.
Summer	Assembling of 4Q fragments completed by international team of scholars working in the Palestine Archeological Museum.
1961, March	Nahal Hever "Cave of Letters" excavated further. About forty more papyrus business documents recovered, dated A.D. 88-132, in Hebrew, Aramaic, Nabatean, and Greek. Cave VIII, "Cave of Horror," also excavated and fragments of Greek Scroll of Minor Prophets (8HevXIIgr) discovered.
Spring	Publication of Wadi Murabba'at manuscripts and artifacts by P. Benoit, O.P., J. T. Milik, and R. de Vaux, O.P. in *Discoveries in the Judaean Desert II: Les Grottes De Murabba'at.*
November 10-20	Psalms Scroll (11QPs^a) opened, and work of analysis begun by J. A. Sanders. Twenty-eight partial columns of the text are preserved, and three more among additional fragments. Thirty-seven Psalms and seven non-canonical compositions included.
1962, March	Fragments recovered from scroll of Ezekiel (11QEzek) studied by W. H. Brownlee.
Spring	Ta'amireh Bedouins discover about forty Samaritan papyrus documents in large cave in Wadi ed-Daliyeh, nine miles north of Jericho.
Fall	Publication of fragments and artifacts from Caves II, III, V-X by M. Baillet, J. T. Milik, and R. de Vaux, O.P. in *Discoveries in the Judaean Desert III: Les 'Petites Grottes' De Qumran.*
1964, January	Five framentary papyrus manuscripts discovered by Israelis in excavation of Masada. They include Gen. 46:7-11; Lev. 4:3-9; Psalms 81-85; a scroll of "Songs of the Sabbath Sacrifices," and five chapters from a first-century B.C. scroll of Ecclesiasticus.
1965	Publication of 11QPs^a by J. A. Sanders in

Discoveries in the Judaean Desert of Jordan IV: The Psalms Scroll of Qumran Cave 11.

Publication of 11QMelch (parts of two columns of a scroll of Melchizedek) by A. S. van der Woude in *Oudtestamentische Studien XIV.*

November	Publication of 1QDan*a,b*, 1QPrayers, 1Q19 and 1Q70 by John C. Trever, "Completion of the Publication of Some Fragments from Qumran Cave I," *Revue de Qumran* 19.
1967, June	Y. Yadin secured the "Temple Scroll" from "Kando." Probably from Cave XI, it is the longest of all the Qumran scrolls (28 feet, 3 inches), with 66 columns of which about seventy per cent is preserved.
1968	Publication by John Allegro of 4Q158—4Q186 in *Discoveries in the Judaean Desert of Jordan V: Qumran Cave 4:I (4Q158–4Q186).*
1969	Y. Yadin published a head-phylactery which may have come from Cave IV: *Tefillin from Qumran (XQPhyl 1-4).*
1970	P. Bar Adon excavates site about nine miles south of Khirbet Qumran near 'Ain Ghuweir where Qumran II period remains appeared. Building 64 x 140 feet uncovered. Small cemetery with Qumran type graves excavated one-half mile to the north.
1971	Publication by J. P. M. van der Ploeg, O.P. and A. S. van der Woude of 11QtgJob in *Le Targum de Job de la Grotte XI de Qumran.*
1976	Publication of excavations at Wadi ed-Daliyeh by Paul and Nancy Lapp in *Annual of the A.S.O.R.* XLI for 1974.
	Publication of Enoch fragments from Cave IV (4QEnoch) by J. T. Milik, *The Books of Enoch: Aramaic Fragments of Qumran Cave 4.*
1977	Publication of "Temple Scroll" (11QTemple) promised by Y. Yadin.

List of Abbreviations

BA	*Biblical Archaeologist*
BASOR	*Bulletin of the American Schools of Oriental Research*
DJD	*Discoveries in the Judaean Desert*
JBL	*Journal of Biblical Literature*
JNES	*Journal of Near Eastern Studies*
JQR	*Jewish Quarterly Review*
PEQ	*Palestine Exploration Quarterly*
RB	*Revue Biblique*
RQ	*Revue de Qumran*
RSV	*Revised Standard Version of the Bible*

Manuscript Designations

Official designation at left includes abbreviations for: Cave number, place found, name of document, and copy number (letters above line). If other than a leather document, material is indicated before the cave number.

Qumran Cave I

1QIs^a—Isaiah "A" Scroll, The Great Isaiah Scroll, The Isaiah Scroll

1QIs^b—Isaiah "B" Scroll, Hebrew University Isaiah Scroll

1QDan^a—Daniel "A" fragments from "matted mass of leather," layers 8 and 9

1QDan^b—Daniel "B" fragments from "matted mass of leather," layers 6 and 7

1QpHab—*Pesher* to Habakkuk, Habakkuk Commentary, Jerusalem Scroll #II, small scroll

1QapGen—1Q20, Genesis Apocryphon, Book of Lamech, Apocalypse of Lamech, Fourth Scroll

1QS—*Serekh ha-Yahad,* Rule of the Community, Manual of Discipline, Sectarian Document, Jerusalem Scroll #I

1QSa—Rule of the Congregation (probably part of 1QS scroll)

1QSb—Collection of Benedictions (probably part of 1QS scroll)

1QPrayers—1Q34*bis,* 1Q34, Liturgical Prayer Scroll, from "matted mass of leather," layers 1-5

pap1Q70*bis*—unidentified papyrus fragment

1Q19*bis*—"The Book of Noah" fragment of 1Q19

1QH—*Hodayot,* Thanksgiving Hymns, Songs of Thanksgiving, Hebrew University Songs Scroll

1QM—War Scroll, "Battle between the Sons of Light and the Sons of Darkness"

Fragments from Other Caves

4Q158-186—*Pesharim* documents from Qumran Cave IV—interpretations of Biblical writings

4QEnoch—Fragments of Book of Enoch from Qumran Cave IV

6QD (6Q15)—"Damascus Document" (see CD below)

11QPs*ᵃ*—Psalms Scroll from Qumran Cave XI

11QEzek—Ezekiel fragments from Qumran Cave XI

11QapPs—Apocryphal Psalms fragments from Qumran Cave XI

11QMelch—Melchizedek Scroll from Qumran Cave XI

11QtgJob—Targum of Job from Qumran Cave XI

11QTemple—Temple Scroll from Qumran Cave XI

5MurXII—Hebrew Scroll of Minor Prophets from fifth Wadi Murabba'at Cave

8HevXII gr—Greek Scroll of Minor Prophets from Nahal Hever Cave VIII

XQPhyl—Phylactery fragments from an unidentified Qumran cave

MasSirSabb—"Songs of the Sabbath Sacrifices," Angelic Liturgy, "sectarian liturgical scroll" from Masada

CD—"Damascus Document," "Zadokite Fragments" from Cairo Genizah; related documents found in Qumran Caves IV and VI

Notes

CHAPTER 1

1. This branch of the Christian Church is usually called Assyrian Orthodox in the United States. See Chapter 3, note 2.

2. Officially he was a monk, secretary of the Monastery, and teacher of the young monks. He did not wish to become a priest, as I was later informed by one of his close friends in Jerusalem.

3. The A.S.O.R., as it is abbreviated, was established at Jerusalem in 1900 (at Baghdad in 1921) to afford opportunities for Biblical study and research in "the lands of the Bible" by graduates of American colleges and universities.

4. For a long time I assumed that the call had come for Burrows, the Director, and that Omar therefore had turned it over to me. In fact, however, Sowmy actually had asked for Brownlee. Since Omar did not find him in his room, he had called me to the telephone. The Syrians, it seems, had thought it more diplomatic first to inquire who was at the School. Knowing that Bishop Stewart at St. George's Cathedral lived close to our School, they had called him the previous day to learn the names of those whom they might call. The Bishop informed them that Burrows had just left and that he did not know who was in charge of the School. He mentioned Brownlee's name, however, because the latter had come to the Bishop's office the day before to obtain a certificate to prove that he was a Christian. For Brownlee's own account see *The Duke Divinity School Bulletin* 21:3 (November, 1956), pp. 68-81.

CHAPTER 2

1. The *keffiyeh* is the Arab headdress, a large cloth tied around by a black goat-hair rope, the *'agal*.

2. At that time Trans-Jordan and Palestine were separate countries.

The Allenby Bridge was the main point of communication between the two, crossing the Jordan River about 7½ miles north of the Dead Sea.

3. It was the second section of what we later called the "Manual of Discipline" (now designated as 1QS). The irregularly broken edge of Column VIII was coiled tightly against the inner turns of leather. See pp. 45-46.

4. A colophon, frequently found at the end of medieval manuscripts, consisted of a symbol or statement about the copyist and often included the circumstances concerning the preparation of the manuscript.

5. Or. 4445.

6. Several Biblical Hebrew manuscripts previously known should have had the distinction of being older. There are some large fragments of scrolls of Jeremiah, Ezekiel, and the Psalms in the Taylor-Schechter collection from the Cairo Genizah in the Cambridge University Library which must be a century, perhaps several centuries, older than the British Museum Codex, as Paul Kahle has shown. Furthermore, it seems quite likely that the Cairo Codex of the Prophets (dated A.D. 895) is at least as old as or older than Or. 4445.

7. Cambridge University Library, Or. 233.

8. "A Biblical Fragment From the Maccabean Age: The Nash Papyrus," *JBL* 56 (September, 1937), pp. 145-176.

9. I failed to mention this fact in my first article, which was written during the summer of 1948. At that time I was under the impression that it was later when the Syrians mentioned knowing that one of the scrolls was Isaiah. My notes and letters written at the time give no contrary information. Brownlee, however, in his version of the incident (*art. cit.,* p. 70), states that the Syrians specified which scroll might be Isaiah and that I indicated this fact to him during our examination of the copied passage. Although I have great respect for Brownlee's memory, I do not believe the Syrians were that specific. That they already knew that the largest scroll was Isaiah, there is no doubt; but they were very cautious about how much they told me at that time, as subsequent events were to show. See pp. 69-70.

10. On the basis of my record of that first interview, as well as my memory of it, another interview in Beirut two months later, and a statement of an American cousin of Ibrahim's, Aziz Souma, I am inclined to agree with Ibrahim's claim that it was he who convinced Metropolitan Samuel that the scrolls were really ancient. Ibrahim is a student of history, having published a number of writings in Syriac, the sacred language of his people.

11. *BA* 11:3 (September, 1948), p. 50.

CHAPTER 3

1. It was Sowmy's marked reactions to my announcement that the passage was from Isaiah that led me to believe that nothing had been said about Isaiah the previous day. See note 9 to Chapter 2.

2. Technically, my reference to "Jacobites" was warranted, for it is a common, though misleading, designation for their church. They were apparently disturbed by the implication that their church was no older than the sixth century, when the energetic work of Jacob Baradaeus (d. 578), a Syrian Monophysite bishop and missionary, greatly extended the influence of the Syrian Monophysite Church. These Syrians sincerely believe that their church represents the original orthodox apostolic church founded in the first century, with Antioch as the center, and thus they refer to their patriarch as the "Patriarch of Antioch."

The term "Jacobite" came to be used by outsiders to distinguish these Syrian Christians from the Nestorians, who were another Eastern "Assyrian" church, formed in the fifth century by followers of Theodore of Mopsuestia and Bishop Nestorius, who had been exiled from Constantinople after the Third Ecumenical Council at Ephesus in A.D. 431. The latter also used the Syriac language for Scriptures and worship.

3. Ira M. Price, *The Ancestry of the English Bible* (rev. ed. 1934).

4. See Chapter 2, note 8.

5. Albright, *op. cit.*, p. 172. Early the next morning I wrote the following to Elizabeth: "I am convinced in my own mind on the matter now, but it may take many months to convince the scholarly world. It is hard for me to believe it possible, but the indications I observed last night point to the Maccabean period for the writing of these manuscripts!! But that dating depends upon the accuracy of Albright's work on the Nash Papyrus. . . . Please keep this confidential, for it might create a premature sensation. If I'm right, it will create a justifiable sensation, but that will have to await further study."

CHAPTER 4

1. Helen Christaki, a widow with five children, was a servant at the School.

2. Twenty-four feet and five-sixteenths inch (7.34 meters) proved later to be a more accurate figure.

3. These tiny uninscribed fragments, together with a few others left over from a later repair task (see Chapter 14), none of them inscribed, are all I possess from the originals.

CHAPTER 5

1. It now seems probable that another document had been attached, perhaps at this point. Two columns (1QSa) of it were secured many months later by the Palestine Archaeological Museum. See p. 150.

2. A large fragment of the cover to this scroll was later recovered from the cave (see p. 150), though there is still some doubt whether it was attached at this point or before some other columns.

3. The description of the process of joining the two parts of the "Manual of Discipline" (1QS) has been elaborated primarily because of

a charge levied by Solomon Zeitlin ("The Idolatry of the Dead Sea Scrolls," *JQR* 48:3 [January, 1958], pp. 243-278). My claim to have joined two scrolls together, he asserts, was an attempt to cover up a deliberate suppression of the so-called "Haftarot Scroll" (see p. 106). He states, "I believe no man had the right to join two scrolls into one without informing the scholarly world that he had done so, otherwise this would constitute a form of scholarly fraud" (p. 244). He presented his paper at the International Congress of Orientalists in Munich on August 30, 1957. Apparently he had failed to read the published statements about the joining of the two parts of the scroll in *BA* 11:3, p. 53, and *BASOR* III (October, 1948), p. 11. He based his claim on a footnote in *BA* 12:2 (May, 1949), p. 26, where I said, "Two of the five [scrolls] were later joined together to make the 'Sectarian Document.' "

In April, 1958, during a visit to the Hebrew University in Jerusalem, where the scroll was on exhibit, I noticed that between Columns 7 and 8 the point of joining had pulled away about an eighth of an inch, revealing clearly the backing of adhesive tape. The evidence is also quite clear on several of my color transparencies taken the morning of February 24, 1948.

4. The notching code on each film shows that it was "Kodak Super-XX Panchromatic" sheet film. Normally I would reject such film for manuscript copying. It was this set of negatives which was used for the final publication in the *Dead Sea Scrolls of St. Mark's Monastery*, Vol. II, Fascicle 2.

5. In the first edition of his *The Dead Sea Scrolls* (1956), John Allegro, in mentioning this experience of mine, said, "However, he seems to have restrained both his impatience and his tongue, for neither then nor at any other time was any mention of the discovery made to the authorities responsible for the control of antiquities in Palestine. . . ." No "authorities" were present that day, but see pp. 59-60. When I wrote to Allegro about this and other misstatements in his book, he sent me an apology and modified this sentence considerably in a subsequent printing (1957), after 40,000 copies of the book had been distributed.

CHAPTER 6

1. In 1950 the I.C.R.E. became the Division of Christian Education of the National Council of the Churches of Christ in the U.S.A.

2. The delay resulted from the broken wires which isolated Jerusalem and cut off our electrical power.

3. These transparencies were made on 6.5 x 9 centimeter Ansco Color sheet film, using a Kodak Medalist II camera with adapters for ground-glass focusing and plate-holders. The Kodak "Ektar" f/3.5 100 millimeter lens on the camera is particularly valuable for such exacting work.

4. These third- and fourth-century A.D. papyrus Biblical manuscripts had been purchased in Cairo, Egypt, in 1930 by A. Chester Beatty and beautifully published under the direction of the British Museum.

5. I had seen and photographed a similar scroll in the Greek Patriarchal Library a few months before. The prominent use of *tagin,* or "crowns," on the tops of certain letters; the extreme contrast between broad, heavy strokes and fine, connecting ones; the pronounced regularity of the height of the letters; and the greatly exaggerated width of letters to fill some lines at the left margin, all impressed me with the modern character of the manuscript.

Through a series of misunderstandings this manuscript became involved in the controversy over the supposed "suppressed scroll of the Haftarot" (see p. 106). I continue to doubt that it had any relation whatever to that matter. See M. Burrows, "Concerning the Dead Sea Scrolls," *JQR* 42:2 (October, 1951), pp. 119-125.

6. I am indebted to Brownlee for helping me reconstruct this incident accurately. Neither of us expected that scroll to become involved in any way in the story of the Dead Sea Scrolls. No one who is familiar with Hebrew paleography would claim a chronological relationship between that scroll and the DSS.

CHAPTER 7

1. The effect of color reproduction on dark manuscripts is similar to but not so great as that of infrared film, which has proved to be indispensable for recovering many obscure parts of the Dead Sea Scroll fragments. Thus a good color transparency may provide a clearer image of an ancient script.

2. Permission to photograph this sacred area surrounding the Dome of the Rock, where Solomon's Temple once stood, was too good an opportunity to pass up, and once again I had been torn away from work on the scrolls.

3. The Edfu Papyri, as they are called, from a Jewish colony in Upper Egypt, were dated largely on the basis of the nature of the names they include. The paleographic consideration was secondary. I was able to examine these papyri carefully in the Bodleian Library, Oxford, in March, 1951.

4. In two letters written the next day, I elaborated this theory. With further study, however, I abandoned it in favor of a date about 100 B.C. for the Isaiah Scroll and have not wavered from this since. It has been interesting to note that several scholars have claimed that same early period of history for the founding of the Qumran community. Even that does not now seem possible on the basis of the accumulated evidence.

5. What I did not know then was that very few Biblical scholars and archeologists had much knowledge of Hebrew paleography. Moreover Hamilton, it needs to be remembered, was facing, with Iliffe, the stupendous task of planning the protection of that valuable Museum from the inevitable strife that was daily intensifying and destined to explode on May 15 at the end of the British Mandate. Preparing to store the valuable exhibits in bombproof shelters and to internationalize the

Museum was occupying every one of their waking moments. The world should be grateful to these men, whose foresight resulted in the saving of all of these priceless records of the past.

CHAPTER 8

1. Although there is no question about my having written the preliminary report (I refer to it twice in my letters and twice in my diary), I have no copy of it today. I have only a vague memory of its contents. During an interview with Anton Kiraz in Bethlehem, April 26, 1958, I was told that the Metropolitan had shown Kiraz "a receipt given him [the Metropolitan] by the A.S.O.R. with two signatures on it . . . some time after February 19, 1948." Perhaps that was the "preliminary report." As far as I know, nothing else in writing was given to the Metropolitan by any of us until March 18, when Dr. Burrows presented him with a copy of the first news release (see pp. 43 and 82).

2. Ugaritic is an alphabetic cuneiform language found on clay tablets discovered at Ras esh-Shamrah in Syria in 1928. Dating from the fourteenth century B.C., the language is that used by the Canaanites and later adopted by the Hebrews.

3. A small liturgical document, written on parchment in an unskilled hand, the Dura Fragment was found in the excavation of the synagogue at Dura on the Euphrates and must date prior to A.D. 256, when the synagogue was destroyed.

4. For his own statement see his *The Dead Sea Scrolls* (1955), p. 29.

5. For the date of the purchase, see pp. 101-102. In my first report (*BA* 11:3, pp. 46-49) I only hinted at this discrepancy in the Syrians' approach, for at the time it seemed wise to avoid undue emphasis upon it. In 1955, Burrows published a more specific statement (*op. cit.*, p. 14). See also Sukenik's record of another approach (Y. Yadin, *The Message of the Scrolls* [1957], p. 25).

6. E. L. Sukenik had secured the jars from a Bethlehem antiquities dealer on December 22, 1947, it was to be learned later. See p. 108.

CHAPTER 9

1. Having sensed their opposition, I had refrained from revealing to them the fact that I had shared the whole story with Director of Antiquities Hamilton on February 27. This statement contradicts the one found in A. Y. Samuel's "The Purchase of the Jerusalem Scrolls" (*BA* 12:2, p. 31), which I prepared on the basis of interviews with him. The date given there was my error. It was on March 19 when the discussion mentioned there occurred. See pp. 85 and 137.

2. In a letter written to my wife the next night, I said: "Any excavations they [the Syrians] might do at the cave would be illegal, unless they first got permission from the Department of Antiquities. Thus, we decided that Mr. Hamilton should be consulted in the matter to know how to proceed."

3. When developed two weeks later, they proved disappointing but usable. The film had defective color-balance.

4. My estimate was much too conservative, for when opened the scroll gave evidence of having more than 700 lines of text.

5. My confidence was not shared by Burrows (see his *The Dead Sea Scrolls* [1955], pp. 226-27). No one could anticipate at that time what a difficult problem would be created by the inner lining of thin white leather, which could be seen from one end and in the large break on one surface. See N. Avigad and Y. Yadin, *A Genesis Apocryphon* (1956), pp. 13-14.

6. It was probably a metallic ink rather than a pure carbon ink, which was used on the other scrolls. Experts claim that this would account for the tendency toward disintegration around the letters, as the manuscript so clearly demonstrates.

7. Ossuaries are rectangular chests cut from soft limestone and used by the Jews for storing the bones of their deceased. They can be dated with considerable confidence to the period from about 40 B.C. to A.D. 70.

8. It was this type of inscription which first convinced E. L. Sukenik of the antiquity of the other similar scrolls in December, 1947, as we learned later. See p. 107.

9. In his first edition of *The Dead Sea Scrolls*, p. 14, Burrows wrote, "Soon thereafter this information [the date of the discovery learned on March 5] was passed on to Mr. Hamilton." Immediately on reading this statement, I urged Burrows to correct the error. My failure to communicate this one point, I knew and I thought he knew, was one of the causes of the misunderstanding that developed later. In March, 1948, I was unaware of the relationship between the date of the discovery and the government antiquities laws. My concern was to get to the cave without acting illegally. Furthermore, at least a week had intervened since the date was revealed, during which I had been under the pressure of re-photographing the scrolls and had suffered several days of illness.

10. I have to rely on my memory and indirect evidence for the date of this visit, for I failed to make note of it in either my diary or letters. By then letters were devoted largely to problems about leaving the country. That the interview must have occurred between March 12 and 20, there is no doubt. The most likely time was on the twelfth, since my first visit to the Museum after Dr. Burrows and I agreed that Hamilton should be consulted occurred on that day. When I discussed the matter with Hamilton in Oxford, during late May of 1958, he showed no recollection of the interview. His instructions to me have remained so indelibly stamped on my mind that there is no question we had the interview. Furthermore, in a letter dated March 20, 1948, I wrote parenthetically: "I have already talked with Hamilton at the Museum about the proper procedure. He has given permission to visit the place to gather up any loose materials left."

From my later correspondence it is evident that during this last interview with Hamilton I raised the question of the Syrians' right to possession of the scrolls. He assured me that there was no question about their ownership, but warned that if they were to excavate the cave it would be illegal. He made his statement about right of ownership, of course, without the knowledge of the recent date of the discovery.

11. The two fragments were returned to the Metropolitan in April, 1949.

12. Unfortunately, it did not occur to us to show this letter to Hamilton. Had we done so the subsequent events might have been quite different. Albright's letter, coming from the world-renowned archeologist and epigrapher, would have immediately convinced Hamilton of the tremendous importance of what I had showed and told him on February 27th, when he gave only a polite response to my pleading for film. As Director of Antiquities, he would doubtless have asked questions about the application of the antiquities laws of the Mandate Government to the discovery; and the recent date of the discovery would have been revealed to him, bringing the discovery under his jurisdiction. So far as' my records reveal, however, I did not see him again after the letter arrived.

CHAPTER 10

1. Some weeks previously, this family with five children, who lived in a quarter west of the school, had received a threatening letter warning them to move within twenty-four hours. Burrows had offered them refuge in the basement of the Director's house. See his *Palestine Is Our Business* (1949), p. 52.

2. The Syrian layman was apparently Anton Kiraz (see p. 110). He attests in an affidavit that he conveyed the Hebrew University request to the Metropolitan but was advised against fulfilling it.

3. Sometime prior to March 5 the Syrians had revealed the fact that some Jews had seen the scrolls "the previous November." No names had been given; but by March 5, as one of my letters indicates, I had assumed that Sukenik was one of them. It later became evident that the Jews referred to were the two librarians whom Magnes sent to the Monastery at the request of Dr. Maurice Brown. See p. 104.

4. At the time the Metropolitan was vague about when Sukenik had seen the scrolls, and I assumed that it was after I had begun work on them. It was to be many months before the date was established. See pp. 108-109.

Shortly after I first saw the scrolls, it occurred to me to seek Sukenik's opinion about their antiquity. I had met him the previous October and had read about his excavation of some tombs on Kiraz's property. When I tried to make the call, however, I found the telephone circuit broken and did not try again.

5. He was referring to the acacia wood box which had been made by the Hebrews, during their wandering in Sinai, to house the stone tablets of the Ten Commandments (Exodus 25:10-16; 37:1-5; 40:20-21). The mystery of the disappearance of the Ark and its tables of stone has long intrigued Jewish and Christian students of the Bible.

6. While preparing the article "The Purchase of the Jerusalem Scrolls" for Metropolitan Samuel the next spring, I inadvertently gave the date for this discussion as February 27, 1948 (cf. *BA* 12:2, p. 31). It should have been March 19. See pp. 123-124.

7. Anton Kiraz, in his affidavit, said that he offered Sukenik, as a substitute for the scrolls, the set of the photographs which the Metropolitan had received from us on March 1. When Kiraz went to the Monastery to get the prints, he says, the Metropolitan refused to let him have them. Kiraz made no further efforts after that to communicate with Sukenik. We, of course, knew nothing yet about the scrolls purchased by Sukenik the previous December. See pp. 106-108.

8. In my first published account I wrote, "Already jubilant over this newest addition to our valuable finds, I was made even more happy when the Metropolitan informed me that Father Butros had left that morning with all the manuscripts, to take them to a place of safety outside of Palestine" (*BA* 11:3, p. 56). Some scholars took these words to mean that I rejoiced over the fact that the scrolls had been smuggled out of the country, an interpretation which never occurred to me as possible from the context of my words (cf. *PEQ*, July — October, 1949, p. 116). Several scholars continued to perpetuate this unfortunate interpretation in their writings. Finally I felt it necessary to make a special visit to Jordan in 1958 to set the record straight. On my arrival in Jerusalem, I was told by an officer of the Jordan Department of Antiquities, to my utter consternation, that the rumor had grown to such proportions that it was then proclaimed that I had personally smuggled all the Dead Sea Scrolls out of the country and carried them to the United States! In fact, he expressed amazement that I had been admitted to Jordan. When he learned the true story, he graciously arranged for a taped radio interview as a means of helping to correct the false rumors.

I was in no position in 1948 to give legal counsel to the Syrians, who must have known far more about the antiquities laws than I did. (Butrus Sowmy had studied law for two years, according to a close friend of his, and his brother was a customs official at Allenby Bridge.) It would have been better, of course, had they secured an export license. It needs to be remembered, however, that in the midst of Palestine's virtual state of anarchy, what was legal or illegal was by that time almost purely academic. Furthermore, respect by the natives for foreign-imposed laws in Palestine had for centuries been only partially maintained.

Chapter 11

1. Some evidence seems to support this description. See G. L. Harding's statement in *DJD I* (1955), p. 6. Some of the roof and sides of the interior of the cave had fallen. There was no large lower entrance at that time, apparently, but only a second, small opening. See Appendix I.

2. In an interview on August 5, 1962, Father Yusif said that he went

to the Syrian monastery by the Jordan River that next day, while George Isha'ya stayed longer at the cave.

3. When I wrote the first account of these experiences that summer (*BA* 11:3), I deliberately telescoped the story told me on February 19 with items added during these later interviews in order to avoid stressing the inaccurate story told me at first. In fact, most of what appears in the third paragraph on p. 47 of that article was gleaned from these later interviews during March, 1948.

4. Several months after this book was first published, Metropolitan Samuel released a romanticized account of some of these same events in *Treasure of Qumran* (1966), pp. 156-163, with numerous variations. Since he gives no documentation, discrepancies should be checked against this documented account. See notes in subsequent chapters where important differences are pointed out.

5. The mystery of the missing export license continued to baffle me. I had paid little attention to the papers given me by Iliffe at the Museum, but placed them with other papers needed for customs. For years I assumed that, on the basis of the official's claim, they gave me no export license. Many years later, in supposedly the same package of papers that accompanied my return trip, I found the license, signed by Hamilton!

CHAPTER 12

1. The major sources for the earliest accounts are, chronologically: A. Y. Samuel, "The Purchase of the Jerusalem Scrolls," *BA* 12:2 (May, 1949), pp. 26-31; G. Lankester Harding, "A Bible Discovery," *The* (London) *Times*, August 9, 1949 (cf. *The Illustrated London News*, October 1, 1949, pp. 494-495); *DJD I* (1955), p. 5; E. L. Sukenik, *The Dead Sea Scrolls of the Hebrew University* (1955), pp. 13-17; John M. Allegro, *The Dead Sea Scrolls* (1956), pp. 15-19; Yigael Yadin, *The Message of the Scrolls* (1957), pp. 15-30; W. H. Brownlee, "Muhammad Ed-Deeb's Own Story of His Scroll Discovery," *JNES* 16:4 (October, 1957), pp. 236-239; J. van der Ploeg, O. P., *The Excavations at Qumran* (tr. by Kevin Smyth, S.J., 1958), pp. 9-13; J. C. Trever, "When Was Qumran Cave I Discovered?" *RQ* 3:1 (February, 1961), pp. 135-141; and W. H. Brownlee, "Edh-Dheeb's Story of His Scroll Discovery," *RQ* 3:4 (October, 1962), pp. 483-494, and 4:3 (October, 1963), pp. 417-420.

2. The following account has been gleaned from repeated interviews with Anton D. Kiraz and other members of the Syrian Orthodox communities in Jerusalem and Bethlehem. Considerable documentation (see below) has been gathered for my files to establish the accuracy of the statements.

3. See *Life* Magazine, December 22, 1947, pp. 75-79.

4. See B. Couroyer, "Histoire d'une tribu semi-nomade de Palestine," *RB* 58:1 (January, 1951), pp. 75-91.

5. Ibrahim Sowmy, customs official in charge of Allenby Bridge from

early 1947 to the end of March, 1948, was frequently troubled by the flow of contraband goods which Bedouins carried across the Jordan several miles south of his post. He was aware of the Ta'amireh activities in this regard, as well as those of the Sawahira and Ibn 'Ubeid tribes. This fact accounts for the origin of the association of smuggling with the early reports concerning the discovery. Apparently, however, smuggling was not the reason for the presence of the Bedouins near 'Ain Feshkha at the time of the discovery.

6. This and other information about the Bedouins has been gleaned from repeated interviews with the three Bedouins during the period from November, 1961 to July, 1964. On the evening of November 24, 1961, Anton Kiraz and J. F. Docmac of Bethlehem questioned two of them for several hours and composed the account from their statements which appears as Appendix I. The following morning sixty-three questions, which I had prepared for the purpose, were addressed to these Bedouins; and the questions as well as their answers were tape-recorded. Several interviews followed during the next six months to secure answers to new questions which arose from an analysis of the recording. On July 29 and again on August 10, 1962, I personally interviewed these Bedouins and their early associates at length, while Kiraz and Docmac (on July 29) served as interpreters. Still further questions have been put to the three Bedouins by Kiraz and reported in letters between October, 1962 and August, 1975.

7. Khalil Musa was the eldest of the trio and very active in subsequent events. He was interviewed twice by me and many times by Kiraz. He has proved most cooperative in supplying information.

The Bedouins insist that no such person as Ahmed Muhammed was involved, as mentioned in early reports. Since Ahmed is associated with edh-Dhib's name (see below) and another relative, Ahmed Abd el-Qadir (both of whom were with Jum'a when they were interviewed by G. L. Harding in 1949), it is easy to account for this error in reporting their names. Kiraz examined Jum'a's identity card (#243419, dated at Jericho January 27, 1957) to be certain of his correct name. Cf. *RQ* 4:3 (October, 1963), p. 418.

8. As a result of the addition of "Hassan" to edh-Dhib's name in reports from Jerusalem during 1963 (*e.g.*, *BA* 26:4 [December, 1963], p. 114, n. 4), I asked Kiraz to check Muhammed's identity card. On July 21, 1964, Kiraz visited him at his camp near el-'Azariyeh (Bethany) and examined the card, which is numbered 5941/218342 and dated in Bethlehem on October 23, 1956. There his name is clearly given as transliterated here.

9. Khalil Musa, during several interviews, stressed the fact that it was the hope for gold in the cave that motivated their searches.

10. In the November 24-25, 1961, interviews Jum'a and Muhammed mentioned that it was "three days later"; but Khalil Musa, when interviewed separately, asserted it was the next morning. Apparently it was the third day (less than two days later), for in an interview with Jum'a on

January 12, 1963, Kiraz was told that the reason they delayed a day was because they had to take all their flocks to 'Ain Feshkha the next day to water them. This was an all-day task which they did every other day, Jum'a explained.

11. He demonstrated the process for me during an interview and in the presence of the other Bedouins on July 29, 1962. Cf. *RQ* 4:3, p. 419.

12. The Bedouins' statement (Appendix I) that the covers also had handles was obviously in error, for no such covers have been found.

13. All the Bedouins interviewed, as well as Father Yusif of St. Mark's, insist on the "greenish" appearance of the cloth; but there seems to be no evidence to explain this description.

14. The excellent state of the preservation of these three MSS, in comparison with all the other MSS from Cave I, argues strongly in favor of this conclusion. See *DJD I*, p. 5, where G. L. Harding drew a similar conclusion.

15. All the Bedouins involved, as well as the merchants who have been interviewed (except Kando, see below), have agreed that only three manuscripts were in the original find. Yusif Saad first made contact with Muhammed and Jum'a in the spring of 1949, and a few days later Harding also interviewed them. In his first report (*The* [London] *Times*, August 9, 1949) Harding states that the Bedouins withdrew *eight* scrolls from the cave at the time of the discovery and divided them equally. In *DJD I*, p. 5, however, Harding states that the Bedouin shepherds took only three scrolls (he assumes they were 1QIs^a, 1QS and 1QpHab) and never returned to the cave for others. Both of these accounts now need to be modified on the basis of the Bedouins' own testimony (see below).

16. In the November, 1961, interviews they mentioned taking the manuscripts and the jars at that time (see Appendix I), but Jum'a and Khalil Musa stated (July 29, 1962) that they went back for the jars at a later time when they decided to try to sell the materials in Bethlehem.

17. Muhammed edh-Dhib's statement in 1956 to Najib Khouri (*JNES* 16:4, p. 236) that in 1945 he found "some rolled leather" in a cave and left it hanging in a bag in his "house" for "more than two years" is obviously inaccurate. See J. C. Trever, "When Was Qumran Cave I Discovered?", *RQ* 3:1 (February, 1961), pp. 135-141. Edh-Dhib has made no such claim in several recent interviews (see Appendix I). If the scrolls were first discovered in November, 1946, as asserted in the November, 1961, interviews, then they must have remained in the Ta'amireh camp for at least three months. That it was in March, 1947, when the scrolls were first taken to Bethlehem now seems apparent from the evidence (see below). See now R. DeVaux, *Archaeology and the Dead Sea Scrolls* (1973), p. vii, where the evidence gathered here is recognized.

18. Discussions with the Bedouins about the breaks in the manuscripts proved fruitless, but they did seem confident that the cover of the Isaiah Scroll broke off and was destroyed during their handling of it.

The writer possesses six very small uninscribed fragments (altogether they make an area less than a square inch) which the Syrian Metropolitan claimed had been a part of the original cover (see p. 42).

19. When 1QS was broken into two parts seems impossible to determine from the evidence. Kando (see below) claimed, in an interview on August 10, 1962, that he delivered four manuscripts to St. Mark's Monastery; but in all the early interviews with the Syrians in 1948-1949 they stated that they had purchased five manuscripts, including the two parts of the 1QS. They seemed much surprised when I told them, on February 24, 1948, that the two parts belonged together (see pp. 45-46, 53). Van der Ploeg, *op. cit.*, pp. 11 and 13, tells of seeing 1QS in two parts in "late July" 1947 shortly after the scrolls were secured by Samuel. Apparently 1QSa and the 1QSb fragments were still in the cave when the other scrolls were sold. If they had been a part of the original 1QS, therefore, they must have become separated in ancient times. See p. 150.

20. The month of March is established from the combined testimony of the Ta'amirehs, Judah Ibrahim 'Ijha (see below), and Metropolitan Samuel. The latter stated, as early as 1948, that he first heard about the scrolls during Holy Week in 1947. To allow for the previous events to which both the Ta'amirehs and 'Ijha testify, the month of March is the most likely time for the first appearance of the scrolls in Bethlehem.

21. The fine state of preservation of the three scrolls then being peddled may account for Salahi's skepticism. The "Fourth Scroll" (1QapGen) was not yet with the others, for when I showed 'Ijha a full-sized photograph of it on August 10, 1962, he was confident that he had never seen it.

22. This date is established by the fact that the Bedouins usually went to Bethlehem on Saturday, their market day, and that it was the following week when Metropolitan Samuel first heard about the scrolls (see below).

23. During interviews with the Syrians in 1948 it was indicated that the Bedouins went first to the Bethlehem Muslim Sheikh (see *BA* 11:3, p. 47) and were told that the scrolls were probably Syriac and thus they should go to the Syrians. Apparently the "sheikh" was none other than 'Ali Subh, as Jum'a has now revealed. 'Ali Subh was interviewed by Kiraz and Docmac on May 16, 1962; being a very old man, he remembered very little about the incident. Kiraz says of the interview, "He only said that Jum'a brought to him 3 scrolls which he called 'books', one larger than the other two. They were the color of earth and not wrapped in anything when he brought them. But Jum'a had told him that originally they were wrapped in cloth and put in jars" (quoted from letter dated May 17, 1962).

24. In an interview with Jum'a on January 12, 1963, Kiraz learned that Khalil Musa joined the others later at Kando's shop.

25. These details were established by Metropolitan Samuel in 1949. See *BA* 12:2, pp. 26-27. The dates for Holy Week are based on the Julian Calendar used by the Syrians.

26. The interview occurred on August 10, 1962, in Bethlehem, with Kiraz serving as interpreter.

27. Although in the interviews of November 24-25, 1961, Jum'a indicated that this and a subsequent visit to the cave took place *after* the sale of the first scrolls to St. Mark's Monastery (i.e., after July 19, 1947), Khalil Musa and Kando (during interviews on August 10, 1962) maintained that these visits to the cave were made *prior to* the sale to St. Mark's. The fact that 1QapGen was included with the scrolls which Kando delivered to St. Mark's is a strong argument in favor of the chronology presented here, for that scroll definitely came from one of these later visits to the cave (see note 31). When Kiraz checked this specific point with Jum'a on January 12, 1963 (his letter to me was sent that same day), Jum'a agreed that Khalil's scrolls were sold to Faidi Salahi several weeks *before* the first scrolls were sold to St. Mark's (see what follows).

28. The interview with Kando took place in his shop on August 10, 1962, with Kiraz as interpreter.

29. Both Kando and Khalil Musa, during separate interviews (August 10, 1962), agreed on this statement.

30. In order to check this assumption, I showed a full-sized photograph of 1QapGen to Muhammed edh-Dhib and Jum'a (July 29, 1962), and neither could remember it. When it was shown later to Khalil Musa, he agreed that it looked like one of the manuscripts he and Isha'ya had secured on their second trip to the cave. When I showed the same picture to Kando, he was quite certain that it was one of the scrolls he had delivered to Metropolitan Samuel. He seemed to think, however, that it was one of the scrolls Jum'a had brought on his first visit. This and other points in Kando's statements, however, indicated that he was somewhat confused about the order of securing those first scrolls. In view of the large number of scrolls and fragments he has handled, it is understandable that he should be vague about the earliest contacts. Since the Bedouins whom I had interviewed had dealt with only a few scrolls, it seems reasonable to suppose that their memories would be more accurate in this matter. The testimonies of Jum'a, Khalil, and Kando, during separate interviews, all agreed that the first group of scrolls had not yet been sold to St. Mark's when Isha'ya made these two trips to Cave I.

31. This information was secured from Jalil Elias 'Abu Sabha, who was a neighbor of Da'ud Musallam in 1947 and who is also a good friend of Khalil Musa. Jalil claims to have seen the scrolls when Da'ud had them. Kiraz interviewed Jalil and reported to me in a letter dated March 3, 1962. Jalil confirmed the essentials of Jum'a's story but claimed that there were at least five scrolls brought to Da'ud. Two of them, he said, were destroyed when the Bedouins tried to soften them with water to open them. Kiraz and I interviewed Jalil in his summer hut on some property he owns north of Bethlehem, on August 10, 1962. His description of the scrolls he saw fit those which Sukenik secured. When I showed him the photograph of 1QapGen, he seemed certain that it was not one of those which he had seen.

32. See below, pp. 106-108. Faidi Salahi died in 1955, but Kiraz arranged for me to visit his home on August 10, 1962. There I was introduced to Mrs. Roginah Marzurqa, who is the widow of an orphan whom Salahi had raised, and had been living with her husband in Salahi's home at that time. She assured me that Salahi received that first group of scrolls from the Ta'amireh Bedouins during the summer of 1947. She added that Sukenik had been a frequent visitor to discuss antiquities with Salahi. She also said that she had recently sold two jars similar to those Sukenik had purchased, except they had no covers. Salahi had secured them from the Ta'amireh Bedouins, but she offered no other information about them. Allegro (*op. cit.*, p. 77; 1964 ed., p. 86) says he purchased a similar complete jar from Salahi in 1953.

33. This date was firmly established during my interviews with the St. Mark's Syrians in 1948 and 1949. See *BA* 12:2, p. 27, where the Metropolitan's reference to the "First Saturday of Tammuz" would be July 5, 1947. See now Samuel, *Treasure of Qumran*, p. 146, where he says, "On the first Saturday of Tammuz, which in the Julian Calendar that year was July 21." But July 21 was a Monday in 1947, and a date so late in July would conflict with the evidence stated by van der Ploeg (*op. cit.*, pp. 7-11), who assumed it was June on the basis of his having seen the scrolls during the "last week of July."

34. The Syrians mentioned "three Bedouins" in connection with this part of the story (see *BA* 12:2, p. 27), but in all recent interviews the Bedouins have maintained that there were just the two who accompanied Isha'ya to Jerusalem.

35. According to Samuel's account (*ibid.*), the Bedouins must have arrived at the Monastery *before* lunch. If so, to equate the story with Jum'a's testimony, Isha'ya must have given the Bedouins an early lunch in order for them to have arrived at St. Mark's before the Metropolitan's lunch.

36. During an interview with Father Yusif on August 5, 1962, the aged priest told me that Isha'ya talked to him about the scrolls at first, for they were close friends. It was he whom Isha'ya was seeking, he claimed, when he brought the Bedouins to the Monastery. Father Yusif was absent from the Monastery at the time, and thus Isha'ya met Father Bulos. It is difficult to evaluate this conflicting testimony, but it is included here for the record. I interviewed Father Bulos on August 6, 1962; he asserted that he did not see the Bedouins but only Isha'ya, who brought the bag of scrolls into the Monastery.

37. This encounter with a Jewish merchant has been a persistent part of the Syrian story, but it is now denied by the Bedouins. Perhaps the Arab-Israel tension might account for the reluctance of the Bedouins to mention the matter now, if it actually did occur.

38. From the early accounts it has been assumed that there was a division of the scrolls at this time and that one Bedouin did not leave his share with Kando. The Metropolitan maintained in all the early interviews that Father Bulos had been certain that there were more scrolls

shown to him at the Monastery gate than the prelate finally secured (see *ibid.*). Perhaps the Metropolitan learned about the scrolls sold to Faidi Salahi and somehow connected them with this part of the story.

39. Samuel was very confident (in interviews during February and March, 1949) that two weeks elapsed before he finally secured the scrolls (see *ibid.*).

40. Butrus Sowmy, in the presence of the Metropolitan late in March, 1948 (according to notes I made at the time), told me that Kando delivered the scrolls after paying the Bedouins their share. Both Jum'a and Kando now have testified that this is the way it happened. (Cf. *ibid.*, pp. 27-28.) Samuel (*Treasure of Qumran*, pp. 146-149) now gives a highly embellished account quite different from what he and Sowmy told me in 1948 and which Samuel asked me to write for him in early 1949 for the May issue of *BA*. The evidence forces me to stand by the story as recorded and documented here.

41. See J. van der Ploeg, *op. cit.*, p. 13. The Metropolitan stated that it was the last week of August (see *BA* 12:2, p. 28); but on the basis of the photographs he took at St. Mark's, van der Ploeg was able to establish the fact that his visit was in late July.

42. He published a book (in 1942) about ancient Syrian monastic life.

43. The 1QapGen scroll was not included. See van der Ploeg, *op. cit.*, p. 11.

44. He died December 30, 1960.

45. *Ibid.*, pp. 9-13. Personal letters from van der Ploeg, which I received in late 1948, further confirm his story.

46. The evidence from reports of the Hebrew University and an affidavit prepared by Anton Kiraz establishes this date for Dr. Brown's visit. Samuel thought (*BA* 12:2, p. 30) it might have occurred in October.

47. Yigael Yadin, *op. cit.*, p. 25.

48. About October 1, according to evidence presented to me by Kiraz, the Metropolitan referred to this offer as they discussed another problem (see below). On several occasions during 1948 and 1949 the Metropolitan mentioned to me that Sassun had made ever increasing offers, but the amounts were never indicated.

49. The title reference to "Antioch" is still retained, despite his residence in Homs. He died in 1957. More recently the Patriarchate was moved to Damascus.

50. I have checked the passports of both the Metropolitan and Kiraz (in February, 1949 and April, 1958, respectively) to determine the accuracy of these terminal dates.

51. This account of Anton Kiraz's claim to partnership with the Metropolitan, through a typically Near Eastern gentleman's agreement, is greatly condensed here to provide only details which I deem essential to the history of the Dead Sea Scrolls. The entire account, however, has

been carefully documented and thoroughly checked from evidences in Kiraz's possession, which I have fully examined during many hours of cross-examination. It is recorded in detail in an affidavit, sworn to, signed, and notarized in my presence in Jerusalem, Jordan, on May 12, 1958. The original copy of the notarized affidavit is in my possession. Compare Samuel's account (*Treasure of Qumran*, p. 155). His evidence to dispute Kiraz's account is meager and unconvincing.

52. Stephan died in May, 1949.

53. The *Haftarot* are selections from the Prophets, organized for reading following the Torah each Sabbath.

54. T. Wechsler, "The Revealed Genizah and the Hidden Genizah," *Ha'olam*, December, 1949 (in Hebrew). I am grateful to Carl Kraeling and Millar Burrows for providing me with an English translation of this article. Anyone who has worked intimately with 1QIs^a and 1QS soon becomes aware, while reading Wechsler's statements, that what he describes as a *Haftarot* scroll is none other than 1QIs^a itself, which his memory, dimmed by passing time and the troubles he experienced in 1948, confused with some features of 1QS. Numerous blank lines, used to indicate paragraph or chapter divisions, as well as many marginal markings, are found on 1QIs^a. What he calls "the scroll of Isaiah" in his article, on the other hand, clearly describes 1QS. See J. C. Trever, "The 'Suppressed' Scroll of the Haftarot," *JQR* 41 (July, 1950), pp. 71-81.

55. See his son's dramatic account: Yigael Yadin, *The Message of the Scrolls* (1957), Part I. Sukenik died in 1952.

56. Every scholar associated with the discovery knows that "Mr. X" was none other than the late Ohan, Jerusalem's well-known antiquities dealer, who was considered by scholars to be the best-informed and most reliable source for ancient artifacts. He died in 1974.

57. The Palestine Archaeological Advisory Board was established in 1920/21 as a provision of the Antiquities Ordinance of the Mandate Government.

58. See G. L. Harding, "The Dead Sea Scrolls," *PEQ*, July-October, 1949, p. 115.

59. Section 6 of the 1929 Antiquities Ordinance reads: "Any person who discovers an antiquity without being furnished with a license to excavate in accordance with Section 9 of this Ordinance shall forthwith give notice of his discovery to the nearest officer of the Department, or to the nearest District Officer or Assistant District Officer, and shall take any other action that may be prescribed by Regulation under this Ordinance."

60. According to testimony given to me personally by Ohan in 1966 and independently to several others who were closely related to the discovery, Sukenik remained that day in Ohan's shop while Ohan went alone to Bethlehem and persuaded Salahi to let him deliver the documents to Sukenik. Sukenik paid £P80 ($324) to Ohan for the manuscripts and expenses, Ohan said. He related also how he and Sukenik had

been the best of friends for over twenty years and during more peaceful times had occasionally gone together to Bethlehem to negotiate for antiquities from Salahi. But see above, note 32. During 1975 I asked Kiraz again to query Mrs. Marzurqa, and in a letter dated August 13 he says she continued to claim that she had witnessed the transaction between Sukenik, Ohan, and Salahi on November 29, 1947.

61. They were the Isaiah Scroll (1QIs^a), the Habakkuk Pesher (1QpHab), and one of the two pieces of the Manual of Discipline (1QS).

62. Kiraz is not quite certain whether this offer was made then or at the beginning of the next meeting. According to Sukenik's various reports, he never did make an offer.

63. This information was checked with Tannourji in March, 1958, in the same office, which is now in Israel. On April 26 I heard the same story from Kiraz in his home in Bethlehem, Jordan. The independent testimony of the two Syrians agreed in almost every detail. Tannourji also testified to Kiraz's references to "his partner." Samuel gives a quite different account of these matters in *BA* 12:2, p. 31, and in his *Treasure of Qumran* (1966), p. 168.

64. When I prepared the article for the May, 1949, *BA* for Metropolitan Samuel, he assured me that it was "late February" when these events occurred. He offered as evidence the claim that I had already given him a set of photographs, which he offered to Sukenik instead. At the time this seemed adequate evidence, and therefore I did not challenge him, despite the fact that Sukenik had insisted on the dates February 4-6 that same morning in New York, where I interviewed him. That the Metropolitan's chronology was in error, there is now no doubt. See pp. 124, 125.

65. On March 19, 1948, the Metropolitan mentioned to me, according to my notes, that Sowmy had been "quite upset" over the negotiations with Sukenik (cf. pp. 83-84).

CHAPTER 13

1. He became the Patriarch in 1957, following the death of Aphram I.

2. The basic text of the Old Testament, used for centuries in schools and synagogues, is called "Masoretic," after the Masoretes, a school of rabbis who were the preservers of the textual tradition. Originating with the efforts of Rabbi Akiba in the early second century, the work reached its zenith in the school of Ben Asher in the ninth and tenth centuries A.D.

3. The Committee for the Revised Standard Version of the Bible adopted fourteen minor readings, attested by this scroll, during their meetings in 1949 to 1951. These readings can be identified by the expression "One ancient MS" in the RSV footnotes to Isaiah. The New English Bible has more recently adopted about fifty readings from this scroll.

4. He died before full appreciation of the antiquity of the scrolls had penetrated British scholarship.

5. My article and the first installment of Burrows' collation appeared in the October issue of *BASOR*. Brownlee's translation was in the December issue. My article on dating the scrolls through paleography and the second installment of Burrows' collation appeared in the February, 1949 issue.

6. *M^egilloth G^enuzoth I* (1948).

7. His copying must have been done in haste, for there were at least twenty-seven errors in his published transcription, most of them omissions of features peculiar to the ancient scroll.

8. This story has been skillfully elaborated in Burrows' splendid book, *The Dead Sea Scrolls* (1955), Chap. II.

9. He left Jerusalem early in November to go to Beirut, where the scrolls had been in a bank vault since March 25. See p. 89.

CHAPTER 14

1. On July 27, 1948, the Metropolitan wrote: "I am glad to let you know that after you left Palestine I was able to get in my possession some other manuscripts, but their date is not so far old as the first ones." In his letter sent from Homs, Syria, on September 14, he mentioned meeting Dr. Sellers in Amman, and added: "The other manuscripts that I bought lately are in the same language but are not as old as the others and they are written on parchments, from the old testament."

2. At the time I assumed that it was one of the Monastery people, but see note 17.

3. At the time, he mentioned November as the date of this visit to the cave; but Sellers had already seen at least some of the fragments on September 1 (see p. 118). During an interview on July 29, 1949, Samuel agreed that it could have been a little earlier than November when the fragments were secured. He mentioned his "poor memory for dates." According to Sellers, moreover, the Metropolitan had told him that Bedouins had brought the fragments as samples of two other manuscripts they were offering to sell. A study of the fragments suggests that the ones which Sellers saw were the loose pieces which were associated with the matted mass which the Bedouins probably were holding back as "other manuscripts." When later I sent photos of the fragments to Sellers, he did not think he had seen the matted mass at the time, but the smaller pieces looked familiar. I had a similar experience in 1958 when a Bedouin showed me a fragment of a supposed Qumran scroll and offered to bring the rest of it if I would purchase the piece. The piece was quite modern, however.

4. Columns 39-54 were rephotographed at that time. Their higher contrast can be observed in Cols. 50-53 of *The Dead Sea Scrolls of St. Mark's Monastery*, edited by Burrows for the A.S.O.R. in 1950.

5. Most scholars date the composition of Daniel in the early half of the second century B.C., sometime before 165 B.C., on the basis of internal evidence.

6. In 1952 a fragment of Ecclesiastes was discovered in Cave IV and probably could claim this distinction with more certainty.

7. This fragment was published in color in *The Interpreter's Bible*, Vol. XII (1957), p. 635, with the permission of the Jordan Department of Antiquities. The reproduction failed, for some reason, to preserve the rich black quality of the script on the original.

8. It has been reported that a fragment of Daniel recovered from Cave IV contains that portion of Chapter 7 where the Aramaic reverts to Hebrew.

9. For a translation of the entire piece, see M. Burrows, *More Light on the Dead Sea Scrolls* (1958), p. 399; also a French translation by J. T. Milik in *DJD I* (1955), pp. 152-155. Jean Carmignac has suggested (*RQ* 4:2 [May, 1963], pp. 271-276) that unit "d" belongs to the lower right of unit "c" (he considers the first line of "d" to be the beginning of line 5 of unit "c"), thus providing parts of the right half of the first column. This is the way it was published (see below, note 20).

10. Proof that all these fragments came from the same scroll cave is established by the fact that one fragment (1Q34) found by the excavators during February, 1949, fits perfectly into a break along the upper edge of the folded fragment which formed layers four and five of the matted mass (unit "d"). Obviously written in the same script and on the same kind of leather, the *shin* and *resh* on its bottom line complete the word '*shr* in the Prayer Scroll fragment. See *DJD I*, Plate 31:34, and p. 152. See below (Chapter 16, note 2).

11. In their introduction to the preliminary publication of this scroll, N. Avigad and Y. Yadin say, "The condition of the scroll was certainly not improved by the fact that for seven years it was shifted about from place to place, without any particular care being devoted to it" (*A Genesis Apocryphon* [1956], p. 12). On the contrary, the scroll was given great care, at least after February, 1948. Between March 1948, and April, 1949, there was no evidence of further deterioration, except for the slightly longer cracks which made possible my removal of the larger fragment. After my work on it in April, 1949, it was most carefully preserved in its special, cotton-padded box. A detailed comparison of the photographs I made of the scroll in Jerusalem in February, 1948, with those published in the above-mentioned volume reveal only very minor evidences of additional deterioration.

12. This measurement included the previously removed fragment (see pp. 74, 78), which was then returned to its former place.

13. See J. C. Trever, "Identification of the Aramaic Fourth Scroll from 'Ain Feshkha," *BASOR* 115 (October, 1949), pp. 8-10. See now N. Avigad and Y. Yadin, *op. cit.*, pp. 16-18.

14. Thus a straight hairline can be seen across the middle of Columns 19-39 in the A.S.O.R. publication of 1QIs^a.

15. At least three recent books by scholars who have been close to the Dead Sea Scroll story have telescoped this "excavation" into the 1947 visits to the cave: John M. Allegro, *The Dead Sea Scrolls* (1956), p. 18 (cf. also pp. 25-27); F. M. Cross, *The Ancient Library of Qumran* (1961), p. 7; and J. van der Ploeg, *op. cit.*, p. 15. They have apparently relied on G. L. Harding's statement in *DJD I*, p. 5; but cf. above, pp. 99-101 and Appendix I. That several visits were made to the cave in 1947 and at least three produced scrolls is, of course, now known to be a fact.

16. He saw them on September 1, 1948, the day the Metropolitan visited the American School in Jerusalem. See pp. 118, 121, and 123 and note 17 below.

17. The evidence seems clear that most of these fragments, if not all of them, were secured by Isha'ya during visits to the cave, shortly after the establishment of the second truce on July 18, 1948. According to Syrian testimony, Isha'ya had been gatekeeper and messenger for the Monastery. (In my files is an early 1949 photograph of the Monastery personnel, showing him in the garb of a monk.) In view of the strong statements I made to Metropolitan Samuel before leaving Jerusalem on April 5, 1948, it is likely that he would have cautioned Isha'ya then about "excavating" (see pp. 94, 123). Apparently after the prelate left Jerusalem for the United States in early November, 1948, Isha'ya and Kando pursued a more aggressive approach to the cave by actual "excavation." At that time Isha'ya was living at the Syrian monastery near the Jordan River, within easy reach of the cave, according to Kiraz, who had also taken refuge there for a few months.

18. *DJD I*, pp. 150-155.

19. The historical fact that the Qumran cave area did not become officially a part of Jordan until December, 1948, lends technical support to his position.

20. "Completion of the Publication of Some Fragments from Qumran Cave I," *RQ* 5:3 (November, 1965), pp. 323-344.

21. *Treasure of Qumran: My Story of the Dead Sea Scrolls* (1966). Apparently the photos were made shortly before the publication.

22. See John C. Trever, "The Future of the Qumran Scrolls," in *A Light Unto My Path: Old Testament Studies in Honor of Jacob M. Myers*, edited by Howard N. Bream *et al.* (1974), pp. 465-474.

23. "1QDan*a*", the Latest of the Qumran Manuscripts," *RQ* 7:2 (April, 1970), pp. 277-286.

CHAPTER 15

1. See Harry M. Orlinsky, "Studies in the St. Mark's Isaiah Scroll," *JBL* 69 (June, 1950), pp. 149-166; John C. Trever, "Isaiah 43:19 According to the First Isaiah Scroll (DSIa)," *BASOR* 121 (February, 1951), pp. 13-16; and notes in *BASOR* 123 (October, 1951), pp. 33-35; 124 (December, 1951), p. 29; and 126 (April, 1952), pp. 26-27.

2. "The Dead Sea Scrolls," *PEQ*, July—October, 1949, pp. 112-116. See above, Chapter 10, note 8.

3. John Malak, prompted by the Metropolitan, on August 31, 1950, sent me a detailed account of his interviews with both Kando and Isha'ya regarding their claims. According to the United States Tax Court decision (36 T.C. 641, p. 5), a "gift" of $4,000 was made to each of them. Kando, in an interview on August 10, 1962, said that Isha'ya, who received the money, absconded with the total amount and has since disappeared. His relatives believe he met a violent death.

4. Dating of the deposit on the basis of the pottery, which was considered to be "late Hellenistic," was too early, as subsequent evidence was to prove.

5. A by-product of atomic research, this age-determination process was developed at the University of Chicago by means of sensitive Geiger counters which would measure the radioactive intensity of the Carbon-14 isotope in ancient organic matter. See Donald Collier, "New Radiocarbon Method for Dating the Past," *BA* 14:1 (February, 1951), pp. 25-29. More recent studies of the process have moved the date back to 24 B.C. ±200 yrs. and added a more precise date of 48 B.C. ±80 yrs. for some palm tree wood from the Qumran community center (*locus* 86, the "pantry"). See F. E. Zeuner, "Notes on Qumran," *PEQ* 92 (1960), pp. 27-28, for the palm wood report. See H. Godwin, *Nature* 195 (1962), p. 984, for the new "half-life" for Carbon 14 of 5730 ±40 yrs. See also J. A. Fitzmyer's somewhat premature statement in *America* 104 (March, 1961), pp. 780-781, where he gives a half-life of 5760.

6. Dr. Solomon Zeitlin of Dropsie College, Philadelphia, remained adamant and vociferous as a spokesman for a medieval dating of all the documents, and he refused to accept the evidence relating the scrolls to the cave. In England G. R. Driver of Oxford and J. L. Teicher of Cambridge also resisted a pre-Christian dating, but less vigorously.

7. The two main requirements were: (1) that the Daniel (and other) fragments be returned to Jerusalem ("adequate compensation" for them was promised); and (2) that the removal of the four major scrolls from the country be legalized by obtaining the proper export license from the Jordan government.

From a strictly legal standpoint, the Jordan government could not press a claim for expropriation of the four scrolls (as Lebanon had successfully done in one case some years before) for the following reasons: (1) the scrolls had been purchased when Palestine was under the British Mandate and were sent to Beirut on March 25, 1948; (2) even though the Mandate Government's antiquities laws had been technically violated at that time, by March, 1948, the administration of many Mandate laws was in a state of chaos, and anarchy existed in Palestine; (3) not until December 1, 1948, when that portion of Palestine was joined with Trans-Jordan to form the "Hashemite Kingdom of the Jordan," was effective government established which could administer the antiquities laws which had continued to be operative in Trans-Jordan; and (4) G. L.

Harding, Director of Antiquities for Jordan, in his letter of January 23, 1950, categorically denied any claim of the Jordan government to rights to the four scrolls in the Metropolitan's possession.

8. Apparently the man died, about 1959, and the manuscript is believed to have been destroyed.

9. See J. C. Trever, "Studies in the Problem of Dating the Dead Sea Scrolls," *Proceedings of the American Philosophical Society* 97:2 (April 30, 1953), pp. 184-193; and the revision of the same article, "The Problems of Dating the Dead Sea Scrolls," *Annual Report of the Smithsonian Institution* (1953), pp. 425-435.

10. Solomon Schechter in 1897 secured some 100,000 fragments, codices, and scrolls from this vast forgotten storeroom in the synagogue of Old Cairo. About 2,000 of the oldest and best fragments have been mounted in glass and carefully filed for easy access.

11. I personally examined the agreement and discussed some of its terms during a visit with the Metropolitan early in December, 1951.

12. In the meantime I had accepted an invitation to become the A. J. Humphreys Professor of Religion at Morris Harvey College in Charleston, West Virginia.

13. For a detailed account of the negotiations, see Y. Yadin, *The Message of the Scrolls* (1957), chap. 3.

14. It is interesting to compare this amount with the price paid in 1949 by the Jordan Department of Antiquities when negotiating with Kando for the remainder of the Cave I fragments — one dinar ($2.80) per square centimeter of inscribed surface. The Isaiah Scroll contains almost 15,100 square centimeters, the "Manual of Discipline" about 3,700, and the "Habakkuk Commentary" a few more than 1,250 — a total of 20,050 square centimeters of inscribed surface. Figuring the then-unopened "Fourth Scroll" at $50,000, the three scrolls thus brought the Metropolitan almost $10 per square centimeter, or about three and one-half times as much as the highest price paid for all the other cave scrolls. The prelate originally paid $97.20 for the scrolls in 1947.

In August, 1962, Metropolitan Samuel told me he had paid federal income taxes of about $87,000 on the amount received. According to the tax decision filed by the Tax Court of the United States on June 30, 1961 (36 T.C. 641), Metropolitan Samuel had amended his trust agreement on October 7, 1952, to provide himself $30,000 cash and $10,000 per year for life. The judge pointed out that, on the basis of life insurance actuarial figures, the total amount received for the scrolls would be exhausted during the Metropolitan's lifetime. The amount received, therefore, was declared personal income and subject to tax. Despite the fact that the trust had been further amended (date not given) to eliminate the annual payments to the Metropolitan, the decision, when appealed by him, was upheld by the Federal Court of Appeals on June 21, 1962 (306 *Federal Reporter*, 2nd Series, pp. 682-689).

CHAPTER 16

1. Phylacteries (called *tephillin* by the Jews) were small leather boxes which were attached to the forehead and arms while morning prayers were recited. They contained minute scrolls inscribed with quotations from the Torah. See Deuteronomy 6:8; Matthew 23:5.

2. The excavators recovered fragments of 1QM and 1QH, which had been among the 1947 finds. They also found small pieces of the larger Deuteronomy fragment (1QDeut*b*), part of which was reported to have come from Isha'ya and part from Kando. Also found by the excavators was a small fragment of the Prayer Scroll (1Q34), larger fragments of which had apparently been secured by Isha'ya during the summer of 1948. A small piece of 1QSb (Col. II) also was sifted from the debris. Larger fragments of this latter document had been secured by Yusif Saad from Kando, along with fragments from 1QIs*b* and some from the "Genesis Apocryphon" (1QapGen). Thus the discovery of all these fragments in the excavation confirmed the fact that the scrolls dug up in 1947, the fragments secured by Isha'ya during the summer of 1948, and those purchased by Yusif Saad from Kando in 1950 all came from Cave I. Lacking only were fragments from 1QIs*a*, 1QpHab, and 1QS to confirm positively the entire original discovery. The circumstances of the discovery of these three (see Appendix I) seem to account for the absence of fragments from them. There is no longer any reason to doubt the relationship of these three to the others, however, especially in view of the fact that 1QS, 1QSa, and 1QSb were all written by the same scribe on the same kind of leather. It is reasonable to believe that these are all parts of a single scroll. How to account for the separation of 1QSa and 1QSb from 1QS, however, remains a mystery.

3. Technically they are called *pesharim*, from the frequent occurrence of the word *pesher*, meaning "interpretation."

4. This excavation seems to have been organized by Isha'ya and Kando almost immediately after Metropolitan Samuel left Jerusalem (ultimately for the United States) early in November, 1948.

5. It is graphically described by John Allegro in *The Dead Sea Scrolls* (1956), pp. 25-34 (2nd ed. 1964, pp. 27-36).

6. These parts are now labeled 1QSa and 1QSb, since their contents do not seem to relate directly to the eleven original columns of that scroll. The script on all of these is identical. These parts may have been attached at one time to the larger scroll at one end or the other, where sewing holes clearly indicate that there had been additional sheets of leather.

7. All these and the artifacts from the cave have been published in D. Barthélemy and J. T. Milik, *DJD I* (1955).

8. Allegro (*op. cit.*, p. 19; 1964 ed., p. 21) related this part of the story in connection with his account of Sukenik's purchase of scrolls late in 1947. It seems apparent that Allegro is in error in placing this event so early. There is no conceivable reason for Kando to have become

frightened at that time; it was to be many months before the authorities began their inquiries about the scrolls. Furthermore, the scrolls' antiquity and value had not yet been established. There is no evidence that Kando had any scrolls in his possession late in 1947. Faidi Salahi seems to have had whatever scrolls and fragments had been secured from the cave about that time, and he was dealing with Sukenik. In early 1949, after his participation in, and perhaps leadership of, the November, 1948 clandestine excavation, Kando would have had considerable reason to take such fatal "precautions." Allegro also errs on the same page in stating that Sukenik dealt with Kando.

9. For details of his adventure, see F. M. Cross, *The Ancient Library of Qumran* (1961), pp. 15-19.

10. Results of these discoveries have now been published in French by P. Benoit, O.P., J. T. Milik, and R. de Vaux in *DJD II* (1961).

11. As late as July, 1956, the Bedouins attempted to sell fragments from this cave.

12. For the story, see F. M. Cross, *op. cit.*, pp. 26-47.

13. For the most recent list, see Joseph A. Fitzmyer, S.J., *The Dead Sea Scrolls Major Publications and Tools for Study*, Sources for Biblical Study 8, Society of Biblical Literature and Scholars Press, 1975. Also see below, note 29.

14. Results of the discoveries in Caves II, III, V-X were published by M. Baillet, J. T. Milik, and R. de Vaux in *DJD III*, 1962.

15. See John Allegro, *The Treasure of the Copper Scroll* (1960; rev. ed. 1964). He is convinced that the scroll represents genuine treasure, but other scholars are equally convinced that it represents mere folklore.

16. For a vivid reconstruction of that community life, see A. D. Tushingham, "The Men Who Hid the Dead Sea Scrolls," *The National Geographic Magazine*, December, 1958, pp. 785-808.

The archeological discoveries at Khirbet Qumran have been best summarized and evaluated by R. de Vaux in his Schweich Lectures before the British Academy (1959): *Archaeology and the Dead Sea Scrolls* (1973).

17. See Yadin's reports in *BA* 24:2 (May, 1961), pp. 34-50; and 24:3 (September, 1961), pp. 86-95.

18. See Y. Aharoni, "Expedition B — The Cave of Horror," *Israel Exploration Journal* 12 (1962), pp. 197-198 (also pp. 201-207).

19. The document has now been published by J. A. Sanders as Volume IV of *DJD* under the title: *The Psalms Scroll of Qumrân Cave 11 (11QPs^a)* (1965). While his more popular treatment of this scroll was in press during 1966, he received a copy of the fragment "E" in fulfillment of a promise Yadin made in connection with his public announcement concerning his receipt of the scroll fragment. Sanders was thus able to add a "postscriptum" to *The Dead Sea Psalms Scroll* (1967). In the meantime, Yadin had published the fragment in *Textus* V (1966) under

the title, "Another Fragment (E) of the Psalms Scroll from Qumran Cave 11 (11QPsᵃ)."

20. See his published results: "The Scroll of Ezekiel from the Eleventh Qumran Cave," *RQ* 4:1 (January, 1963), pp. 11-28.

21. 11QapPs was published by J. van der Ploeg in *RB* 72 (1965), pp. 210-217, and 11QMelch by A. S. van der Woude in *Oudtestamentische Studien* 14 (1965), pp. 354-373. See also note 29 below.

22. See the preliminary report, F. M. Cross, "The Discovery of the Samaria Papyri," *BA* 26:4 (December, 1963), pp. 109-121; and Paul W. Lapp and Nancy L. Lapp, *Discoveries in the Wâdī ed-Dâliyeh, Annual of the A.S.O.R.* 41 (1974).

23. See Y. Yadin, "The Excavation of Masada 1963/64: Preliminary Report," in *Israel Exploration Journal* 15 (1965), pp. 103-114.

24. "The Temple Scroll," *BA* 30:4 (December, 1967), pp. 135-139.

25. The existence of such a text is mentioned in the Palestinian Talmud (*Sanhedrin* 29a) as having been written by Ahithophel, a servant of David; but Yadin says that internal evidence of the Temple Scroll would date its composition in the first century B.C.

26. Yadin's volume on "The Temple Scroll" is promised for 1977.

27. It has been beautifully published by Yadin in *Tefillin from Qumran (XQPhyl 1-4)* (1969).

28. Reported in *Eretz-Israel* X (1971), pp. 72-79.

29. John Allegro, *DJD V: Qumrân Cave 4, I (4Q158-4Q186)* (1968) (it includes twenty-eight assembled *Pesharim* — Biblical interpretation — documents and a few related fragments); but see also J. Strugnell's additions and corrections in "Notes en Marge du Volume V . . . ," *RQ* 26 (1970), pp. 163-276. Also, J. T. Milik, ed., *The Books of Enoch: Aramaic Fragments of Qumrân Cave 4* (1976); this volume, published independently of the *DJD* series, includes seven Cave 4 Enoch fragmentary scrolls and the closely related "Astronomical Book of Enoch" (4 copies) and a scroll of the "Book of Giants." The Cave XI Aramaic Targum of Job also was published independently by J. P. M. van der Ploeg, O.P., and A. S. van der Woude, *Le Targum de Job de la Grotte XI de Qumrân* (1971).

30. In the meantime, the unpublished Samuel scroll materials from Cave IV have been shared with the "Bishops' Committee of the Confraternity of Christian Doctrine" by Frank Cross, an "Associate Editor." *The New American Bible* (1970) includes almost one hundred references to 4QSamᵃ, ᵇ, ᵃⁿᵈ ᶜ, as revealed in the notes of the St. Anthony's Guild edition.

CHAPTER 17

1. For a more detailed description of the community, its organization, beliefs, and customs, along with translations of manuscripts, two paperback volumes are especially helpful: Geza Vermes, *The Dead Sea*

Scrolls in English (rev. ed. 1968); and Theodore H. Gaster, *The Dead Sea Scriptures* (rev. ed. 1964). For a systematic treatment of the Qumran theology see Helmer Ringgren, *The Faith of Qumran: Theology of the Dead Sea Scrolls* (1963). A splendid brief summary by G. Vermes has just appeared in *The Interpreter's Dictionary of the Bible*, Supplementary Volume (1976), pp. 210-219. See also pp. 438-441 and 585 f.

2. For the latest tally see James A. Sanders, "The Dead Sea Scrolls — A Quarter Century of Study," *BA* 36:4 (December, 1973), p. 136.

3. Frank M. Cross, *The Ancient Library of Qumran* (1961), p. 179. Chapter 4 is a valuable summary of the textual contributions from Qumran. Two other more recent studies should be mentioned: William H. Brownlee, *The Meaning of the Qumrân Scrolls for the Bible* (1964); and F. M. Cross and Shemaryahu Talmon, eds., *Qumran and the History of the Biblical Text* (1975).

4. For a summary of his research see Joseph A. Fitzmyer, *The Genesis Apocryphon of Qumran Cave I, A Commentary* (rev. ed. 1971), especially pp. 14-29. The quotes are from pages 20 and 22 respectively.

5. For a detailed summary of Qumran exegetical methods see G. Vermes, "Interpretation, History of: At Qumran and in the Targums," *Interpreter's Dictionary of the Bible*, Supplementary Volume, pp. 438-441.

6. See above, Chapter 16, notes 24 and 26.

7. Qumran in this respect is a clear prototype of modern sectarian movements such as the Mormons, the Jehovah's Witnesses, the Seventh Day Adventists, and others whose convictions stem from writings by their founders accepted as authoritative.

8. Excellent summaries of the relation of the Qumran community to the New Testament are: Krister Stendahl, ed., *The Scrolls and the New Testament* (1957); and Millar Burrows, *More Light on the Dead Sea Scrolls*, Part II (1958); Matthew Black, *The Scrolls and Christian Origins* (1961); and William Brownlee, *The Meaning of the Qumrân Scrolls for the Bible* (1964), chapters 5 and 6. More recently William S. LaSor has published a fine summary of the issues involved in his *The Dead Sea Scrolls and the New Testament*, 1972.

9. In 1972 José O'Callaghan published in *Biblica* (53 [1972], pp. 91-100) an article in which he claims to have identified three very small papyrus fragments from Qumran Cave VII as pieces of scrolls of the Gospel of Mark and the Epistle of James. Carlo Martini supported the claim in the same issue. The very fragmentary pieces were immediately examined by many other scholars and these suggestions were seriously questioned. Confirmation has not been established to date.

CHAPTER 18

1. For further study of the nature of the community see Chapter 17 and note 1.

2. In Daniel, it is true, the author uses expressions that suggest a long time hence; see chapter 9, especially verses 24-27; 10:14; chapter 11; and 12:4, 9-13. It has been clearly demonstrated, however, that in Daniel these passages provide a literary device to transcend the time from the Persian period in which the stories about Daniel take place to the crisis of 168 B.C. when the author was writing. Compare Daniel 12:2-13 with Revelation 22:10-12 to see the contrast.

3. Mark 9:1; compare Matthew 10:23 and Luke 22:18; see also Mark 13:30.

4. Note the contrast between these verses in Genesis 8 and those in 9:11-15, which represent a much later (about 500 B.C.) elaboration of the original account very probably written in the 10th century B.C. In Genesis 8:21-22 God's statement is unequivocal, while in 9:11 and 15 it refers only to destruction by means of a flood.

5. A Christian who accepts the nature of God as revealed in Jesus Christ (cf. I John 4:7-17) should be especially sensitive to this basic theme of redemption as God's method of working in history.

6. For a valuable exercise in studying the nature of apocalyptic literature I would recommend to the layman the article on "The Apocalyptic Literature" (pp. 1106-1109) in *The Interpreter's One-Volume Commentary on the Bible* (1971) along with its commentaries on Daniel and Revelation.

7. Compare, however, 1QS X:17-18, "I will not return to a man the recompense of evil. With good will I pursue a man. For the judgment of every living being is with God, and it is he who will make each man's recompense complete."

8. It was the less rigid and more broadly focused faith of some Pharisees which managed to survive Roman oppression and eventuate in modern Judaism.

9. Jesus quoted here from Isaiah 29:13, which in the Isaiah Scroll (1QIs*ᵃ*) differs a little from the traditional Masoretic Hebrew. The New Testament, which is followed here, uses a Greek reading that differs from both Hebrew versions as well as the Septuagint Greek usually found in such quotations. Thus four different textual variants are known for this verse and suggest that it was quoted freely. Jesus was using it obviously in criticism of the Pharisees' emphasis upon the traditional interpretations of the Law (*Halakhoth*), to which they gave divine authority.

10. The last three paragraphs have been adapted from the author's article, "The Qumran Covenanters and Their Use of Scripture," *The Personalist* 39 (Spring, 1958), pp. 135-137.

APPENDIX I

1. The evidence from the interviews would allow for a date as late as January or February, 1947.

Index

Price, Ira M., 199, 210
Psalms, apocryphal (11QapPs), 157, 233
Psalms fragments (1Q), 149; (11Q), 155 f., 232 f.; (Hev), 140 f.; (Mas), 158, 204; (Taylor-Schechter), 209
Psalms *pesher* fragments (1Q), 149

Qumran Caves
  Cave I (1Q), 9, 25, 69 ff., 76 f., 83 ff., 87 f., 92, 94, 98 ff., 118 f., 123, 132 f., 138, 148 f., 164, 191 ff., 196 f., 199 f., 202 f., 214, 221, 227 f., 231 f.
  Cave II (2Q), 151, 201, 204, 232
  Cave III (3Q), 151, 155, 204, 232
  Cave IV (4Q), 152 f., 158 f., 164, 166, 202, 204, 227, 232
  Cave V (5Q), 153, 202, 204, 232
  Cave VI (6Q), 153, 202, 204, 232
  Caves VII-X (7Q-10Q), 154 f., 202, 204, 232, 234
  Cave XI (11Q), 155, 156, 158 f., 203, 232 f.
Qumran cemeteries, 150, 154 f.
Qumran community, 152 ff., 163, 167, 169 ff., 176 ff., 181 ff., 195, 212
Qumran, Khirbet, 150 ff., 157 ff., 161 f., 174 f., 191, 196, 199, 201 ff., 232
Qumran, Wadi, 150 ff., 176

Raad, C., 61, 66, 68, 70, 72 f., 75, 81, 88
Rimawi, Abdullah, 19, 27, 29 f.
Ras Feshkha, 97
Revised Standard Version of the Bible, 115, 159 f., 225
Ringgren, Helmer, 234
Romans, 150, 154, 156, 163, 170, 173 f., 178, 186, 195, 235
Rule of the Community, *see* Manual of Discipline
Rule of the Congregation (1QSa), 184

Saad, Yusif, 11, 149 f., 199f., 219, 231
Sadducees, 161
St. Mark's Monastery, 10, 16, 22, 29, 31, 52ff., 65, 67 ff., 77, 81 ff., 96 f., 101 ff., 115, 117 ff., 138, 146, 149, 192 f., 197 f., 220 f., 226
St. Mark's scrolls
  discovery, 25, 99, 101, 191 ff., 197, 219, 221
  exhibited, 142, 144, 200

preservation, 134, 145
purchase, 25, 69, 102, 193, 202
publication, 83, 93 f.
safety of, 53, 60, 82 f., 85, 89
sale of, 101 f., 109 f., 118, 136 ff., 198, 202, 230
title, problem of, 137 ff., 144 f., 229
trust agreement, 144, 230
  see also Genesis Apocryphon, Habakkuk Commentary, Isaiah Scroll "A," Manual of Discipline
Salahi, Faidi, 100, 102, 107 f., 193 f., 194, 197 f., 220 ff., 232
Samaritan manuscripts, 104, 157, 165, 204, 233
Samaritan Pentateuch, 166
Samuel, Athanasius Y., 10, 31 ff., 39 ff., 52 ff., 64 f., 69 ff., 74, 78, 81 ff., 93 f., 97, 101 ff., 108 f., 115 ff., 121 ff., 132 ff., 136 ff., 143 f., 147, 192 f., 197 ff., 213, 215 ff., 226, 228 ff.
Samuel fragments (1Q), 149; (4Q), 166, 169, 233
Sanders, J.A., 156, 204, 232, 234
Sassun, 104 f., 223
Sawahira Bedouins, 218
Schechter, Solomon, 209, 230
Sectarian document, *see* Manual of Discipline
Sellers, Ovid, 118 f., 121 f., 132 f., 137, 199, 226
Septuagint, 152, 156, 166 ff., 201, 204
Shahin, Khalil Eskander, 100 ff., 138 f., 149 f., 151, 158, 192 f., 197, 205, 219 f., 228 ff.
Shamoun, George Isha'ya, 92, 100 ff., 119, 138 f., 192 f., 197 ff., 217, 222, 228 f., 231
Shrine of the Book, 134
Simon Maccabeus, 162
Songs of Thanksgiving Scroll, *see* *Hodayot* Scroll
Songs of the Sabbath Sacrifices, 134 f., 140 f., 158, 204
Sons of Darkness, 173, 177 f., 182, 186
Sons of Light, 173, 177 f., 186
Souma, Aziz, 121, 209
Sowmy, Butrus, 16, 21 ff., 31 ff., 39 ff., 52 ff., 69 f., 74, 81 ff., 93, 98, 110, 112, 115, 117, 121, 124, 198 f., 208 f., 223
Sowmy, Ibrahim, 22 ff., 77, 98, 112, 209, 217

Sowmy, Karim, 112
Strugnell, J., 233
Stendahl, Krister, 234
Stephan, Stephan Hanna, 103, 106
Stewart, Bishop, 91, 110, 208
Sukenik, Eliezer L., 84, 97, 102, 106 ff., 114 ff., 118, 124 f., 137 f., 145, 147, 194, 197 ff., 203, 214 f., 222, 224, 231 f.
Syriac Gospels, 53 f., 87
Syriac New Testament, 145, 166

Ta'amireh Bedouins, 98 f., 108, 150 ff., 157 f., 191, 194, 196 ff., 218 ff.
Talmon, Shemaryahu, 234
Tamimi, Anwar, 78, 80, 86 f., 91
Tannourji, Malak, 109 f., 225
Teacher of community, 162, 167, 170 f., 185, 187
Teicher, J.L., 114, 229
Temple Scroll, 158, 170, 172, 205, 233
tephillin, see phylacteries
Testament of Levi fragments (1Q), 149, 163, 172
Testament of Naphtali (4Q), 163, 172
Timotheus, 196
Tischendorf, Constantine, 24 f., 34, 44, 193
Tobit fragments (4Q), 172
Torah codex (Or. 4445), 24, 209
Torah scrolls, 54, 121 f., 212
Tushingham, A.D., 232

United States Junior Chamber of Commerce, 145
University of Chicago, 142, 200

Uzziah, 163, 195

Valley of Achor, *see* Buqei'a
van der Ploeg, J., 103, 157, 197, 205, 217, 222 f., 228, 233
van der Woude, A.S., 157, 205, 233
Vermes, Geza, 233 f.
Vespasian, 163, 173, 178
Vester, Bertha, 64
Vincent, L.H., 103

Wadi ed-Daliyeh, *see* ed-Daliyeh, Wadi
Wadi Murabba'at, *see* Murabba'at, Wadi
Walters Art Gallery, 142, 200
War Scroll (1QM), 108, 116, 163, 178, 198, 231
Wechsler, Tovia, 106, 197, 224
Worcester Art Museum, 144, 201

"X," Mr., *see* Ohan

Yadin, Yigael, 134, 147, 156 ff., 172, 202 f., 205, 214, 223 f., 227, 230, 232 f.
Yale Gallery of Fine Arts, 39, 127
Yale University, 126, 142
Yonan, Norman M., 144
Yusif, Father, 69, 84, 92, 103, 123, 197, 216 f., 219, 222

Zadokites, 162
Zealots, 158, 161, 174
Zeitlin, Solomon, 211, 229
Zephaniah *pesher* fragments (1Q), 149
Zeuner, F.E., 229

Maps show the principle sites and areas mentioned in THE DEAD SEA SCROLLS, ca. 1948.

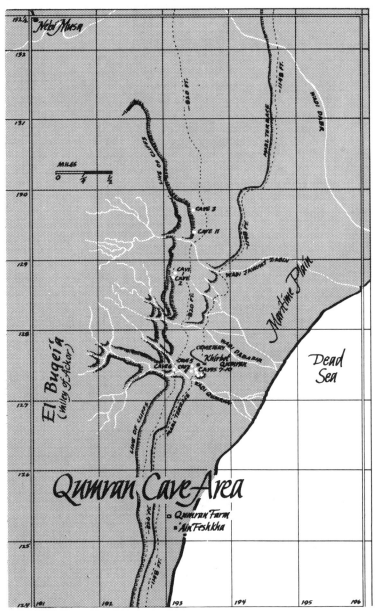

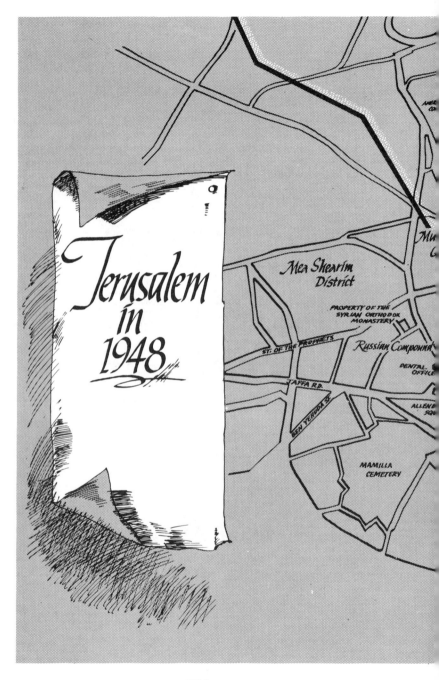

Jerusalem in 1948

Mea Shearim District

PROPERTY OF THE SYRIAN ORTHODOX MONASTERY

ST. OF THE PROPHETS

Russian Compound

DENTAL OFFICE

JAFFA R.P.

BEN YEHUDA S.

ALLENB SQ.

MAMILLA CEMETERY

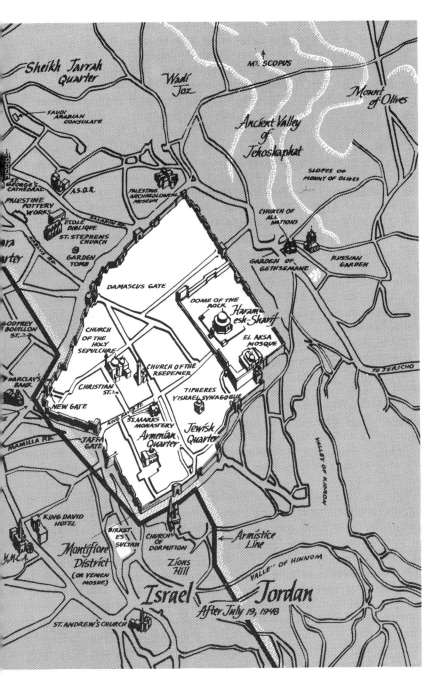

Sheikh Jarrah Quarter

Wadi Joz

MT. SCOPUS

Mount of Olives

SAUDI ARABIAN CONSULATE

Ancient Valley of Jehoshaphat

SLOPES OF MOUNT OF OLIVES

GEORGE'S CATHEDRAL

A.S.O.R.

PALESTINE ARCHAEOLOGICAL MUSEUM

CHURCH OF ALL NATIONS

PALESTINE POTTERY WORKS

ECOLE BIBLIQUE

ST. STEPHENS CHURCH

RUSSIAN GARDEN

Quarter

GARDEN TOMB

GARDEN OF GETHSEMANE

DAMASCUS GATE

GODFREY BOUILLON ST.

CHURCH OF THE HOLY SEPULCHRE

DOME OF THE ROCK

Haram esh-Sharif

EL AKSA MOSQUE

BARCLAY'S BANK

CHURCH OF THE REEDEMER

TO JERICHO

CHRISTIAN ST.

NEW GATE

TIPHERES YISRAEL SYNAGOGUE

KING DAVID ST.

ST. MARKS MONASTERY

Jewish Quarter

JAFFA GATE

Armenian Quarter

MAMILLA RD.

VALLEY OF KIDRON

KING DAVID HOTEL

BIRKET ES SULTAN

CHURCH OF DORMITION

Armistice Line

Y.M.C.A.

Montifiore District

(OR YEMEN MOSQUE)

ZIONS HILL

VALLEY OF HINNOM

Israel

Jordan

After July 19, 1948

ST. ANDREW'S CHURCH

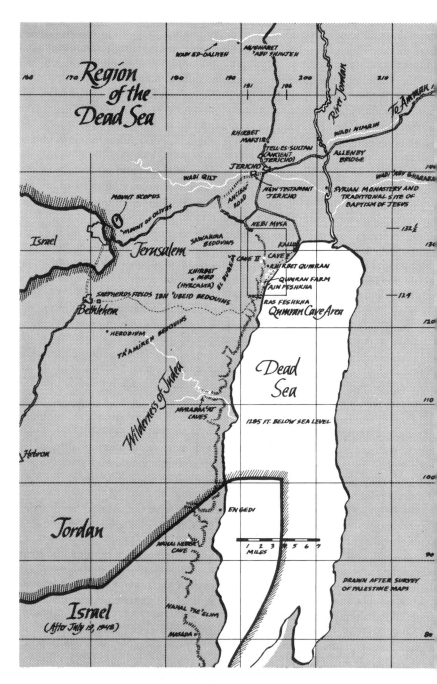

Region
of the
Dead Sea

WADI ED-QALIYEN
MUGHARET 'ABU SHINJEH
KHIRBET MAFJIR
TELL-ES-SULTAN (ANCIENT JERICHO)
JERICHO
Rive Jordan
WADI NIMRIN
To Amman!
ALLENBY BRIDGE
WADI 'ABU SHARABA
WADI QILT
ANCIENT ROAD
NEW TESTAMENT JERICHO
SYRIAN MONASTERY AND TRADITIONAL SITE OF BAPTISM OF JESUS
MOUNT SCOPUS
MOUNT OF OLIVES
NEBI MUSA
Israel
SAWAHIRA BEDOUINS
KALIA
CAVE II CAVE I
KHIRBET QUMRAN
Jerusalem
EL BUQEI'A
QUMRAN FARM
'AIN FESHKHA
KHIRBET MIRD (HYRCANIA)
IBN 'UBEID BEDOUINS
RAS FESHKHA
Qumran Cave Area
SHEPHERDS FIELDS
Bethlehem
HERODIUM
TA'AMIREH BEDOUINS

Dead
Sea

Wilderness of Judea

1285 FT. BELOW SEA LEVEL

MURABBA'AT CAVES

Hebron

Jordan

EN GEDI

NAHAL HEVER CAVE

1 2 3 4 5 6 7
MILES

Israel
(After July 19, 1948)

DRAWN AFTER SURVEY OF PALESTINE MAPS

NAHAL TSE'ELIM

MASADA